CAMBRIDGE STUDIES IN LATIN AMERICAN
AND IBERIAN LITERATURE 6

Bello and Bolívar

As Andrés Bello predicted in 1823, the glory of Simón Bolívar has continued to grow since the Spanish American Revolution. The Revolution is still viewed as an almost mythical quest, and the name of the Libertador has become synonymous with the region's hopes for integration. In this book, the official history of the Revolution – the heroic history of Bolívar – is replaced by the account of Bello, who was first Bolívar's teacher and later his critic. Through a detailed study of the manuscripts of Bello's unfinished poem *América*, Antonio Cussen reconstructs Bello's version of the Revolution and seeks to understand its political and cultural consequences. The author argues that Bello recorded the disintegration of the Augustan model of power and intimated the inevitable approach of liberalism with a certain longing for the classical culture of his youth.

Bello and Bolívar

Poetry and politics in the Spanish American Revolution

ANTONIO CUSSEN

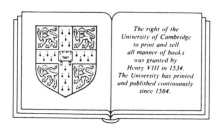

The right of the
University of Cambridge
to print and sell
all manner of books
was granted by
Henry VIII in 1534.
The University has printed
and published continuously
since 1584.

CAMBRIDGE UNIVERSITY PRESS
CAMBRIDGE
NEW YORK   PORT CHESTER   MELBOURNE   SYDNEY

Published by the Press Syndicate of the University of Cambridge
The Pitt Building, Trumpington Street, Cambridge CB2 1RP
40 West 20th Street, New York, NY 10011, USA
10 Stamford Road, Oakleigh, Melbourne 3166, Australia

© Cambridge University Press 1992

First published 1992

Printed in the United States of America

Library of Congress Cataloging-in-Publication Data
Cussen, Antonio.
Bello and Bolívar: Poetry and politics in the Spanish
American Revolution / Antonio Cussen.
p.   cm. – (Cambridge studies in Latin American and Iberian
literature ; 6)
Includes bibliographical references and index.
ISBN 0-521-41248-x (hardback)
1. Bello, Andrés, 1781–1865. Alocución a la Poesía.   2. Latin
America – History – Wars of Independence, 1806–1830 – Literature and
the wars.   3. Bello, Andrés, 1781–1865 – Political and social views.
4. Bolívar, Simón, 1783–1830. I. Title. II. Series.
PQ8549.B3A7436   1992
861 – dc20   91-10546
                                                                   CIP

British Library Cataloguing in Publication Data
Cussen, Antonio
Bello and Bolívar: Poetry and politics in the
Spanish American Revolution – (Cambridge
studies in Latin American and Iberian literature, 6)
1. South America, history, 1809–1830.   Bello, Andrés 1781–
1865.   Bolívar, Simón 1783–1830
I. Title
980.02

ISBN 0-521-41248-x hardback

For my parents

Contents

Acknowledgments

My interest in Bello and Bolívar began during my years as a graduate student at the University of California at Berkeley, when Michel Foucault led me to look at poetry as an archive that often includes secret meditations on power. I owe much to Luis Monguió for pointing out the need to study Bello's poetry in the light of Virgil and to G. Arnold Chapman, Francine Masiello, Tulio Halperin Donghi, Gwen Kirkpatrick, and Florence Verducci, who made valuable suggestions regarding my dissertation, which was an earlier draft of this book.

In Santiago, Chile, I spent many hours discussing Bello with the late Alamiro de Avila, who gave many helpful hints about Bello's London years and made valuable comments on the manuscript. With the generous assistance of Haverford College I made two trips to Caracas, where I met several distinguished scholars who guided me in my work. I have particularly fond memories of my discussions with Ildefonso Leal and Arturo Ardao. At the Casa de Bello in Caracas I spent many hours talking about Bello and Bolívar with Pedro Grases and Oscar Sambrano and was able to examine the manuscripts of Bello's poems, which allowed me to date them and suggest a chronology for his political and cultural evolution during the London years.

At Haverford I had many useful discussions with students and colleagues. I would especially like to thank Israel Burshatin, Richard Luman, and John Spielman for their editorial suggestions. I also benefited from the help of Serena Black, Jorge Edwards, Amy Einsohn, Julie Greenblatt, Enrique Pupo-Walker, Mario Lobo, and Mary Racine and from the comments of the anonymous readers of the manuscript. This book's errors and omissions are, of course, my own.

Finally, I wish to express my gratitude to my children for their interest in my work and to Celia for her generosity of heart and mind.

Introduction

On April 19, 1810, after learning that the armies of Napoleon Bonaparte were in control of the Iberian Peninsula, the people of Caracas moved to oust the local Spanish officials and to form their own governing junta. The Venezuelans were fearful of French aggression, and in June they sent a diplomatic mission to London in search of an ally. The mission was headed by Simón Bolívar; its secretary was Andrés Bello. Bolívar returned the same year to Venezuela, where he helped transform the grievances of the Caracas junta into a decisive call for independence. Bello, for his part, remained in London until 1829. As a leading voice in three London journals – *El Censor Americano, La Biblioteca Americana,* and *El Repertorio Americano* – he became one of the most accomplished members of the Spanish-speaking intelligentsia, whose headquarters during this period were in London. And in his unfinished poem *América* (1811–26), Bello recorded a version of a crisis whose repercussions are still felt throughout the American continent.

In Spanish America, Bello and Bolívar are often invoked as the representatives of the Americanist ideal, the union of all the Spanish-speaking countries on the continent. We often hear how Bolívar with his sword and Bello with his pen gave political and cultural independence to the continent. The alliance of the two founding fathers forms one of the most enduring myths of the Spanish American Revolution, and we seem to cling to that myth all the more strenuously the more we realize that the Revolution's promises of freedom and well-being failed to materialize.

In this book I look closely at Bello's poems, particularly the fragments of *América,* which are among the principal sources of this myth. Poetry was always the medium that linked Bello and Bolívar. In the years before the Revolution, both attended the neoclassical literary gatherings of colonial Caracas, where they

xi

and their friends could assume the disguises of Horace, Virgil, and Maecenas and attempt to replicate the glories of the Augustan principate. Still undisturbed by romanticism and republicanism, they could then play out their pastoral fantasies by imitating and translating the Roman poets or by acting out the more severe role of critic or patron. After 1810, once the events of the Revolution separated them, Bello expressed in poetry his most compelling thoughts on the Libertador; and in the scattered documents that reveal Bolívar's passion for poetry, we discover his reactions to the lines of his old friend.

The evidence presented in this book is mostly Bello's, and therefore the story is told from his perspective. I have made no attempt to temper his claims and his often impassioned allusions to Bolívar, and if the tone is partial it reflects primarily the partial feelings of Bello. I have traced his thoughts on Bolívar and the Revolution throughout his long life, from Caracas to London to Santiago, where he lived for thirty-six years, until his death. But my main effort has been to reconstruct Bello's version of the Spanish American Revolution during his London years. I have therefore tried to replace the official history of the Revolution – the heroic history of Bolívar – by the account of a poet who was recording his thoughts and feelings on the Revolution from a distant and perhaps privileged vantage point.

I like to think of Bello's *América* as an archive of undiscovered statements about the Spanish American Revolution. Read in isolation, these statements do not speak to us: they are like old files in a corner collecting dust. But once we evoke their historical context, they become vibrant testimonies, documents that illuminate the past. Poems, however, are not ordinary documents. They not only yield historical information that satisfies our positivistic anxieties; they also furnish a wealth of information that enables us to perceive the sensibility of an era. Poems, especially poems written in times of revolution, are also an intense response to a generalized crisis of meaning; we can find in them the roots of a culture that is being threatened and transformed.

Bello's reputation as a poet has suffered because readers have tried to see in him what he clearly was not, a romantic poet, a contemporary of Wordsworth and Coleridge. When Bello arrived in London in 1810, he began to write a philosophic and didactic poem in imitation of Virgil's *Georgics,* a genre that was completely out of style in England. Like other Spanish American authors before and after him, he was following a literary model that was hopelessly out-of-date in northern countries. But his Virgilian lines were describing one of the most radical and profound upheavals of the day, a revolution that shook and altered the West. Bello may well be a prime representative of the conflict between past and present – a characteristic of Spanish American letters. It is his *destiempo,* this clash of a classical voice with a world that is inexorably subverting all the major strongholds of classical culture, that constitutes the peculiar appeal of his poetry.

PART I

Caracas (1781–1810)

1

Augustan Caracas

Oh Happy Age! Oh times like those alone
By fate reserv'd for Great *Augustus'* Throne!

John Dryden

Andrés Bello was born in 1781 to a family of modest means. All eight of his great-grandparents had emigrated from the Canary Islands at the beginning of the eighteenth century. They had left behind a life of poverty and had advanced considerably in the social echelon since their arrival in Venezuela. Some of Bello's ancestors were construction workers, and his paternal grandfather was a shoemaker; but his mother's father – Juan Pedro López – was a painter of distinction in colonial Caracas. Bello's father, Bartolomé Bello, was both a lawyer and a musician. He married Ana López in 1781 and Andrés was the first of eight children. The poet grew up in the house of his grandfather López, who had at his death in 1787 a mortgaged house and three slaves.[1]

Bello was fortunate to have as his tutor the Mercedarian friar Cristóbal Quesada, who was well versed in the Roman and Spanish classics and sensitive to the beauties of poetry. When he was fifteen, Bello worked on a translation, which has not survived, of book 5 of the *Aeneid*. In 1797 he entered into the last year of the preparatory course at the Royal and Pontifical University of Caracas, where he was perfecting his already proficient Latin. The course was devoted entirely to Christian doctrine and to oral and written fluency in the language of Rome. From seven until nine-thirty each morning, and in the afternoons from two to four, the presbyter José Antonio Montenegro examined the works of Virgil and Cicero and the Council of Trent. In addition, he urged his students to go to confession, and on Saturdays he explained Christian doctrine.[2]

At sixteen Bello had already achieved a certain notoriety as an extremely diligent student, and he was asked to become the tutor of Simón Bolívar, a descendant of Simón de Bolívar, one of the earliest conquistadors of Venezuela. Bolívar's parents had accumulated an immense fortune, including several ranches of cacao and indigo, cattle, four houses in Caracas – fully furnished and with slaves – nine houses in La Guaira, the whole valley of Aroa, and the mines of Cocorote. Bello gave lessons in geography and belles lettres to Bolívar, who was twenty months his junior, but these lessons did not last long since his student embarked for Europe to spend time at the court of Charles IV. Bello later reported that Bolívar was restless and not a conscientious student, but that these faults were offset by extraordinary talents. Restless he was; at age twelve, already an orphan, Bolívar had gone to court to defend his rights to change his residence from that of his uncle to that of his sister.[3]

In 1797 the British took possession of the island of Trinidad, only a few miles off the mainland, and the Spaniards were in constant fear of renewed threats of British or French expansion. Of greater concern, however, was the revolutionary plot led by Manuel Gual and José María España in the same year. Under the influence of a Spanish radical, these men had organized a conspiracy in La Guaira, the main port of Venezuela, with the ultimate objective of establishing republican institutions. In vain Spain had tried to establish a *cordon sanitaire* that would effectively isolate the peninsula and its colonies from revolutionary France. Despite the careful watch of the Crown and the Inquisition, printed material proclaiming the rights of man crossed the Pyrenees and the Atlantic Ocean and led to several unsuccessful conspiracies, La Guaira's probably being the most serious.[4]

The new intellectual currents had also reached Caracas. Some of Bello's professors at the University of Caracas were praising the new science and the benefits of trade and agriculture; some were introducing the principles of mechanics and mathematics by way of François Jaquier, an eighteenth-century French philosopher and mathematician who tried to simplify scholastic jargon and to accommodate ideas of the Enlightenment. Thus, one of Bello's professors, Rafael Escalona, could freely lecture on Newton, Locke, and Condillac. But this was the voice of the minority; most of the faculty of the University of Caracas held to orthodox Thomism and only grudgingly allowed some mention of the new science. So when Bello took his final exams, in May 1800, he had to put his syllogisms to use and prove in Latin several Aristotelian axioms. An applicant for a degree had to swear to maintain the Immaculate Conception and neither to teach nor to practice regicide or tyrannicide. Bello was also required to present documents proving that he was of the white race.[5]

As the eighteenth century came to an end, the rate of change began to increase in colonial Caracas. Perhaps nothing symbolizes better the clash between old and new ideas than the sojourn of Alexander von Humboldt and Aimé Bonpland in Caracas from November 1799 to January 1800. Years later, Humboldt published his impressions of Venezuela in *Voyage aux régions équinoxiales du Nouveau Continent* (Paris, 1814). He divided the territory of the country into three zones, which paralleled the three stages of human society: the life of the wild hunter in the forests of the Orinoco, the pastoral life in the savannas, or *llanos,* and the agricultural life in the high valleys and at the foot of the coastal mountains. The coast of Venezuela, and its proximity to Europe, had encouraged Humboldt to envisage the growth of trade, and the islands in the mouth of the Orinoco were transformed in his vision to enclaves of high agricultural productivity and constant domestic and international commerce.

In Caracas Humboldt also saw a lively interest in learning, including a knowledge of French and Italian literature, as well as a predilection for music. He was surprised, however, not to find a printing press. Nor did he find much curiosity among the *caraqueños* about the natural landscape. Of the forty thousand people who lived in Caracas in 1799, Humboldt and Bonpland could not find anyone who had reached the summit of La Silla: "Accustomed to a uniform and domestic life, they dread fatigue, and sudden changes of climate. It would seem as if they live not to enjoy life, but only to prolong its duration."[6] Bello was one of the few *caraqueños* who accompanied Humboldt and Bonpland on their expedition to La Silla in the first days of 1800, though he did not reach the summit. Humboldt took an interest in the young man and considered his devotion to learning excessive, given his frail disposition.

The German naturalist noticed the characteristic Hispanic passion for genealogy, yet also observed that this passion did not transform the Creole aristocracy into a group that insulted and offended, which was the case – he said – of most European aristocracies. He also distinguished two species of noble Creoles: those descended from Spaniards who had recently held positions of high distinction in the imperial bureaucracy and those descended from the conquistadors. Yet, as Humboldt observed, all whites, noble or not, enjoyed a certain equality following the axiom that *"todo blanco es caballero."*[7]

It was this equality among whites that allowed Bello to develop close friendships with the *mantuanos,* the name given to members of the highest aristocracy in Caracas. Bello was particularly fond of the *mantuano* José Ignacio Ustáriz, a fellow student of philosophy who along with his brothers liked to play the role of patron of the arts. At the Ustáriz house, Bello found a library of Roman and Spanish classics and also a selection of modern European books. The study of modern foreign languages was not generally encouraged in Caracas: Bello would later recall that on one occasion a priest had seen him reading a tragedy of Racine's and had observed that it was a pity that he had learned French. Soon afterward Bello began to study English by translating Locke's *Essay Concerning Human Understanding.*[8]

In 1800 Bello graduated with a bachelor's degree from the University of Caracas. He enrolled in the School of Medicine and the School of Law, hoping to obtain higher degrees. But after one year he had to abandon his studies, probably for financial reasons, and decided to apply for the vacant position of second officer of the captaincy general's secretariat, a high position in the imperial bureaucracy, especially considering that the young applicant had been born on American soil – a Creole. The man who recommended Bello, Pedro González Ortega, wrote about him: "I have seen several of his works, both translations of classical authors and his original writings, though of less importance, in which one can recognize an uncommon talent and ideas that combine an extensive knowledge and valuable discernment." Bello was given the post and became a close assistant to the captain general, Manuel de Guevara y Vasconcelos. He was extremely diligent in his tasks, writing official documents and translating articles from English and French journals.[9]

Vasconcelos had arrived in Caracas in April 1799. A man of solid administrative and military credentials, he was determined to rule the vast provinces of Venezuela with a firm hand and wasted no time in venting his full force on those daring to proclaim republican ideals, the rights of man, or any such French ideas. Scarcely a month after his arrival he had ordered the execution of José María España, which was carried out with fanfare and exemplary cruelty: España was hanged in Caracas's Plaza Mayor, and for a long time inbound travelers disembarking at the port of La Guaira could see his head in an iron cage. The remaining parts of José María España's body were divided and placed in Macuto, El Vigía, Quita-Calzón, and La Cumbre.[10]

This kind of display was far from customary in the colonies; the extreme punishment corresponded to the extreme rarity of the crime. Day-to-day life in colonial Caracas, at least among the elite, was marked, rather, by an almost placid and pastoral pace. Vasconcelos had an interest in the arts and frequently invited *caraqueños* to his home for Sunday gatherings, adorned by poetry and dance. These events were attended by local dignitaries, and they became for the captain general a source of secret intelligence that expedited his duties.

Vasconcelos enjoyed a moment of great triumph in the spring of 1804 when he hosted the arrival of an expedition led by Francisco Balmis and financed by the Spanish Crown, the purpose of which was to distribute an antivariolic vaccine to all corners of the Spanish Empire. In the colonies, as well as in the Spanish metropolis, there was still much resistance to new ideas and new practices, and the success of the vaccine expedition depended on the attention it elicited from the notables of Caracas. Vasconcelos therefore celebrated the arrival of Balmis with serenades, parties, and ecclesiastical acts; and in one of the festivities Andrés Bello, the captain general's secretary, delivered a poem entitled "Oda a la vacuna."[11]

The great Charles, Bello said, has distributed the vaccine throughout the empire, reenacting the efforts of the Crown since the Indies were first discovered. The navigator had then learned of new routes and brought to America the skills and arts of the Old World. A thousand riches were distributed throughout both hemispheres with the advent of trade, and the Christian gospel put an end to the sanguinary rites that offended the Supreme Being. The great work of royal tenderness seemed complete, but a plague brought desolation to the new colonies. The palace and the hut were in mourning; the old perished with the young. The most indissoluble ties were broken: the wife fled the husband, and the slave his master. But through the intervention of Providence, and in a pastoral setting, Jenner discovered the vaccine. King Charles gave to the earth the gifts of heaven, agriculture started feeling the salutary effects of science, and the poet and his audience were transported to the beautiful days of the golden age.

In the "Oda" Bello drew heavily on Virgil's *Georgics,* especially in his attempt to blend poetry with science and politics. Like its model, the "Oda" begins with a long proem, a dedication addressed to the poet's patron:

> Vasconcelos ilustre, en cuyas manos
> el gran monarca del imperio ibero
> las peligrosas riendas deposita
> de una parte preciosa de sus pueblos;
> tú que, de la corona asegurando
> en tus vastas provincias los derechos,
> nuestra paz estableces, nuestra dicha
> sobre inmobles y sólidos cimientos;
> iris afortunado que las negras
> nubes que oscurecían nuestro cielo
> con sabias providencias ahuyentaste,
> el orden, la quietud restituyendo.[12]

> (Illustrious Vasconcelos, in whose hands the great monarch of the Spanish Empire has placed the dangerous reins of a precious part of his lands; you who, after ensuring the rights of the Crown in your vast provinces, establish our peace and our happiness on solid, unmovable foundations; fortunate rainbow who dispelled the black clouds that darkened our skies with wise measures, restoring order and tranquillity.)

Again following the example of Virgil, Bello closes the proem to his ode by describing the superhuman aura that sur-

rounds the leader. Though the poem is dedicated to Vasconcelos, the ultimate beneficiary is not the intermediary of the
king but the king himself. The poet tells his Maecenas:

> digno representante del gran Carlos,
> recibe en nombre suyo el justo incienso
> de gratitud, que a su persona augusta,
> tributa la ternura de los pueblos;
> y pueda por tu medio levantarse
> nuestra unánime voz al trono excelso,
> donde, cual numen bienhechor, derrama
> toda especie de bien sobre su imperio;
> sí, Venezuela exenta del horrible
> azote destructor, que, en otro tiempo
> sus hijos devoraba, es quien te envía
> por mi tímido labio sus acentos.   (ll. 17–28)

(worthy representative of the great Charles, receive in his name the just incense of gratitude,
which is a tribute of tenderness from these lands
to his august person; and may our unanimous
voice be raised through you to the lofty throne
which, as a benign divine power, pours all forms
of goodness upon the empire. Yes, Venezuela
free from the destructive scourge, which for-
merly devoured her children, sends you her
songs through my timid lips.)

In referring to the "*persona augusta*" of the monarch, Bello
was following the standard practice of using the epithet *augusto*
in a royal setting. Elsewhere in the "Oda a la vacuna" the Spanish queen is addressed as "augusta Luisa," and in Bello's dra-
matic poem "Venezuela consolada," also written to celebrate the
vaccine expedition, we find King Charles invoked as "augusto
Carlos." The epithet had been used for centuries among European monarchs, an echo of the man who had changed the
course of Western politics by cloaking his power in a religious,
superhuman aura. Poets were especially fond of making the
connection between the epithet and its eponym. As we shall see,
in his old age Bello referred explicitly to this connection.

In Spain the epithet *augusto* often had the meaning of "venerable" or "majestic." In the eighteenth century it still preserved
these meanings, but it was most commonly used in two very
specific ways: to refer to the Eucharist (*el augusto sacramento*,
sometimes used in the superlative) and, by extension, to the

Church or to the emperor. The *Diccionario de la lengua castellana,* published by the Real Academia Española in honor of the first Bourbon monarch, supported its definition of the epithet with the following example: "Si no se conserva lo augusto de la majestad, no habrá diferencia entre el Príncipe y el vasallo" (If the august traits of majesty are not preserved, there will be no difference between the Prince and his subject).[13] In Bello's Caracas days the epithet was found mainly in association with the Crown and the Church. *Augusto* designated the dividing line between the powerful and the powerless, the rulers and the ruled.

In the "Oda a la vacuna" the religious aura of *augusto* is enhanced by expressions that emphasize the divine origin of the monarch, who appears closer to God than to mortals: "incense," "divine power," "lofty throne." The spiritual and secular unity of the empire is embodied in a Crown that is sanctioned by God – its subjects can only thank with a "unanimous voice" the munificence of the king. The tone is the established form of adulation, the expected declaration of allegiance to the ruler. It is the kind of verse written by all young, aspiring courtiers who expect to receive the benefits of patronage.[14]

Promonarchic sentiments were strong in the Spanish world at the end of the eighteenth century, and both conservative and reformist forces vied to link the Spanish Crown with the principate. After the rebellion of Gual and España, for example, the bishop of Caracas, Juan Antonio de la Virgen María y Viana, delivered a homily whose epigraph was a line of Saint Peter (1.2.v.17): "Deum timete; Regem honorificate" (Fear God; honor the King). Characterizing the search for freedom as a snare of the Prince of Darkness, similar to Adam's notion of primitive freedom and to the temptation of the serpent, Bishop Viana told the *caraqueños* that they should record the maxim of the Prince of the Apostles, which is the fear of God, and honor, reverence, total submission, and obedience to sovereigns and to the sacrosanct laws they establish. Viana was convinced of the superior power of kings, next to God, and said that even Christ respected Pilate as a superior power consecrated by God. The traditional Christian support for monarchy should be the model of behavior for those who, finding nothing but joy, peace, and quiet, wish to snatch from the sacred temples of their monarchs the Crown that God himself has given them. Republicanism, as the bishop reminded the most distinguished members of the Caracas nobility, is the voice of the devil, and a devouring fire will consume the land if such evil is not restrained.[15]

The Church was not always ready to extol the Crown in these terms, but in times of crisis, when republican ideals threatened the integrity of the empire, variations of Bishop Viana's homily were often delivered. The principate, with more specific references to the court of Augustus, was also a favorite allusion of the new generation of poets and politicians who had come to power in Madrid in the last decade of the eighteenth century. The young men who gathered around the illustrious humanist Gaspar Melchor de Jovellanos, named secretary of state and justice in 1795, were eager to exalt a model of power in which the monarch, with the aid of a wise minister, brings wealth to the empire, peace to the people, and emoluments to the poets. In the first of his epistles, addressed to Manuel Godoy, Charles IV's right-hand man, the poet Juan Meléndez Valdés invokes the Muses, who once ensured the immortality of Augustus and his prime minister: "Así dura inmortal, de olvido ajena, / La memoria de Augusto y su valido" (Thus lasts forever, beyond oblivion, the memory of Augustus and his minister).[16] Meléndez Valdés goes on to evoke Augustan Rome, when the arts and sciences were cultivated, and then contrasts that time with Spain's present circumstances:

> Mas hoy mísero yace [el ingenio], y oprimido
> Del error gime y tiembla, que orgulloso
> Mofándole camina el cuello erguido.
> No lo sufráis, señor; mas, poderoso,
> El monstruo derrocad que guerra impía
> A la santa verdad mueve envidioso.   (*BAE*, 63: 200)

> (But now genius lies in misery, and moans and trembles oppressed by error, who walks proudly with his head held high and mocks him. Do not bear it, sir; instead, overthrow with your power the jealous monster who wages an impious war against holy truth.)

Here Meléndez Valdés is calling for the overthrow of the Spanish Inquisition, the bastion of the traditionalists.[17] The Spanish poet presents the Augustan principate as an ideal moment of royal authority and munificence, yet at the same time he tries to disentangle the intimate alliance between the Church and the Crown, which traditional spokesmen of the Church like Bishop Viana wished to emphasize.

Among the Spanish poets of the late eighteenth century Augustus had acquired a prestige that is hard to find in other places and other times. The Roman *princeps* was placed in regions so high that even the praises of the Roman Augustan poets paled in comparison. In 1798, for instance, Nicasio Alvarez de Cienfuegos published a version of Horace's "Regulus" ode (3.5) that begins:

> Alzase Jove, a su augusta planta
> Truena el Olimpo retemblante. ¡El cielo
> Es el trono del dios! pronuncia Augusto,
> Y a Britania y a Persia omnipotente
> En el imperio encierra.
> ¡César, César es Dios sobre la tierra!
>   (*BAE*, 67: 14)

> (Jove rises; shuddering Olympus thunders at his august feet. Heaven is the throne of the god! proclaims Augustus, and he encloses Britain and almighty Persia in his empire. Caesar, Caesar is God on earth!)

For Cienfuegos, Augustus is above Jupiter: Caesar is God, while Jove is merely a god. Horace had not gone that far. He granted to Jove the kingdom of heaven and to Augustus power over the earth; he also allowed Augustus to appear as a god ("divus Augustus"). But in Horace's poem Augustus's divinity was presented in conditional terms; it was predicated on his successful conquest of the Britons and the Parthians. As Howard D. Weinbrot has observed: "Augustanism rises and falls with royalism and absolutism."[18] At the turn of the nineteenth century, the monarchic propaganda in imperial Spain was at its height, and the figure of Augustus was therefore exalted.

The proem of the "Oda a la vacuna" finishes with Bello thanking the king for putting an end to the "destructive scourge." The primary meaning of this expression is clearly the plague, which the vaccine will cure, but the absence of any medical terminology in Bello's periphrasis suggests that the "destructive scourge" is also the plague of civil and international conflicts brought about by the French Revolution. Just as Vasconcelos is thanked for putting an end to the local republican threats of Venezuela, the "black clouds," Charles IV is thanked for putting an end to the expansion of revolutionary ideas. The vaccine thus becomes in Bello's poem a metaphor for the cure of all plagues. We already see in this youthful poem Bello's tendency to present in thinly disguised figurative language the political issues of the day. Like most poems by Bello and faithful to the spirit of the Roman Augustan poets, the "Oda a la vacuna" is a political poem, one meant to have public resonance.

Bello's proem gives us an image of his understanding of the Spanish Crown scarcely four years before the Bourbons were forced to abdicate their rights to Napoleon. His special brand of Augustanism was a typical product of a young Creole who had come of age at the end of the eighteenth century. It is a product of the political and aesthetic convictions of the age, and also of the rigorous classical and Catholic upbringing of the subjects of the Spanish Crown.

At age twenty-two Bello held attitudes and opinions that reflected the main beliefs and tensions of the Spanish world of his time. Like Bishop Viana, Bello viewed the republican rebellion as a scourge that had threatened the peaceful order of the empire and disturbed the solid foundations of the monarchy. Both the poet and the bishop extolled the Spanish monarch as an almighty figure: he rules over all, from the highest conceivable altitude. Viana had used the language of the Bible and of the Church fathers; Bello, the language of Virgil. These languages were not in any way incompatible. Indeed, the simultaneous birth of the Roman Empire and Christianity reinforced the mutual dependence between these two languages.

At the same time in the "Oda a la vacuna" Bello takes up some of the favorite themes of Spanish poets like Meléndez Valdés. He wished to advance the new ideas that were in the air at the University of Caracas and the universities of Spain: human perfectibility, economic trade, and above all *agricultura*, the development of the land, a word that had a new, enlightened ring. Unlike Bishop Viana, who presented the colonies as a kind of isolated paradise, Bello wished to promote trade with the rest of the world, and argued that through trade and agriculture Venezuela might return to the golden age:

> La agricultura ya de nuevos brazos
> los beneficios siente, y a los bellos
> días del siglo de oro, nos traslada;
> ya no teme esta tierra que el comercio
> entre sus ricos dones le conduzca
> el mayor de los males europeos;
> y a los bajeles extranjeros, abre
> con presuroso júbilo sus puertos.
>
> (ll. 241–8)

(Agriculture now feels the benefits of new hands and transports us to the beautiful days of the golden age; this land no longer fears that trade will bring her the greatest of all European evils among its rich gifts, and with eager joy she opens her ports to foreign vessels.)

But such lines are exceptional in the poem; they are Bello's timid attempt to put forth a note of change or reform. And fearing that these thoughts may present too strong a break with the Edenic isolation of the colonies, Bello prefaces them with the concept of trade in the classical vein of Horace and Virgil, and contrasts the vaccine expedition with "ambition" crossing the seas. It is as if Bello, fearing to come too close to the new currents of thought, sets them within a framework that exaggerates the classical worldview dear to the empire. The "Oda a la vacuna" placed Bello in line with Jovellanos's desire for reform, but in his poem there is not even a hint of criticism of the Church. In fact, he expressly defends the role of the Church since the Spanish conquest of America:

> No más allí con sanguinarios ritos
> el nombre se ultrajó del Ser Supremo,
> ni las inanimadas producciones
> del cincel, le usurparon nuestro incienso;
> con el nombre español, por todas partes,
> la luz se difundió del evangelio,
> y fue con los pendones de Castilla
> la cruz plantada en el indiano suelo.
>
> (ll. 65–72)

(The name of the Supreme Being was no longer profaned there by sanguinary rites; nor did the lifeless products of the chisel usurp our incense;

the light of the gospel and the Spanish name
were spread everywhere; and it was with the
banners of Castile that the cross was planted on
Indian soil.)

In poems such as "Oda a la vacuna" and the allegorical scene
"Venezuela consolada," which develops similar ideas but with a
diction closer to Calderón's, Bello's intention is unmistakable:
these are panegyrics to the monarch, and the subtle intrusions
of eighteenth-century concepts are surrounded by overt, de-
clamatory expressions of support for the cause of Crown and
Church. The colonies are rich and peaceful lands, and since the
Conquest they have benefited from the evangelical zeal of the
Crown.

In writing adulatory exercises in praise of Charles IV, the
youthful Bello was carrying on a tradition of long standing. His
was a poetry of enlightened values, often didactic, with a strong
conviction that the monarch must spread knowledge and the
benefits of scientific progress among his subjects. Bello dis-
celos for restoring the solid, unmovable columns of the empire,
he was invoking the power of Spanish rule, a power derived
from the coherence and awesome antiquity of its myths.

2

Revolt

Así (¡cosa por cierto bien extraña!) lo que debía tro-
carse en una insurrección de independencia em-
pezaba por una explosión de fidelidad al monarca.

Miguel Luis Amunátegui

Bello's Caracas poems show the success of a time-proven educational model. Under the guidance of Virgil and Horace, the
young poet develops themes venerated by an imperial power:
he talks about the countryside; he dwells on moral virtue; and
in the face of a grave crisis, he can dream about the mythic
season of abundance, the *alegre imagen del dorado siglo*" (the
happy image of the golden age; *OC*, 1: 17). But unlike Horace
and Virgil, Bello develops a poetic world that is virtually isolated from the risks and corruption of court life, as can be seen
in "Mis deseos," a free adaptation of Horace's satire "Hoc erat
in votis" that omits the contrast of court and country central to
the original:

> ¿Sabes, rubia, qué gracia solicito
> cuando de ofrendas cubro los altares?
> No ricos muebles, no soberbios lares,
> ni una mesa que adule al apetito.
>
> De Aragua a las orillas un distrito
> que me tribute fáciles manjares,
> do vecino a mis rústicos hogares
> entre peñascos corra un arroyito.
>
> (*OC*, 1: 7)

(Blonde girl, do you know what favors I ask
when I cover the altars with offerings? Neither
rich furniture nor a superb home, nor a table
that flatters my appetite. [I ask for] a region on
the borders of the Aragua valley, which honors
me with easy food, where next to my rustic
dwelling a small brook runs among large rocks.)

The emerging worldview is pastoral and peaceful: the young poet seeks in Aragua a region that will provide him with "*fáciles manjares*" (the Virgilian *facile victus* of book 3 of the *Georgics*) and with the shade of a palm tree. With the first words of Horace's satire as an epigraph, as a kind of inspiration, Bello proceeds to write a charming sonnet that dissolves the tensions of Horace's complex satire.

What most clearly separates the poems is their treatment of city life. For Horace, life in the city is unavoidable; there he goes pushing through the crowd to see his patron Maecenas and the silent "gods" of the court of Augustus. He runs into moneylenders and government bureaucrats, who urge him to carry out his scribal duties and who insult him, envious as they are of his privileged access to the rulers of Rome. Horace is trapped by the city, and the constant shifts in tone and perspective evoke urban agitation, not rural tranquillity.

The contrast between Augustan Rome and colonial Caracas is all too obvious. Instead of a city of 1 million people from many lands who speak many languages, one finds in Caracas a city of forty thousand prolonging a placid peace of three centuries. In Bello's sonnet there is no prevailing force pulling him away from his valley; the metropolis is absent, and the hustle and tension of city life are unknown. The "city" one found in the provinces of Venezuela was surrounded by luscious fields, and the fortunate few could enjoy the pleasures of town and country. This at least was the view of Bello, who wrote a motto for his friend Bolívar: "Ruris deliciis urbana adjuncta commoditas" (Urban comfort united to the pleasures of the countryside).[1]

In July 1808 the captaincy of Venezuela received an issue of the London *Times* that disrupted Bello's pastoral fantasies. The *Times* announced the abdication of Charles IV and of his son Ferdinand at Bayonne and the nomination of Joseph Bonaparte as emperor of Spain. Bello translated the articles and delivered them to Juan de Casas, the interim successor of the recently deceased Vasconcelos. De Casas called a meeting of prominent men of Caracas. The articles in the *Times*, these men agreed, were patent lies designed to stir the rebellion of Spanish Americans. Not even the copious documents of the resignation could convince them of the reports' authenticity. But two weeks later, on July 15, envoys from Joseph Bonaparte arrived and confirmed the news. The people of Caracas, after hearing about the events of Bayonne, rushed to praise their monarch. Ten thousand *caraqueños* gathered around the captaincy's palace shouting, "¡Viva Fernando VII! ¡Muera Napoleón!" Joseph's envoys were chased out of Venezuela by a band of fanatical royalists.[2]

The events of Bayonne and the ensuing Spanish uprising shattered the long-standing peace in the colonies. In Caracas the interim captain general, feeling the need to dissipate rumors, imported a printing press and began to publish the *Gazeta de Caracas*. As the *redactor* of the journal, Bello wrote articles that informed his compatriots about the Napoleonic Wars. A feeling of exhilaration filled the pages of the *Gazeta;* the crisis of the Bourbons was portrayed as the beginning of a new era in which Spaniards and Spanish Americans would have the same rights. Bello commented extensively on the call made by the junta of Seville to name delegates for the meeting of the Cortes at Cádiz; he also quoted from the prospectus of the journal *El Voto del Pueblo Español,* which called for freedom of the press. For the *Gazeta* Bello also translated documents published in journals from Great Britain and the British colonies. These journals arrived in Caracas as a result of the increasing contact and trade with the British Antilles and especially with Curaçao, which sent several commercial and diplomatic missions to different regions in Venezuela.[3]

In the years of crisis that surrounded the fall of the Bourbons, Bello continued attending the literary gatherings of the *mantuanos.* At the sumptuous banquets Bolívar organized after his return from Europe in 1807, Bello impressed the future warrior with his translation of the fifth book of the *Aeneid.* In another session the young poet read his translation of Voltaire's *Zulima.* According to Bello, Bolívar was an authority in literary matters and a devoted reader of Voltaire. But Bolívar was not pleased with Bello's choice of Voltaire's play about aborted rebellion and filial devotion, themes at odds with the mood of these gatherings. In truth, the *mantuanos'* neoclassic literary meetings were increasingly marked by the rhetoric of conspiracy. Side by side with Virgil and Horace were the works of the

French encyclopedists. And the conformity of pastoral verse began to give way to the angry, dry, disenchanted language of Tacitus. At these meetings Bello was in a delicate position. His employment in the captaincy general and at the *Gazeta* was a statement of support for the juntas of Spain, a statement that no *mantuano*, and no *caraqueño* of literary inclinations for that matter, would have wanted to make. Thus, when Bello became ill in February 1809, no one wanted to state his allegiance to the monarchy by replacing him as the *redactor* of the *Gazeta*. At Bolívar's gatherings Bello seems to have played mainly a literary role, avoiding political postures that would compromise his position in the captaincy general.

In 1808 the revolutionary aspirations of the youngest and most rebellious *mantuanos* had found both an opportunity and a new obstacle, as the events of Bayonne left the Spanish Crown vacant but also kindled the *caraqueños'* love for their monarch. Vicente Emparán, the new captain general, managed to hold the reins of power while the Spanish cause was still strong. But he was soon suspected by both Spaniards and Creoles of favoring the cause of Napoleon and, in the absence of news from Spain, opposition to Emparán became intense. On April 1, 1810, a group of *mantuanos* attempted to form a junta, but an officer, Diego Jalón, discovered the plot. When word reached Bello, he was left in a quandary about whether to inform his superior Emparán. To speak out might bring a strong reprisal against his friends and acquaintances, in addition to the shame of being instrumental in the denunciation. If he kept silent, he would become a coconspirator. Bello decided not to inform Emparán until April 5. His delay incited Emparán's fury, though it may well have tempered the reprisal: Simón Bolívar was sentenced to leave Caracas and to stay on a family farm.[4]

On April 17, two Spanish envoys arrived in Caracas with devastating news: except for Cádiz and the island of León, the Spanish peninsula was in the hands of Napoleon. They also brought a manifesto of the Regency, the conservative body acting in the name of Ferdinand VII, which promised a new era of liberty and representation in the Cortes. The manifesto, drafted by the poet Quintana, announced: "From this moment, Spanish Americans, you see yourselves elevated to the dignity of free men; you are no longer as you were before, bowed under a yoke made heavier the further you were from the center of power; looked upon with indifference; harassed by greed; and destroyed by ignorance."⁵ Quintana's rhetoric notwithstanding, in an attached decree the Regency curtailed freedom of trade and restricted the representation of the Creoles in the Spanish Cortes.

Two days later, on April 19, Emparán was overthrown and the people of Caracas formed the "supreme junta entrusted with preserving the rights of Ferdinand VII." This was an ambiguous revolution, motivated by the conservative fears of the old Creoles and the radical aspirations of the younger generation. The first declarations were a curious composite of moderate claims and loud condemnations. And it was left to Bello to create a language, and a logic, that would express this state of affairs. His response to the Regency is a daring document that voices the frustrations of the more radical Creoles – but it also satisfies the aspirations of conservatives to preserve the links with the Spanish monarchy. Bello writes that the *caraqueños* have abundantly shown their allegiance to the "beloved sovereign, Ferdinand VII." But this does not mean that they will be obedient to substitute institutions that have no legal foundation. Despite the initial encouragement of equality offered by the junta of Seville, Bello continues, Spanish Americans now see only signs of favoritism for the "unfortunate relics of Spain." The system devised by the Cortes for electing deputies is wholly inadequate because the elections are to be carried out by the *cabildos,* or local colonial assemblies, which are not representative of public opinion. For these and other reasons Bello asks, "Is it not clear that the liberty and fraternity that are cackled about are voices devoid of meaning, are illusory promises and, in a word, the banal artifice with which our infancy and our chains have been prolonged for three centuries?"

Caracas has deposed the representatives of the metropolis, Bello says, for two reasons: the Venezuelans can no longer relinquish their rights, and they are convinced that the captain general has sworn allegiance to the French government. Thus, he concludes, "In short, we do not recognize the new Council of the Regency; but if Spain is saved, we shall be the first to show allegiance to a government that is constituted on legitimate and fair foundations." The letter closes with an expression of support for the Spanish war against Napoleon (*OC*, 10: 411–18).[6]

At the outbreak of the Spanish American Revolution, one sees Bello stretching his rhetorical skills so as to absorb two essentially antithetical positions, legitimacy and rebellion. Ferdinand's absence from Spain allowed Bello to preserve the fiction that this was a temporary revolt and that the monarchy and the empire would be reconstituted in more equitable terms upon the return of the monarch. This fiction, or hope, sprang from the new idealism that Bello read in the journals of Cádiz and Seville and was apparent in the manifesto of the Regency.

It is remarkable that Quintana's manifesto and Bello's response – the two documents that set in motion the Spanish American Revolution – were written by two poets who were in perfect agreement. Both wanted a new empire based on the moderate implementation of the ideals of the age. If anything, Quintana was much more daring than Bello in demanding this change. In 1806 the Spanish poet had written a poem to celebrate the return of Balmis and the vaccine expedition in which he spoke to America as the innocent and virginal victim of Spanish rapacity. But Napoleon's invasion had so drastically changed the relationship between Spaniards and Spanish Americans that Quintana drafted the manifesto of the conservative Spanish Regency, while Bello, who only a few years before had such an exalted image of the Spanish monarch, was the first Spanish American to challenge openly the legitimacy of the Regency and deplore the rhetoric that camouflaged the old chains.

Uprisings similar to the ones in Caracas would follow in Buenos Aires, Santiago, and Bogotá. Claiming that the colonies owed allegiance to the Spanish Crown, and not to Spain, the people of Spanish America declared that, in the absence of the Spanish monarch, the colonies were free to sever political, administrative, and economic ties with the provisional governments of Spain. It is absurd to interpret the Caracas revolution, as Gil Fortoul does, as pure pantomime. Many older *mantuanos* and many Creoles, including Bello, sincerely believed in the oath of the junta: "to keep, fulfill, execute, and ensure that all and any orders of the Supreme Sovereign Authority of these provinces are kept, fulfilled, and executed, in the name of our King and Lord Ferdinand VII (may God protect him), unjustly held captive in the traitorous French nation. We shall uphold the rights of our country, our King, and our religion."[7] These lines expressed the sincere feelings of a large majority of Spanish Americans.

For the young *mantuanos*, however, this was formulaic language intended to appease the fears of the conservative members of the junta. Bolívar and his friends, inflamed by the rhetoric of the French Revolution, were determined to stop at nothing in order to attain the goals of independence and republicanism, which usually meant the same thing. Humboldt attributed this passion for freedom to Venezuela's geography; the combination of a long coastline and the protected nature of the sea of the Antilles favored legal and illegal trade. He was quick to add the political implications of this phenomenon: "Can we wonder, that this facility of commercial intercourse with the inhabitants of free America, and the agitated nations of Europe, should have augmented in conjunction, in the provinces united under the Capitania-General of Venezuela, opulence, knowledge, and that restless desire of a local government, which is blended with the love of liberty and republican forms?"[8]

With no Spanish support and with the imminent risk of a French invasion, Caracas was in need of an ally. The Caracas junta thus decided to send Simón Bolívar and Luis López Méndez on a diplomatic mission to London; their primary purpose was to seek the protection of Great Britain in case of French aggression. The two envoys requested that Andrés Bello be included in the mission, and on June 5, Juan Germán Roscio, the secretary of foreign affairs of the junta, approved the request. Since Roscio's response is all of this transaction that is on record, the reasons for the envoys' request is a matter of conjecture. However, it is safe to presume that Bello's duties in the captaincy general made him one of the very few *caraqueños* experienced in diplomacy. He had been active in the trade negotiations with Curaçao, and his correspondence illustrates that his English was at least adequate. The choice of Bello might also have been encouraged by Roscio himself or by other moderate members of the junta. It is noteworthy that the foreign secretary of the junta confided in Bello more than in Bolívar and López Méndez. Indeed, the letters of Roscio to Bello – first published by Amunátegui – are among the most comprehensive documents of the events in Caracas between 1810 and 1812. On June 9, 1810, the envoys embarked on the *Wellington* at La Guaira; Bello had had only a few days to prepare for his trip, and he spent his time gathering documents of the captaincy that could be useful for the diplomatic mission.[9]

Shortly after Bello left Caracas, the *Gazeta* announced the imminent publication of the *Calendario manual y guía universal de forasteros en Venezuela para el año 1810*. As Juan Vicente González and, more recently, Pedro Grases have shown, the document's summary of Venezuela's history, the *Resumen de la historia de Venezuela*, that filled forty of the sixty pages of the *Calendario*, was written by Bello, probably between 1809 and the first months of 1810. In the *Resumen* Bello outlined his intellectual and political affinities: an enlightened monarchy and expansion of the free-trade legislation that had marked the reign of Charles III.

Far from seeing the events since 1808 as a step toward the independence of the colonies, Bello's *Resumen* interpreted the popular revolts throughout the empire as proof of the indissoluble bonds between Spain and Spanish America. The *Resumen* is at a basic level a favorable account of the progress of Spanish intervention in Venezuela, from the hardships of the conquest to the present unity of the empire in its struggle against Napoleon:

Three centuries of unshakable loyalty on all occasions should no doubt suffice to prove the reciprocal ties that would make each hemisphere inseparable from the other. But circumstances allowed Venezuela the satisfaction of being the first country of the New World where the vow of eternal hatred was sworn spontaneously and unanimously against the Tyrant who sought to break such close links. Venezuela gave the definitive and most relevant proof of the inhabitants' conviction that their happiness and tranquility depended on maintaining relations to which all America owes her preservation and growth for so many centuries. The date July 15, 1808, will complete the circular seal of Venezuela and will always recall the pure patriotism with which, as an act of eternal condemnation of treachery, she vowed to the Crown of Castile that this precious piece of her patrimony would be preserved whole, faithful, and peaceful.[10]

Alongside this expression of support for the Spanish revolt against the Napoleonic invasion, the *Resumen* states that this support has to be matched by a reevaluation of the role of the colonies in the empire. The essential message is that freedom of trade, not only with all the points of the empire but with friendly nations as well, has become imperative. Comparing Venezuela at the end of the eighteenth century to a child reaching maturity, Bello argues that the monopolistic control of trade imposed during Venezuela's childhood is no longer appropriate.

In his preface to Bello's historical works (*OC*, 19) Mariano Picón Salas has examined the georgic strain of the *Resumen*. Although the richer centers of Spanish American colonial courtly life were based on a mining economy, he says that in the *Resumen* Bello displays his conviction that agriculture has been and should continue to be the essence of Venezuela. Picón Salas asks the reader to perceive in the *Resumen* the Virgilian laboriousness and moderation of the countryside. Yet, according to Bello, one should distinguish two stages in Venezuela's agricultural life. The first stage, from 1722 to 1788, was marked by the progress achieved under the protection of the Compañía Guipuzcoana; at this time Basques and *canarios* brought new vigor to the "delightful valleys of Aragua" and increased the population and wealth of the region: "From la Victoria to Valencia there was only one scene to be found, that of happiness and abundance; and the traveler found himself charmed by the pleasures of country life and was welcomed everywhere with the warmest hospitality." With the end of the Compañía Guipuzcoana's monopoly in 1788, Venezuela's "infancy" ended, and Bello severely criticizes the monopolists' attempts to hinder Venezuela's natural development. In light of the subsequent struggle of the Creoles to break down the trade barriers maintained or imposed by Spanish authorities, Bello wishes to recover the spirit of the last year of Charles III, when Venezuela considerably expanded its trade: "The year 1788 will always be etched in the annals that celebrate the political regeneration of Venezuela, and it shall always be inseparably linked with the memory of the Monarch and the Minister who, with an august munificence, broke down the barriers that opposed progress" (*OC*, 23: 51).

Thus, we may amend Picón Salas's reading of the *Resumen* to observe how Bello adapts Venezuelan reality to the Virgilian model. The stage of Venezuela's infancy corresponds to the closed economy and pure customs of the old agricultural times, drawn from the end of book 2 of the *Georgics*. This is a simple, morally uncorrupt world, very distant from city life. It does not exist during the golden age, but it corresponds to the regions visited by Astrea before she abandoned the world. Next comes what might be called the adolescence of Venezuela, to preserve Bello's analogy, marked by an avid desire to know and trade with the world. There is no classical parallel to this stage – for Virgil and Horace, as Bello well knew, considered navigation inherently dangerous, a product of human greed. The Virgilian parallel returns when Bello invokes the monarch and preserves virtually intact the structure of the *Georgics:* the writer praises the minister and the monarch for their interest in agriculture.[11]

In the *Resumen* Bello preserves the Augustan model used in "Oda a la vacuna," but a significant change has occurred. In the "Oda a la vacuna" the names of Charles IV, Luisa, and even Godoy are mentioned, but in the *Resumen* no living member of the Spanish royal family is named, and the only monarch recalled with admiration is Charles III. Here the court of Spain is ruled by a lofty monarch advised by an unnamed minister who sometimes allows the "*clamores*" of the people to reach the king. The system of power described in the *Resumen* preserves the Augustanism of the "Oda a la vacuna," but it has been considerably stripped of its flattery. It is as if Bello sought to neutralize flattery by relegating the royal epithet to the philanthropic designs of the institution of monarchy.

On the eve of the Spanish American Revolution, Bello stood as a man of the late Enlightenment. He calls for freedom of trade in his poems, his memoranda, and his *Resumen*. But in poetry and in politics the stronghold of the Augustan model still prevails, and Horace and Virgil remain the sources of inspiration. (Three of the six extant poems dating from Bello's Caracas period are adaptations, imitations, or translations of these Latin poets.) Though tempered by hopes of greater participation by the colonies in imperial politics, his political ideas are Augustan. Along with Jovellanos, Bello could dispense with the excessive adulation that had characterized the last years of Charles IV's reign, but his faith in the preeminence of Rome's political model remained unshaken. In short, the Bello who left Caracas was still a neoclassical poet and a monarchist.

Bello had adopted neither the dark, guilty voice of Tacitus nor the rebellious language of Voltaire's better plays. But he had read them and had decided that the Virgilian source had to be stripped of the apotheosis of the monarch; there would be no more incense and heavenly thrones in Bello's own work. That he learned these lessons at such a late date he could blame on the excessive protection under which Spain had protracted the infancy of the colonies.

In conversations with his biographer, Miguel Luis Amunátegui, Bello looked back in detail at the events that launched the Spanish American Independence and gave special significance to one date: July 15, 1808, the day when the people of Caracas proclaimed their loud support for Ferdinand and their hatred for Napoleon. Bello saw himself as part of the groundswell of revolt against French tyranny. But as Napoleon scored new victories and as the different local governments that represented Ferdinand lost legitimacy and increased their arrogance toward the colonies, Bello expressed the sharp discontent felt by all Creoles. From July 15, 1808, to the formation of the junta on April 19, 1810, Venezuelans repeatedly and explicitly declared their allegiance to the Spanish monarch. But within the moderate claims of the Caracas junta, the voice of the young *mantuanos* was loud. They would soon become the leaders of public opinion and be the first Spanish Americans to declare formal independence from Spain. As Bello and Bolívar crossed the Atlantic, they had diverging dreams: one wished to reform the Spanish Empire, the other to liberate the New World. Everything conspired in Bolívar's favor. He had the elegance, the tenacity, the rhetoric. His was the winning cause.

PART II

London (1810–1829)

3

Independence

Bello, el que lo supo todo, Virgilio sin Augusto y pintor de nuestra zona.

Cecilio Acosta

When the members of the Venezuelan mission reached England, they found a British intelligentsia divided into two factions, those who supported Spanish American independence and those who thought its time had not yet come. The undisputed leader of the independentist cause was Francisco de Miranda, whose dream was to liberate the continent and give it the name of Colombia. Known as the "Precursor" of the Spanish American Revolution, Miranda had left Venezuela in the 1770s and fought in the North American and French revolutions. With a small fund provided by the British government, he made two unsuccessful attempts in 1806 to liberate the Spanish possessions in America. After the failed expedition, he had come into the London limelight as a radical, some thought Jacobin, advocate of Spanish American independence. His association with James Mill and Jeremy Bentham contributed to this reputation.

In 1809 Mill, with Miranda's supervision, published "Emancipation of Spanish America" in the *Edinburgh Review*. The main purpose of the article was to press for British support for Miranda's cause and to present a plan intended to disassociate Miranda from French radicalism. The occasion of the article was a review of Viscardo's *Lettres aux Espagnols Américains*, the famous pamphlet written by an exiled Jesuit that called for the emancipation of the colonies. Mill quickly gets to the main argument. Spain, he says, is irredeemably lost to Napoleon, and Great Britain must assist the people of Spanish America in their unanimous desire for independence. He then presents a vision of instant freedom and happiness, of vast advancement in world trade and communication that will be brought about by the creation of a canal joining the Pacific and Atlantic oceans. After sketching Miranda's first projects of emancipation, Mill presents evidence of the general's moderation, such as his repeated warning against adopting French principles that would jeopardize freedom.

According to Mill, the present state of affairs has made Spanish American emancipation inevitable. The fate of Spain is sealed; it is in the hands of Napoleon. The only question remaining for Britain is whether it will take Spanish America for itself or give it to Bonaparte; whether Spanish America will become free under the auspices of British protection or will become enslaved to the French monarchy. Having established the inevitability of Spanish American independence, Mill goes on to discuss the manner in which it is to be effected. The constitution Mill proposes for Spanish America, inspired by the ideas of Miranda and Bentham, will require a minimum of change in existing institutions. The *cabildos* are seen as the main vehicle for the rise of representative government. Yet despite the great admiration Spanish Americans show for republican forms, Mill believes that they should not follow the example of the United States, but should instead form a great monarchy, headed by a king, a consul, or an Inca, the term preferred by Miranda.[1]

A second group of intellectuals opposed the "inevitability" argument made by Mill and Miranda. They did not completely reject the idea of independence, but they thought the time for such a drastic change had not yet come. Led by Lord Holland, a member of the Whig party who had strong links with Jovellanos, this group was interested primarily in the regeneration of Spain, not in the disintegration of the Spanish Empire. The principal members of this group were Lord Holland's factotum, Dr. John Allen, who had accompanied him on prolonged visits to Spain, and José Blanco White, a Spanish defrocked priest who, disappointed with the Cortes, had abandoned fatherland and religion, settled in London, and would soon embrace the Church of England. In 1810, with the financial support of the British government but guided by the ideas of Lord Holland, Blanco White started publishing his journal *El Español,* in which he promoted the principles of free trade and political moderation, and warned against constitutions that were not based on experience.[2]

Dr. John Allen answered Mill in the April 1810 issue of the *Edinburgh Review.* Allen's article was a review of Alexander von Humboldt's *Essai politique sur le Royaume de la Nouvelle Espagne,* a book that presented to the European public a complex view of the richest colonial center, where the free-trade ideals of the Enlightenment were in tension with colonial trade monopolies. Allen discusses at length the deleterious effects of protectionism and government intervention in the economic affairs of New Spain. A further obstacle to prosperity, he explains, is Spanish America's caste system, and he predicts that the tensions among different castes are likely to increase, rather than diminish, if the colonies become independent. He also warns against ambitious men (i.e., Miranda) who seek independence for their own glory.

Allen's article was translated by Blanco White in the fourth volume of *El Español,* published in July 1810. In that issue he also celebrates the moderate nature of the Caracas junta and vehemently criticizes the Spanish Cortes for shortsightedness. Unless the Cortes accept the formation of Spanish American juntas and justify them as spontaneous manifestations of allegiance to Ferdinand, parallel to those of Cádiz or Seville, and unless the Cortes abolish the heavy protectionist burden on the colonies' trade, Blanco White warns, the rift between Spain and the American colonies will be permanent.

Addressing the more vehemently anti-Spanish American members of the Cortes, Blanco White asks that they consider the likely results of a civil war: wouldn't a war only exacerbate the pressing social and economic problems of the present? But although he acknowledges that independence is a natural desire for a continent so distant from the center of power and one that is amassing so much wealth, he argues against complete independence of the colonies *at the present time.* For him, the paramount issue is Spain and its independence from Napoleon, and an independent Spanish America would leave Spain without resources at a time of utmost need.[3]

Bolívar's mission arrived in Liverpool on July 10 and soon moved on to London. The Venezuelans immediately arranged for a meeting with Lord Wellesley, the foreign secretary, who received the envoys at his private residence (Apsley House) on July 16. There are two versions of this meeting. In one version, told by Amunátegui, Bolívar presented to Lord Wellesley not only the credentials but also the instructions given by the Caracas junta to the envoys. And then, in perfect French, he gave an eloquent speech on his people's hopes and desires for complete emancipation from Spain. After Bolívar had finished, Wellesley noted that the presentation contradicted the instructions of the Caracas junta. For the junta, which was governing Venezuela as the representative of Ferdinand VII, had instructed the envoys to seek Britain's mediation in order to avoid a rupture with the Spanish government. Bolívar could not respond to Wellesley's consternation. According to Amunátegui, he had gone to the meeting without much preparation and afterward told Bello how sorry he was not to have read the instructions that had been written with so much wisdom and penetration.

The second version of the meeting appears in the minutes taken by Bello. According to this source, Lord Wellesley first pointed out that the junta of Caracas had erroneously assumed that Spain was irredeemably lost to Napoleon. Given the present improvement of the Spanish cause, he wished to know whether the events of April 19 were a response to some specific dissatisfaction with the metropolis or, in effect, a declaration of independence. Bolívar gave a summary of the main events since July 1808, stating that the junta was created in order to wrest power from the Spanish authorities who had openly revealed their affection for the Bonapartes; he concluded with a declaration of the Regency's illegitimacy. Wellesley was quick to interpret Bolívar's response as an admission of Venezuela's independence and said that such an act threatened the integrity of the Spanish Empire and was against Britain's own interests. Bolívar replied that Venezuela would continue assisting the Spaniards, and as proof of this, he handed Wellesley his credentials and instructions. As he read, the foreign secretary observed that Venezuela was not satisfied with its representation in the Cortes and that the envoys were required to act in agreement with the laws of the monarchy. Bolívar did not respond to these charges, and after a brief intervention by López Méndez, the discussion resumed. Wellesley now strongly urged a recognition of the Regency and offered Britain's assistance in bringing about changes in the composition of the Cortes. But the envoys rejected these proposals. More arguments were given by both sides, but the positions had been established; there was to be no agreement on the central issue, the recognition of the Regency.

Venezuelan scholars have objected to Amunátegui's version of the meeting as a fabrication, and Pedro Grases has advanced the notion that this version contradicts Bello's minutes of the meeting. Bello's minutes do offer a more complete description of the discussion, but the two versions are, in essence, compatible: both show Bolívar defending a course of action that is interpreted by Wellesley as equivalent to a declaration of independence; both show Wellesley stressing the contradictions between Bolívar's words and the instructions of the Caracas junta; and, finally, both stress Bolívar's inability to respond to these charges. These coincidences are not surprising. Both versions were derived, after all, from one source: Bello.[4]

To save the mission from disaster, Bello harnessed all his rhetorical and diplomatic abilities. Realizing that the British government could only accept language that in some way supported the integrity of the Spanish Empire, he drafted a memorandum that insisted on the junta's allegiance to Ferdinand VII: "The solemn declarations of that government include . . . the assurance that Venezuela, far from aspiring to break the ties that have brought her close to the metropolis, has only wanted to take the steps necessary for the protection from the dangers that threatened her. Although she is free from the Council of Regency, she is no less faithful to her monarch nor less interested in the success of Spain's holy war."[5]

While the negotiations followed their course, the Venezuelans were in the London limelight, under the escort of Miranda. The envoys had been warned that their countryman's opinions contravened the monarchic principles that the Caracas junta was defending, but on July 19 Miranda received the envoys at his home on Grafton Street. As his guests, they began visiting members of the British nobility and the intelligentsia. Richard Wellesley, the son of the foreign secretary, saw them frequently; they visited Hampton Court, the Greenwich Observatory, and the Kew Botanical Gardens; they met the duke of Gloucester, the educator Lancaster, and the philanthropist Wilberforce.[6]

At the end of August the envoys learned that the Regency had ordered a naval blockade of Venezuela. Bolívar, believing that his presence was more valuable in Caracas, left on September 16 on a British military ship to prepare the way for the arrival of Miranda, who embarked a month later on a civilian boat (OC, 25: 28). When Miranda reached Caracas, there was already considerable agitation. The Gazeta had started publishing on November 23 a series of articles by William Burke, an Irishman with close links to Miranda who had left for Caracas from New York as soon as he heard about the creation of the junta. Under the title Derechos de la América del Sur y de México, Burke published more than fifteen articles that proclaimed freedom of trade, democracy, religious tolerance, and independence.[7] Burke's ideas were influential in the Sociedad Patriótica, a forum for the more ardent Creoles. Originally formed in August 1810 as the Sociedad Patriótica de Agricultura y Economía, this institution was taken over by the partisans of full emancipation from Spain. Miranda and Bolívar became leaders in these nightly meetings, whose mixed audiences scandalized many caraqueños: not only all the castes but also women were allowed to participate. The style and rhetoric were copied from the clubs of the French Revolution.

Both in the newly formed Congress and in the Sociedad Patriótica, the momentum for independence increased throughout the first half of 1811. Much of the debate centered on the appropriate form of government: Miranda presented a plan by which two Incas would be elected every ten years; Roscio, the foreign secretary of the junta and Bello's friend, refused to consider such ideas. Some members were fearful of breaking with Spain and insisted on preserving the oath of April 19; others, already excited by the prospect of revolution, praised anarchy.

A substantial majority in Congress favored the United States model, and as July 4 approached the suggestion was made that the Venezuelans declare their independence on the same day as their "Anglo-Saxon brothers." But there were still doubts: Should they not first form a confederation and then declare independence? And what about the provinces of Coro, Maracaibo, and Guayana, which had not recognized the junta and the Congress? Would they not be further estranged once independence was declared? Would the United States and Great Britain recognize the sovereignty of Venezuela? Would the people, accustomed to a monarch sanctioned by God, accept a federal republic? Such questions were asked and discussed in Congress, and the fears of change were not totally dispelled by Miranda. But in the Sociedad Patriótica patience had run out, as is evident in the eloquent speech Simón Bolívar gave on July 3, which closed with these words: "The patriotic junta respects, as it must, the national Congress, but the Congress must listen to the patriotic junta, the focus of all revolutionary interests. Let us lay without fear the cornerstone of South American freedom. To waver is to be lost!" A delegation of the Sociedad Patriótica visited Congress on July 4, and on July 5, 1811, Venezuela became the first Spanish American nation to declare its complete independence from Spain.[8]

Meanwhile, Bello and López Méndez were living in Miranda's house, which had become the London headquarters of Spanish American emancipation. This house was also the center of a Masonic lodge called Logia Lautaro – sometimes known as Gran Reunión Americana or Sociedad de Caballeros Racionales – whose primary purpose was to promote the struggle against the Spanish despots. Late in 1811 a ship carrying a mail pouch from Bello and López Méndez was intercepted by the royalist forces. Therein was a document which shows that both men were part of the Sociedad de Caballeros Racionales. Probably as a result of these political-Masonic activities, Bello met the future liberator of Argentina and Chile, José de San Martín.[9]

Bello spent many hours reading the books in Miranda's library, a collection of nearly six thousand volumes. The collection was very rich in Roman classics; it included more than thirty volumes of Cicero, several editions of Julius Caesar's *Gallic Wars,* and Tacitus's *Opera,* accompanied by English, Spanish, French, and Italian translations of his works; there were three different editions of Lucretius, five of Horace, and seven of Virgil. The library also contained all the major modern British authors, including Bacon, Hobbes, Milton, Locke, Dryden,

Pope, Hume, Gibbon, Adam Smith (in a Spanish version published in Valladolid in 1794), and Bentham. The complete works of the philosophes were also there: seventy volumes of Voltaire, thirty-five of Rousseau, and twenty-three of Condillac. The many volumes of Spanish literature included Tomás Antonio Sánchez's *Colección de poesías castellanas anteriores al siglo XV*, a work that, according to Pedro Grases, Bello began consulting soon after his arrival in London and that became the starting point of his philological reconstruction of the *Cid*. Miranda also had more than two hundred volumes of classical Greek literature. Bello, observing that all educated Londoners had access to this literature in the original language, decided to teach himself Greek. An extant edition of Aeschylus, with Bello's copious annotations in Latin, attests to his success.[10]

The duchess of Abrantes once heard Napoleon say that Miranda had a sacred fire in his soul. And she added that Miranda's face brightened as soon as he began to speak, which he did with inconceivable rapidity.[11] Bello also succumbed to Miranda's charm; there is little doubt that the general's energetic personality and culture were responsible for Bello's moderately radical position. In the letter to the Caracas junta in support of Miranda's return, Bello concludes his most impassioned paragraph: "How diligently we have seen him helping us with his intelligence, with his books, with his faculties, with his connections!" (*OC*, 11: 66).[12]

Despite his affinity for Miranda, Bello stepped out of his circle and soon after his arrival in London became a close friend of Blanco White, who was swiftly becoming the leading spokesman of the Holland group in Spanish American affairs. Amunátegui tells us that by January 1811 the two writers were already in contact and in agreement on political matters, which later extended to literary matters as well.[13] *El Español* began to publish regular accounts and commentaries about events in Caracas, and since several of these articles bear the trace of someone who has firsthand knowledge of the events and issues under discussion, it is very possible that Bello helped Blanco White in his publishing venture.[14] In any event, the articles of *El Español* that deal with Caracas show a view of the independence process that is virtually identical to the one stamped in Bello's poetry of 1811–12.

The core of *El Español*'s position is that Spanish Americans are mistaken if they declare their independence and adopt the model of the United States: "A declaration of absolute independence could compromise the nascent happiness of southern America. The example set by the United States is not suitable to her circumstances." The United States, the article continues, was formed by people of different origins who were unified in their hatred of European domination; these people had first crossed the ocean in order to find independence. This is not the case of Spanish America, which is full of rich and powerful Europeans, full of employees of the Spanish bureaucracy who expect raises and promotions, full of people who are passionately attached to regular employment because they have no knowledge of industry, full of men who "motivated by passion and pride will destroy everything before paying attention even to the word *independence*." *El Español* goes on to state that the United States had the support of France and Spain, whereas Spanish America cannot rely on a European ally at the present moment. The existing degree of freedom in the United States at the time of its independence is another point of contrast with Spanish America. Before the American Revolution there was a well-developed internal government that did not depend on the central government except for matters of war and peace. Not so with Spanish America, which has not yet passed the novitiate of freedom. *El Español* warns the colonies not to accelerate the natural political process: "Liberty is a fragile plant that weakens and perishes when it is forced to produce fruit too early."[15]

While Blanco White sat writing these words on July 11, 1811, he was unaware that independence was no longer a project but a reality. As he intimated in his article, the proclamation of independence soon led to violence. On that same July 11 a large group of *canarios* staged a mutiny on the outskirts of Caracas to protest Venezuela's independence. They were immediately apprehended, and seventeen men were put to death. Roscio wrote to Bello about both the declaration of independence and the ensuing bloodshed, which he justified as the necessary price for the consolidation of the new freedom. The divisions between royalists and patriots were so sharp, Roscio wrote, that only Miranda seemed to have the necessary expertise to consolidate independence.

The news from Caracas confirmed Great Britain's worst apprehension, that a new French-style revolution was under way. Lord Holland's group had already told Blanco in October 1810 that the colonies must be warned against Miranda's project to form independent republics. And Holland's confederates were quick to attack the new course of events. In November 1811 John Allen published a continuation of his review of Humboldt in the *Edinburgh Review*. There he condemned Venezuela's independence and attacked Miranda for having destroyed with his Jacobin principles the first junta of Caracas. He proposed a flexible system of government with completely free trade and independent legislative bodies in each country of Spanish America.[16]

James Mill, disturbed by the bad press directed at his friend Miranda, wrote to Bello at the end of 1811 urging him to write an article in the *Morning Chronicle* that would contradict the accounts of the Caracas killings. Bello took no action, and a second letter followed: "I would earnestly recommend it to you to have the story effectually contradicted." But Bello could not contradict what he knew was true. There had been bloodshed, Roscio had told him (*OC*, 25: 40).

After the declaration of independence, the Venezuelans began to work on their constitution. The legislators responsible for drafting the document were all very close to Bello: Francisco Isnardy, with whom Bello had planned to publish the journal *El Lucero;* Francisco Javier Ustáriz, the elder brother of Ignacio; and Juan Germán Roscio. The constitution called for the establishment of a federal republic closely patterned on the United States model, though it also included long passages of political philosophy drawn from French thinkers. In Congress, Miranda strongly opposed the project, as did Bolívar in the Sociedad Patriótica. Both men favored a centralized government. Despite their objections, the constitution was ratified in December 1811. Miranda argued that the constitution "is not in agreement with the population, the habits and customs of these countries" and warned that the federalist experiment would cause division and threaten independence.[17]

The Constitution of Venezuela was sent to London, and in 1812 Bello published it along with a collection of documents of the first republic. Included in the volume are some "Preliminary Remarks," which have been attributed to Bello by Carlos Pi

Sunyer.[18] All the documents appear in Spanish and English, and the finely bound book was given a bilingual title: *Documentos interesantes relativos a Caracas / Interesting Documents Relating to Caracas*. In his remarks Bello attempts to justify the establishment of an independent republic, but he also subtly points to a possible reconciliation between Spain and Spanish America.

He begins by stating the great significance of the present world crisis: "Old and entire empires have been dissolved, and have lost their political being, whilst new ones have sprung up out of their ashes." In defense of the 1811 declaration of independence Bello presents four arguments: (1) Spanish Americans have not had adequate representation in government. (2) Spanish colonial legislation has favored the creation of trade monopolies that affect the very foundations of Spanish American society. (3) The demands of the American representatives at the courts of Cádiz have been met with the indifference of the Spanish government. (4) According to Locke, legitimate government is derived from the consensus of the people; if the acting authority is not benefiting the common good, the people can assume power.

Yet Bello also presents ideas that lead the reader to understand that things could have been, and even still might be, different. He laments that the Spanish government has been deaf to "the just cries and appeals of a well-deserving moiety of the nation" (or in the Spanish version, "una parte benemérita de la Monarquía"). Then Bello suggests a hope, however faint, of reconciliation: "There was wanting a healing and cementing principle of benevolence, nor is there *up to the present day,* a proper measure of redress or of conciliation, on record [my emphasis]." Here there is no sense of an irrevocable breach, no echoes of the ardent rhetoric of William Burke or the Sociedad Patriótica. The tone is one of a great loss. Bello refers the reader to a manifesto included in *Interesting Documents* for an appreciation of the declaration of Venezuela's independence as a measure of last resort: "Imperious causes have compelled her to this step, to this last alternative." Later, somewhat enigmatically, Bello recalls Montesquieu's statement that nations can be saved only by the restoration of lost principles. Venezuela, Bello says, has elected its representatives "in order to get out of the orphan state in which they were plunged." By this logic, the

Venezuelan republic serves only to restore the principles lost with the fall of the Spanish monarchy.

In sum, the "Preliminary Remarks" represent Bello's almost desperate attempt to reconcile two contradictory positions: the skepticism of Blanco White and the emancipatory rhetoric of Miranda. In the end, however, he chooses the road of independence:

A sense of common interests, and the general effect of patriotic feeling has produced the change, has called forth the energies of the people; and he must be callous to the glowings of humanity who can contemplate without pleasure, this great effusion of enlightened patriotic spirit, which already gleams from one extreme to the other of the Columbian continent, and irradiates a people, heretofore buried in the deepest gloom.

Bello closes his remarks by asking Britain for support. He believes this course is both a duty and an opportunity for Britain to expand its market for manufactured goods.[19]

An examination of the few existing prose documents from Bello's first London years reveals a man deeply attracted to Miranda's personality but fearful of the consequences of complete independence. Though Bello's "Preliminary Remarks" defend the independent republic of Venezuela, the word *republic* never appears. Unlike Blanco White, Bello could sometimes share the excitement of Miranda's cause, but his enthusiasm was colored by deep apprehensions. More than anything, Bello saw himself as someone outside the process who could dispassionately give advice and direction, as someone willing to explore the underlying conflicts of the Spanish American crisis. To appreciate his position more fully, we must turn to the poetic documents from Bello's early London years.

On the first page of his poetic manuscripts (sheet 2), most likely written in 1811, Bello addresses a central question about independence: what is the appropriate form of government for the new country?[20] Using the commonplace trope of the legislator as a farmer who tends the delicate plant of freedom, Bello repeats the advice given to the new lawmakers in *El Español:* do not imitate blindly the example of the United States; seek instead the peculiar traits of Venezuelans, their traditions and customs. Like a prudent farmer, each legislator must become

an expert on the climate and topography of his particular par-
cel of land:

> Tú que pides al suelo ora materias
> en que se ocupe artífice ingenioso,
> ora sustancias que a los hombres nutran,
> antes que todo observa del terreno
> el clima y temple: si abrigado yace
> en un valle profundo, o si la espalda
> de un monte ocupa; si colinas breves
> acá y allá se elevan con suave
> ascenso, o de una plana superficie
> se ofrece la apariencia, do en invierno
> hacen mansión las aguas e inficionan
> con vapores morbíficos el aire;
> cómo reciba de la luz dorada
> la vital influencia, y a cuál punto
> mire del orbe etéreo; si se cruzan
> sobre su faz arroyos cristalinos,
> o si sediento en el verano invoca
> las aguas de los cielos; y cuál sea
> de antiguos labradores la costumbre,
> y qué nativas plantas alimente.   (OC, 2: 3–4)

(You who look to the soil for the theme of the
ingenious artificer or for the substances that
may nourish men, first examine the climate and
the atmospheric conditions of the terrain;
whether it lies protected in a deep valley, or it
occupies the backside of a mountain; whether
small hills rise softly here and there or a plain
appears, where during winter the waters gather
and pollute the air with sickening vapors.
[Examine] how the terrain can receive the vital
influence of the golden light, and at what point
of the ethereal orb does it gaze; whether the
crystalline brooks cross each other on its surface, or whether in summer, thirsty, it calls for
the waters of the skies, and [examine] what
might be the customs of the peasants of old and
which native plants it nourishes.)

The idea that the political forms of government must be
derived from a country's particular culture and history is, of
course, a commonplace of the Enlightenment, a stock concept
known to any reader of Montesquieu. Here Bello casts that

thought in a close imitation of Virgil's *Georgics,* a text whose traces we noted earlier in the "Oda a la vacuna" and the *Resumen de la historia de Venezuela.* But whereas Virgil begins his poem with an elaborate address to Maecenas and Caesar (ll. 1– 42) before describing the farmer's attention to the condition of the terrain, Bello simply omits the address to the leaders and offers a version of Virgil's lines 50 to 53:

> ac prius ignotum ferro quam scindimus aequor,
> ventos et varium caeli praediscere morem
> cura sit ac patrios cultusque habitusque locorum,
> et quid quaeque ferat regio et quid quaeque
>   recuset.

> (But before we break up the untried surface with the plow, it is important to forecast the winds and the changing moods of the sky and learn about the ancestral modes of cultivation and the conditions of places, and also about what each region produces and each does not.)

Like Virgil, Bello addresses the farmer in a strongly didactic tone and in the second person: the farmer is the recipient of the poet's knowledge. But whereas Virgil has dedicated his poem to Maecenas and lavishly offered Caesar a place among the stars, Bello skips over the dedication to the patron and the deification of the ruler. His poem instead opens with a simple "*Tú,*" an address to the farmer-legislator-reader who is considering the conditions of the soil and the customs of the land.

In a second passage on sheet 2, Bello draws on the *Laus Italiae* of book 2 of the *Georgics,* a passage in praise of the natural beauty of Italy, and again omits mention of an Augustus. In this instance Bello follows the example of the British Augustans, who praised their own land instead of Italy, and he begins to sing the beauties of the torrid zone. In this manuscript, probably written in 1811, we find for the first time the expressions "*tórrida zona,*" "*americana,*" and "*colombiano*":

> En las húmedas vegas
> [illegible] crece de la tórrida zona,
> tiñe de negra púrpura el cacao
> sus cóncavas mazorcas.
> Allí sus blancas flores el arbusto
> de Arabia desenvuelve; allí sus hojas
> el plátano lustroso; allí su tallo

nectáreo erige la otaytina caña;
ni el trigo americano sus espigas
ve malograr, ni el algodón sus copas.
Mas el dorado trigo, y el cambure
de africana extracción, y los frutales
que debe a Europa el suelo colombiano
menos ardiente habitación reclaman.[21]

([It] grows in the damp riverbanks of the torrid zone; the cacao darkens its concave beans with black purple. There the shrub of Arabia unfolds its white flowers, there the shining banana tree raises its leaves and the sugarcane its nectar-filled stem; neither the American wheat sees its ears spoiled, nor cotton its fruits. But the golden wheat and the *cambure* of African origin and the fruit trees which the Colombian soil owes to Europe require a less ardent dwelling.)

In this fragment the terms "torrid zone," "American," and "Colombian" are both linked and differentiated. The torrid zone comprises all those areas around the globe that lie between the two temperate zones. Though Bello attempts to include other regions of the torrid zone, like Arabia, he is chiefly describing the land and the flora he knows best, those of Venezuela. "American" is here used mainly to distinguish the American wheat, which is originally from Mexico and can be grown in the torrid zone, from the European wheat, which needs milder climates. Finally, "Colombian" is here used generically, as the land of Columbus, but it inevitably brings to mind the term favored by Miranda to describe independent Spanish America. Bello's use of the term connotes his allegiance to an independent "Colombia," but one that – at least in Miranda's plans – should closely follow the existing political customs and not be at war with its colonizers. As Bello acknowledges, a "debt" is owed to Europe by the Colombian land. If independence was to be the road, then Miranda's constitutional plans should be preferred to the United States model.

Virgil majestically closes his praise of Italy with the praise of the Decii, the Marii, the Camilli, the Scipios, and finally Augustus Caesar ("*et te, maxime Caesar*," 2.170), whom he extols for being victorious on the shores of Asia and for keeping the Indians off the citadels of Rome (2.171–2). In Bello's fragment, however, no names are mentioned. The allusions to the greatness of Spanish America, and even to its independence, are not attributed to any leader.

Bello's first London poems exemplify the same density of political allusion that was already present in the "Oda a la vacuna." But in that youthful poem, the Virgilian model could easily be filled with a divine monarch; now the Virgilian model is called upon to denote the absence of that monarch – for the first two books of the *Georgics* were more than sources or inspirations for Bello's poems. Virgil's words, metaphors, and ideas became the raw material from which the Venezuelan poet tried to shape his political and aesthetic thinking. Other poets before Bello had used the Roman model for their poetic ventures; indeed, since the time of Quintilian the study of Virgil had been so narrowly equated with the process of education itself that a poet was expected to follow the *Eclogues* or the *Georgics* or the *Aeneid*. What is peculiar to Bello is his attempt to preserve the Virgilian model at a time when all the aesthetic and political qualities that had become associated with it over eighteen centuries were crumbling before his eyes.

4

The reconquest

¡Dios, qué buen vasallo, si oviese buen señor!
El Poema de Mío Cid

The first republic of Venezuela did not last long. The threats of the Regency and the verbal attacks by the Spanish authorities in Puerto Rico turned to action in March 1812, as General Domingo Monteverde disembarked in Coro and advanced toward Caracas. Though the Spanish forces were small, fewer than five hundred men, an accident of nature would assist their cause. On March 26, while most *caraqueños* were attending the mass of Holy Thursday, an earthquake rumbled for more than one minute and laid low many of the city's buildings and churches, leaving many worshipers buried under the rubble. Royalist priests seized the occasion to mobilize the people to the cause of the Crown. The earthquake was a divine punishment inflicted on the people of Venezuela, they preached; the *caraqueños* had first moved away from Spanish authority on Holy Thursday, 1810, so on Holy Thursday, 1812, God punished their faithlessness. These arguments were persuasive to a people stunned by terror, but the royalist message moved the patriots to rage. Bolívar mounted the ruins of a church and addressed these words to the monarchist José Domingo Díaz: "If nature opposes us we will fight against her and make her obey us."[1]

The earthquake of Caracas shattered the wavering federalist experiment. Former patriots and freed slaves began to fill the ranks of the royalists, and the country erupted in civil war. The warnings of Blanco White and Lord Holland's group had not been heeded, and the era of violence they feared had now arrived. Bello was moved to present a tragic version of the first stage of the Revolution in a poem in Latin hexameters that compares the fate of the Aztec Empire to that of the Spanish

Empire. The poem appears at the end of the second letter that
Fray Servando Teresa de Mier, the Mexican polemicist and advocate of the independence cause, sent to Blanco White as part
of the debate about emancipation the two men carried out between 1811 and 1812.[2] But Bello's oracular hexameters seem
much closer to Blanco White's dire predictions than to Mier's
optimism. In contrast to the melancholy note sounded in Bello's
endorsement of independence in *Interesting Official Documents*,
the Latin poem interprets the Revolution as a fatal event that
will bring about destruction and civil war.

In his first letter to Blanco White, Mier had recalled a prophecy of Bartolomé de Las Casas. Spain, so the prophecy went,
would be punished in a way that paralleled the destruction of
America during the Conquest. The fulfillment of this prophecy
was now at hand, Mier explained: France would now destroy
Spain as Spain had destroyed Mexico. In both historical episodes, Mier found the same resignations based on the same
deceits, the same happiness and protection promised by the
same destructive tyrants. Either there was no God in heaven to
avenge the crimes of the Spaniards, he concluded, or the Colombians would be set free from the Spaniards and their kings.

Referring to Mier and Las Casas's prophecy, Bello begins by
asking whether the fates decided that Tenochtitlan would be
subjected to another empire. The conquest of the Spaniards is
presented as a series of savage acts, compared with which even
the wrath of Achilles seems tame. You will see the great city
collapsing ("videres / . . . ruere altam funditus urbem"), Bello
says, at the hands of the Spaniard who does justice to his Van-
dalic origin. But the day will come when those crimes are
atoned, and just as strength suddenly failed the Aztecs, it will
also fail the Spaniards when the French fall upon them:

> Immo autem simili miraberis ordine casus
> Evolvi: hic etiam captivus fraude mala Rex;
> Intrataeque dolis urbes, admissus et hostis
> In iura hospitii, atque ipsa in penetralia regni
> Perfidus: hic etiam amentes discordia cives
> Prodidit, et patriam insidiis obiecit apertam.
>
> (In fact, more than that, you will be stunned to
> see how the disasters unfold in a similar se-

quence. Here again the King is made prisoner
by an evil trick; the cities are deceitfully taken,
and the enemy admitted against the laws of
friendship, a traitor at the very center of the
realm. Here again civil war abandons the mind-
less citizens and hurls the country open to
treachery.)

The parallel closely follows the one established by Mier, but
offers a sharply different outcome. Whereas Mier ended his
account of the prophecy with a loud and hopeful note about
independence, Bello asserts that the events of Bayonne opened
the doors to civil war ("*discordia*") and treachery. The poet concludes that the destruction of the Spanish Empire cannot be
explained simply by the strength of the French. The gods, and
especially Nemesis, are here at work; one can feel the approach
of the fates and ineluctable time. Another historical dimension
is embedded in the poem, as Bello closely follows the language
and imagery of the fall of Troy in book 2 of the *Aeneid*. Bello
uses Virgilian phrases like "*preaecipitesque trahit silvas*" and
"*hominumque labores*" to reinforce the inevitability of this chain
of collapsing empires – Troy, Mexico, Spain.[3]

Bello's version of the Revolution in 1812 is remarkably close
to Miranda's. The general had surrendered at the end of June
and had obtained a permit to leave Venezuela, but a group of
young patriot officers, led by Bolívar, detained him and handed
him over to the Spaniards. (Bolívar, in turn, was allowed to
leave.) Writing from the dungeons to which he had been confined after he surrendered to the Spanish forces in July 1812,
the general explained that, despite some victories, the state of
the nation was calamitous; there was no food in Caracas and La
Guaira, and the Spaniards had effectively freed and mobilized
the slaves against the patriots. By surrendering, Miranda had
sought to restore peace, to repair the damage brought about by
the earthquake, and finally to reconcile Americans and Spaniards in order to avert what he described as the "perilous movements of a devastating civil war."[4]

By 1813 Bello saw the independence movement as a failed
experiment. In June of that year he wrote to Spain's ambassador to England and enclosed a letter to the Spanish Regency

seeking amnesty for himself. This document provides us with some rare autobiographical information about Bello during the first years of the Revolution:

The petitioner had no role in the movements and schemes that led to the Revolution; no collusion with the promoters of the first junta; not even the slightest false step while the legitimate government stood in Caracas.

The second junta was established in Caracas in April 1810 under circumstances that easily commanded the approval of the most faithful subjects. The sad state of the metropolis, the moderate system that seemed to characterize the first measures taken by the revolutionary junta, and its declared adherence to the legitimate sovereign of Spain – if such circumstances are not sufficient to clear of all blame the conduct of those who continued in their assignments and took on new ones, they at least should allow it to be considered the product of an error in judgment.   (*OC*, 23: 56–7)

The Spanish ambassador forwarded Bello's request to the Regency in Cádiz on July 7, and on July 28 the Regency sent Bello's request to General Monteverde. By the time Bello's application crossed the Atlantic, however, Monteverde was no longer in power. The reconquest had scarcely lasted one year, and now Caracas was again controlled by the patriots, who, led by Bolívar, entered the city in August 1813.

The Venezuelans had learned from the mistakes of the federal experiment, and they set out to create a centralized government. Francisco Javier Ustáriz suggested that the executive and legislative bodies be in the hands of one man, thus avoiding the rapid erosion of power that contributed to the destruction of the first republic. Though republican principles were preserved, Bolívar was entrusted with full dictatorial powers, and in October he was named Libertador de Venezuela. Bolívar imprisoned Spaniards and *canarios* suspected of royalist leanings and began to negotiate with Monteverde the terms for an exchange of prisoners. The Spanish general still controlled Puerto Cabello, whose jails were filled with the patriots who had fallen with Miranda, but he refused to negotiate on any terms with Bolívar. The two bands – patriots and royalists – were decisively split, and both sides displayed an intense ferocity, a *guerra a muerte*.

Bello's disappointment with the Revolution was at this time so complete that he even began to long for the return of Ferdinand, the "captive" of fate:[5]

> No para siempre encarceló la Parca
> a su triste cautivo, que el candado
> quebrante al fin del arca
> funérea, y de sus hierros desatado
> su forma en otras formas convertida
> pace otra vez las auras de la vida.
>   (*OC*, 2: 27–8, ll. 278–83)

(Fate did not imprison her sad captive forever; may he break at last the lock of the death chamber, and, after freeing himself from his chains, his shape transformed into new shapes, may he breathe again the gentle breezes of life.)

In this passage, which appears on sheet 6, Bello returns to book 2 of the *Georgics* as his model, using the section that immediately follows the praise of the fatherland. But this time a surrogate of Augustus does appear, in the hope that Ferdinand will escape from Napoleon's prison and restore the monarchy. Ferdinand, however, is not invoked with the images of pomp and apotheosis that Virgil accords Caesar in his proem. Indeed, it is precisely the human condition of the monarch that Bello wishes to emphasize. Bello assumes the mantle of a new Virgil, but his is a human version of monarchy, one far removed from the awesome, divine power that he had celebrated in the "Oda a la vacuna."

In the poetic fragments from 1813 (sheets 5, 6, and 7), Bello seems to be withdrawing from his Americanist stance. The lexicon of Miranda's ideal – American, Colombian, torrid zone – gives way to a description of the natural bountifulness of the New World in terms of Roman mythology:

> o de quien largo premio el hombre espera,
> como la caña de nectaria savia,
> la rubia Ceres o el café de Arabia.
> Como el maíz dorado,
> como tu cara vil, Baco festivo.[6]

(or from whom man expects a large reward, like the sugarcane with its nectarean sap, blonde Ceres or the coffee of Arabia. Like golden corn, like your evil face, festive Bacchus.)

On another manuscript sheet from 1813 or 1814, Bello compares the Revolution to a fire that is raging out of control:

> Mas derribado el alto bosque y seco
> sea el incendio en tal región prendido
> de do lo empuje a las demás el viento.
> Antes habrás, empero, prevenido
> una barrera al rápido elemento
> en torno despejando
> toda materia que cebarle pueda.
> Si no, desenfrenado irá talando
> por montes y por campos la arboleda
> y ni la verde selva será parte
> a sujetarlo, ni del hombre el arte . . .
>
> (OC, 2: 61–3, ll. 664–74)

(But once the lofty and dry forest has been
felled, let a fire be started, which the wind will
blow to all other regions. Before, however, you
must have placed a barrier to the quick element,
clearing all around any material that could fuel
it. If not, it will go unleashed, laying low trees
through mountains and fields, and neither the
green jungle nor the skill of man will be able to
control it.)

Bello's earlier metaphor of freedom as a plant to be cultivated
by the prudent farmer-legislator is now replaced by the image
of revolutionary fervor as fire spreading from Caracas to other
regions of Spanish America. If allowed to burn uncontrolled,
this fire will destroy everything. The passage is inspired by
Virgil's advice to the farmers in lines 84 and 85 of book 1 of the
Georgics: "saepe etiam sterilis incendere profuit agros / atque
levem stipulam crepitantibus urere flammis" (It is often useful
to burn the barren fields and to burn the light straw with crack-
ling flames). But when the farmer is careless, when political
leaders are reckless, Bello warns, they unleash an apocalyptic
conflagration:

> ¡Cielos! ¿qué torbellino de humareda
> la luz embarga, y nube sobre nube
> aglomerando, en parte espira sube
> por el éter inmenso? Cual si el bando
> de espíritus rebeldes que al Infierno
> precipitado fue, de nuevo alzando
> sedicioso pendón contra el Eterno
> la adamantina cárcel quebrantara,

y el Abismo en bostezos vomitara
huestes de fuego armadas que impusiesen
montes a montes y a escalar subiesen
el alcázar Empíreo. Mas en cuanto
la parda noche descogió su manto
crece el horror: del Avila eminente
se ve ardiendo en mil partes la floresta.

(OC, 2: 63–4, ll. 675–89)

(Heavens! what a whirlwind of smoke shuts out
the light, and heaping cloud upon cloud, rises in
a spire through the immense ether. It is as if the
band of rebel spirits that was hurled into hell
were breaking the adamantine jail, raising once
again the seditious banner against the Almighty;
as if the Abyss were vomiting hosts armed with
fire who placed mountains upon mountains in
order to climb to the empyrean fortress. But as
soon as the dark night unfolds her mantle, horror grows. One can see the forest of the eminent
Mount Avila blazing in a thousand places.)

Having failed to take the necessary steps to guarantee an
orderly constitution, the first republic has turned an Edenic
Venezuela into an inferno, where "rebel spirits" lift the banner
of sedition against the Almighty. Rejecting historical precision
for poetic pathos, Bello here evokes the events of his ravished
homeland with greater particularity than in his other early
poems about the Revolution. Mount Avila, the highest of Caracas, is ablaze, and the night is "*parda*" (replacing the more neu-
tral "*negra*" of a prior version), an adjective that alludes to the
pardos, whose traditional racial resentment against the Creoles
was ignited by the royalist José Tomás Boves into a racial war.
In Miltonic language, Bello suggests that the Revolution has
become a clash of hellish forces. He attacks the *pardos*, it is true,
but these forces only escalate a conflict between the hellish
hosts of the royalists and patriots.

In his longing for the restitution of Ferdinand, his letter to
the Regency in 1813, and the poems he wrote that year, Bello
continues to accept the principles that provoked the Revolution
of April 19, 1810. But unlike most Venezuelans, who in retro-
spect saw the creation of the junta as a step toward complete
independence, Bello took to heart the letter of his oath of allegiance to Ferdinand. It is true that he was captivated by Miran-

da and, given the intransigence of the Cortes and Spain's sub-
jection to Napoleon, he hoped that the general could improve
the desperate condition in which the colonies found themselves
in 1810. But Bello had deep misgivings about the independence process, and the ongoing civil war, which he anticipated
in the Latin poem, was even more violent than his worst fears.

Whatever hopes Bello had for a moderate and clement period that would seal the wounds of war were dashed by Ferdinand's restoration of absolute power in 1814, and above all by
the ruthless reconquest of Spanish America carried out by
Pablo Morillo between 1815 and 1817. Bello, following Blanco
White and Lord Holland, had wished to see a modern Spanish
Empire, a kind of commonwealth of regions free to trade with
the rest of the world and united under the aegis of a constitutional monarchy. But they were alone in the view, which was
anathema to the radical strain of patriots. Nor could they find
allies on either of the two sides that dominated peninsular politics: they disliked the orthodoxy and the absolutism of the
serviles and also were disturbed by the *liberales* (the "*perseguidos y
perseguidores liberales*," as Blanco called them in a letter to Bello),
who despite their generous claims had refused to accept the
equal rights of Spanish Americans. Men like Bello and Blanco
White had welcomed the moderate language put forward by
the Caracas junta of 1810, in which they saw a possible end to
the old model of empire. But in the first experiments of the
Spanish American Revolution they witnessed the persistent
misguided effort to adapt political models that were the-
oretically attractive but ill-suited to the temperament and traditions of the colonies. At the same time, both Lord Holland and
Blanco White were critical of the Cortes's failure to respond
adequately to the claims of Spanish America, and they cen-
sured the utopian nature of the liberal constitution of 1812.[7]
By 1814 both Bello and his friends in the Holland circle had
given up hope for a peaceful reconciliation among the warring
sections of the Spanish Empire and turned their attention to
philology.

Bello's contact with the Holland circle was strengthened by a
mutual interest in a topic of great currency among the most
enlightened members of the Spanish intelligentsia: the medieval roots of constitutional monarchy. The works of Jovellanos

and Martínez Marina revealed that, contrary to the arguments of the recalcitrant members of the Cortes, the *serviles*, the absolute monarchy that had ruled the Spanish Empire since the sixteenth century had supplanted an older tradition in which the Cortes limited the power of the monarch. Spanish circumstances and experience were thus only recently absolutist. Spain's medieval past could serve as a precedent for a modern constitution in which the legislature would check the executive.[8]

Bello's correspondence with Blanco White and – indirectly, through Blanco White – with John Allen suggests that Bello's research on medieval Spanish history and epic took place between 1814 and 1822. And it may well have started, as Grases has indicated, with the reading of Tomás Antonio Sánchez's edition of the *Cid* in 1810 in Miranda's library. In 1814 Bello appears to have spent many hours at the British Museum. Fourteen of his notebooks, with long extracts on philological and historical matters concerning medieval epic,[9] are in the library of the University of Chile. Bello made much progress, and by 1816 and 1817 he was capable of carrying on complex historical and philological discussions with one of the greatest Spanish philologists of the day, Bartolomé José Gallardo.

But Bello's interest in the medieval period was not narrowly academic. Disappointed with the experiment of the first republic, Bello hoped to discover a form of government that would constitute a viable alternative to the long tradition of Spanish absolute rule. Like Jovellanos and Blanco White, he was looking for a model that controlled the excesses of the ruler – a limited monarchy much like the one the British had enjoyed since 1688. Quite possibly, Bello's medieval studies were also guided by his desire to find some legitimacy for his belief in constitutional monarchy. He chose as his principal project the reconstruction of the *Cid*, hoping at least to provide an approximation of a more complete version of the poem than that of Tomás Antonio Sánchez, the first modern edition of the *Cid*, published in 1779. Bello wished to reconstruct the lost beginning of the poem and especially the missing scenes of the Jura de Santa Gadea, which would show that in the origins of the Spanish epic the monarch was strictly controlled by his subjects.[10]

Tomás Antonio Sánchez's edition of the *Cid* had transcribed the only extant manuscript, copied by Per Abat, which starts with the Cid's exile. In Bello's eyes it was clear that the beginning of the manuscript was a continuation of a longer episode. So Bello set out to prove that the *Cid* could be at least partially reconstructed by studying the Spanish medieval chronicles, which he believed had faithfully transcribed large portions of the poem. In London he did not have access to the *Crónica de veinte reyes,* which more clearly than any other work reveals the indebtedness of the chronicles to the poem. But he did consult and transcribe numerous passages of the *Crónica del Cid* published by Velorado in 1512.

Bello's studies of medieval rhyme and metrics enabled him to perceive the precise structure of the *Cid,* which he defined thus: "strophes with a single rhyming scheme, consisting of long assonant lines, with a varying number of syllables, divided by a caesura." He would then look at the *Crónica del Cid* in search of passages that had a similar structure and from them reconstruct some sections of the original version of the poem.

The Jura de Santa Gadea, in which the Cid forces King Alphonse to swear that he was innocent of the death of his brother King Sancho, was one of the key missing scenes in the extant poem, so Bello set out to reconstruct it on the basis of the *Crónica del Cid.* This is how the *Crónica* described the second oath applied by the Cid:

El Cid preguntó la segunda vez al Rey Don Alfonso e a los otros buenos omes diziendo: "Vos venides jurar por la muerte de mi señor el Rey Don Sancho, que nin lo matastes, nin fuestes en consejarlo?" Respondió el Rey e los doze cavalleros que con él juraron: "*Sí juramos.*" E dixo el Cid: "Si vos ende sopistes parte o mandado, tal muerte murades como morió mi señor el Rey Don Sancho. Villano vos mate, ca fijo dalgo non; de otra tierra venga, que non de León." Respondió el Rey: "*Amen,*" e mudósele la color.

(For the second time the Cid asked King Alphonse and the other good men: "You come to swear that you neither killed my Lord King don Sancho nor were a part of the plot?" The King and the twelve knights who swore with him answered: "*Yes, we swear.*" And the Cid said: "If you heard of any report or order, you will die like my Lord don Sancho. A commoner will kill you, not a hidalgo; he will come from another land, not from León." The King answered, "*Amen,*" and the color of his face changed.)

On the basis of this passage, Bello proposed this segment for the *Cid:*

> Es ora Mío Cid el que en buen ora nasció,
> Preguntó al Rey don Alfonso e a los doze buenos
>   omes:
> ¿Vos venides jurar por la muerte de mi señor,
> Que non lo matastes nin fuestes end consejador?
> Repuso el Rey e los doze, *ansí juramos nos.*
> Hi responde Mío Cid; oiredes lo que fabló:
> Si parte o mandado ende sopistes vos,
> Tal muerte murades como morió mi señor:
> Villano vos mate ca fijodalgo non:
> De otra tierra venga que non sea de León.
> Respondió el Rey *Amén,* e mudós'le la color.

Bello's comments on this passage read: "This is grand, sublime. None of the insolence, the bragging, the boasting that later, and even in our days, has dulled this beautiful ideal of the Castilian champion of the poem."[11] In this passage of the Jura de Santa Gadea Bello found what he called "this beautiful ideal," a popular hero's forceful but restrained control of the monarch – neither absolutism nor republicanism.

With the defeat of Miranda, Bello seems to have reconsidered his mild sympathy for the radical cause. There is no more mention of his Masonic affiliation, he diminishes his contacts with Mill and Bentham, and for the next ten years he gravitates toward the moderate ideas held by Lord Holland, Allen, and Blanco White: specifically, toward a model of controlled monarchy whose origins could be traced back to the medieval Spanish Cortes and, as Bello discovered, to the founding text of the Spanish nation, the *Poema de Mío Cid.*

During Bello's early years in London, the *Georgics* was the fundamental model for his poetic enterprises. He began his project by writing a Spanish version of the opening of book 1 of Virgil's poem but a version that omitted any allusion to Augustus's apotheosis. Quite the opposite occurred in his Cid studies. Noticing that there was an omission at the beginning of the *Cid,* he attempted to reconstruct it. And instead of doing away with a divinely inspired monarchy, he rediscovered a medieval antecedent to limited monarchy. Bello is careful to handle poetic and political origins and guides us to the roots of his convictions. Poetry for him is invested with that legitimizing force in which the customs of a people are engraved. It is the source of wisdom, and the source of political guidance. As he would say in 1823 in "Alocución a la Poesía":

> maestra de los pueblos y los reyes,
> cantaste al mundo las primeras leyes.

> (teacher of peoples and kings, you sang the first
> laws to the world.)

5

The decided revolution

The South Americans then clearly saw they had nothing to expect either from the nation or from the king; the decided revolution may in consequence date its origin from this period.

Outline of the Revolution in Spanish America,
published in 1817, "By a South American"

Bello's poetic manuscripts from 1814 and 1815, during the reconquest of Spanish America, show him struggling with the same themes as in his earlier manuscripts: the nature of the soil, the plants of the torrid zone. But the georgic tone is interrupted in a fragment on sheet 18, written in 1815–16, that Bello later used in the "Alocución a la Poesía" as a transition between the description of nature and the poem's section on war:

> Mas iah! ¿prefieres de la guerra impía
> los horrores decir, y al son del parche
> que los maternos pechos estremece
> pintar las huestes que furiosas corren
> a destrucción, y al suelo hinchan de luto?
> ¡Oh si ofrecieses menos triste tema,
> a bélicos cantares, patria mía!
> (*OC*, 2: 95, ll. 1306–12)

> (Do you prefer to speak instead of the horrors of the impious war, and at the sound of the drum that makes the mothers' breast tremble show the hosts that furiously rush toward destruction and cause the soil to swell with mourning? Oh, my country! If only your war songs were filled with themes less sad.)

Once again Bello portrays the Revolution as a civil war, using the Virgilian qualifier "*impía*" to emphasize the essential breach of higher laws. The bands, or "*huestes*," are blind destructive forces that have so completely overtaken the poet's attention that his georgic fantasies have been preempted. But Bello can no longer be the distant observer who is torn by a conflict that he considers essentially tragic. He must take sides. On the same manuscript sheet are variants that give a new dimension to his song:

> ¡Oh! si también no diese
> a tu voz canto . . .
>
> América a tu voz
>
> ¡Oh si fértil tema a tus cantares
> también aquí mi Patria a tu alabanza
>
> ¿Qué clima, qué desierto no han bañado
> de sangre ajena y pro[pia,]
> de ibera sangre, y sangre de sus hijos
>
> (ll. 1311–12)

(Oh! If I did not also give voice to your song

To your voice, America

Oh! If a rich theme to your songs
[were not] also my country's praise

What region, what desert have they not soaked
with their own and with foreign blood, with the
blood of Iberia and the blood of her sons?)

In earlier manuscript sheets Bello had evoked America, Colombia, and the torrid zone in a pacific context, and he had talked about the botanic peculiarities of the New World. When he wrote about America, it was to describe a bountiful land that compared favorably with any other region of the world in its natural beauty and variety. But now "América" appears for the first time in the context of war, near the word "Patria." Bello appears to take an Americanist stance when he equates foreign blood and Iberian blood ("*sangre ajena*" and "*ibera sangre*"), which open the last two lines, although the last line establishes the intimate connection between patriots and foreigners. The war is not a civil war between brothers, not between Romulus and Remus, but a war between a mother and her children, a war that sheds the blood of the Iberian mother and that of her American offspring. In this fragment one sees traces of the hard choice: Spanish or American. The wars of independence have acquired a new meaning for Bello: they are a struggle for an American, as distinct from a Spanish, identity. Like most Spanish Americans, Bello felt his patriotic impulse kindled when Ferdinand's troops reconquered the liberated territories and imposed a law that allowed no clemencies.

The theme of nature is now supplanted by the theme of war; the georgic mode by the epic mode; and allegory by direct statement. Fire is no longer the product of infernal rebel forces; now, as in these lines addressed to Morillo, fire is the flame of freedom for which great patriots have died:

> ¿Piensas que apagarás con sangre el fuego
> de libertad en tantas almas grandes?
> De Cotopaxi ve a extinguir la hoguera
> que ceban las entrañas de los Andes.
> Mira correr la sangre de Rovira,
> a quien lamentan Mérida y Pamplona,
> y la de Freites derramada mira
> heroico defensor de Barcelona.
> (*OC*, 2: 107–8, ll. 1481–8)

(Do you believe that blood will put out the fire of freedom of so many great souls? Go and extinguish the bonfire of Cotopaxi fed with the Andes' entrails. Look at the flowing blood of Rovira mourned by Merida and Pamplona, and look at the spilled blood of Freites, Barcelona's heroic defender.)

Freedom remains nonetheless an essentially uncontrollable element: the "bonfire fed with the Andes' entrails" is a thinly disguised reference to the civil tensions between Bolívar and Castillo in Cartagena that contributed to Morillo's victory in 1815. As this passage illustrates, Bello now openly incorporates history into his poetry, preferring the blunt impact of bare names to the suggestive imprecision of georgic metaphors and allegorical allusions.

Other verses on this manuscript sheet (sheet 23) describe events from the death of Ricaurte, on March 25, 1814, to the fall of Barcelona, the Venezuelan port, on April 7, 1817. Throughout, Bello evinces unequivocal sympathy for the cause of the patriots. His disenchantment with Ferdinand may have started as early as 1814, once the immigrant Spanish liberals began to arrive in London, proving that Ferdinand's mood was one of vengeance rather than reconciliation. But it was reinforced by the atrocities of Morillo's reconquest of Venezuela and Nueva Granada.

Further evidence of Bello's increasing commitment to the Americanist cause is found in the letters he sent in 1815 to the governments of Buenos Aires and Cundinamarca, in which he offers his services, hoping that he might be able to live again in Spanish America. In 1815 we also find him in the company of a Venezuelan patriot, Manuel Palacio Fajardo, with whom he collaborated on two projects. The first of these was a long letter that Palacio Fajardo sent to the government of Cartagena; the second was a book, the *Outline of the Revolution in Spanish America.*

The significance of Palacio Fajardo in Bello's life was such that we should look at him closely. Born in the Province of Barinas between 1784 and 1787, Palacio Fajardo completed his studies in Bogotá, where he obtained doctorates in law and medicine. He returned to Venezuela in 1811, was elected to Congress by his province, and became an ardent spokesman for complete independence. With the implacable logic of a Jacobin, he saw the imminent dangers of the first republic and more than once advocated dictatorial powers for the executive. He was also the most zealous advocate in Congress of the execution of the rebel *canarios.*

Palacio Fajardo was led by one guiding idea: that the emancipation of Spanish America could not be achieved without international help. After the fall of the first republic, he went to Cartagena and then set out on a mission to find an ally. He arrived in Baltimore at the end of 1812 and was received by Madison and Monroe. His descriptions of the vast regions of prosperity and of the cultivated inhabitants of Spanish America were met with skepticism. Word of the disaster of the first republic had reached the United States government, and the Venezuelan envoy received a response that he termed "glacial." Palacio Fajardo then approached the French ambassador in Washington, Serurier, who advised him to go to France in order to meet with Napoleon. But by the time the Venezuelan patriot reached France in March 1813, the Russian campaign had damaged the emperor's fortunes. Palacio Fajardo sent memoranda describing the conditions of Spanish America and the popular support for Napoleon, but it was too late. The emperor was fighting his last battles and could not divert his scarce resources from France. Upon the fall of Bonaparte and the restoration of the Bourbons in 1814, Palacio Fajardo undertook conversations with some of the generals of the deposed regime. He was caught by the authorities and imprisoned, and only through the intercession of Humboldt and Bonpland was he freed and allowed to leave for London. He arrived there at the end of 1814 and for the next two years maintained correspondence with Bonpland.

In 1815 Palacio Fajardo sent a letter to the government of Cartagena in which he justified his failed diplomatic mission. This letter, now preserved in the Archivo del Libertador, was written by Bello.[1] There is evidence that the two Venezuelans were part of the small group of Spanish Americans then in London, which included the secretary of the mission from Nueva Granada, Juan García del Río; the envoy from Chile, Antonio José de Irisarri; and the Mexican freethinker José María Fagoaga. Servando Teresa de Mier was also part of this group, and after he left London with the expedition of the Spaniard Mina to liberate Mexico, he evoked the Spanish American circle in a letter to Fagoaga: "a thousand kind regards to Palacios [sic], García, Bello and Irisarri."[2]

Bello soon assisted Palacio in a much more important project, a book-length account of the Revolution published in 1817 as *Outline of the Revolution in Spanish America; or an Account of the Origin, Progress, and Actual State of the War Carried on Between Spain and Spanish America; Containing the Principal Facts Which Have Marked the Struggle*. Signed "By a South American," the book provided Europeans and Americans with a detailed account of the Revolution at one of its most critical stages. The volume was reviewed immediately after publication in the *Quarterly Review*, the leading Tory journal; a New York edition and a French translation also appeared in 1817, followed by a German translation in 1818 and a second French edition in 1819.

Most external evidence indicates that Palacio Fajardo had the leading hand in the *Outline*. Pi Sunyer shows that the accounts with Longman's, the publisher of the *Outline*, were settled in Palacio Fajardo's name. In May 1819, after Palacio's death, the *Correo del Orinoco* published an obituary that mentioned the *Outline* as his work. In Bello's circle, furthermore, the work was

generally recognized as belonging to Palacio Fajardo. Blanco
White wrote to Bello in 1820 about the "book of the deceased
Palacios [sic]" and in a review of H. M. Brackenridge's *Voyage to*
South America in *El Censor Americano,* the journal edited by
Irisarri and Bello in 1820, homage is paid to Palacio Fajardo as
the author of the *Outline.*[3]

One piece of contemporary evidence, however, contradicts
this attribution of authorship. *Strictures of a Voyage to South Amer-*
ica, a book published in 1820 in Baltimore by the "secretary to
the [late] mission to La Plata" and conceived as a criticism of
Brackenridge's work, includes the following passage on page
108: "Since I am correcting erroneous impressions, I may as
well repeat a caution on the authorship of the '*Outline,*' already
mentioned. D. Andres Bello and Jonte were its authors; receiving articles from South American agents in London."[4] This
contemporary claim of Bello's authorship has led critics to hy-
pothesize that Bello at least assisted Palacio in preparing the
Outline. Indeed, all the scholars who have insisted on Palacio
Fajardo's authorship have noted the undeniable presence of
Bello in the work, or have noted inconsistencies between the
Outline and the words and deeds of Palacio Fajardo.[5]

Despite the external evidence that favors Palacio's authorship, internal evidence points to Bello as the true author of
the *Outline.* The tone and the language are Bello's, and the
arguments and even the details ratify and develop Bello's ideas
about the end of the Spanish Empire, ideas that appear scattered in his letters, articles, biographical confessions, and
poems. The content of the *Outline* belies what we know of Palacio Fajardo's life and works. Especially striking are the contradictions between the *Outline* and an account about the Revolution written in 1813 by Palacio Fajardo in collaboration with L.
Delpech, *Rapport sur ce qui s'est passé depuis la guerre d'Espagne aux*
Colonies Espagnoles du Nouveau Monde et leur situation actuelle.[6]
We know that Bello drafted for Palacio Fajardo the letter in
Spanish to the government of Cartagena; I believe that he also
conceived and composed the *Outline.*

Let us first look at how the author of the *Outline* explains the
events of the Spanish American Revolution and the evidence he
presents to justify his assertions. The work opens with a short
preface in which the author states that his main concern will be

the "simple relation of facts." He says that he himself has witnessed many of the events discussed in the work, and of those
he has not witnessed he has received trustworthy reports. He
has also consulted the newspapers printed in Spanish America
and other works published in London, including Mier's *La historia de la Revolución de México* (published under the pseudonym
José Guerra), Walton's *Exposé to the Prince Regent of England*,
Blanco White's articles in *El Español*, and De Pradt's *De Colonies
et de l'Amérique*. The author then says that some readers may
feel that his narrative is incomplete since it omits "the relation
of some of those revolting cruelties which stain the history of
every such contest," but he believes he has included enough of
them that a just idea may be formed of the spirit that has
prevailed during the war. The author closes the preface with an
apology for the Spanish idioms that may be found in his work.

What follows is a hundred-page general discussion of the
Revolution. After a brief description of territorial divisions, the
author explains the nature of the legal contract that has bound
Spanish America to Spain since the time of Charles V. With
frequent references to the Recopilación de Indias, he sets out to
show that the newly discovered regions were attached to the
Crown of Spain and in principle shared the same rights as the
inhabitants of the metropolis (pp. 1–9).[7] He then writes about
the 13 million inhabitants of the continental portion of Spanish
America. He says that the Indians and Negroes have retained
their customs, while the Creoles have acquired theirs from the
Spaniards. Ignorance reigned in these territories, except in cities like México, Lima, and Santa Fé de Bogotá, where medicine
and the natural sciences "are pursued with much success" (pp.
9–10).[8]

The Spanish government severely restricted the trade between the new regions and foreign countries and even among
the different portions of Spanish America – order was ensured
by isolation. The court of Madrid needed to maintain only a
small number of troops on the new continent in order to assert
its power. The Creoles were "cordially attached to the mother
country," and the Indians were unable to free themselves.
There were, nevertheless, four important insurrections in the
eighteenth century. The first was the midcentury rebellion
against the company of Guipuscoa, which held a monopoly on

trade in Venezuela. In 1780 the insurrection of Tupac-Amaru in Peru was motivated by the "abject state" of the Indians owing to unfair taxation and labor practices. This insurrection was extended over three hundred leagues, but it was ultimately suppressed by troops from Buenos Aires and Lima. Tupac-Amaru and other leaders "were put to death in a shocking manner." According to the author, during this insurrection "the greatest number of the people" had in the end turned to the side of the Spaniards, despite their desire to see a change in the administration. This same discontent with Spanish authorities, though not with the king, surfaced in the 1781 insurrection in Nueva Granada, when seventeen thousand men marched toward Bogotá shouting, "Long live the king, but death to our bad governors." In contrast to these insurrections, the rebellion of Gual and España, inspired by the principles of the French Revolution, included only a few Creoles and Spaniards. In this attempted rebellion, as in the attacks of Miranda against Venezuela in 1806 and of Whitelock against Buenos Aires in 1807, the author attributes much significance to the support offered by the British government (pp. 10–18).

The author then lists a series of grievances that the Spanish Americans held against the court of Madrid. Among these were the arbitrary power of the viceroys and captains general, the air of superiority displayed by all Spaniards, the imposition of trade barriers, and the almost total lack of participation by the Creoles in local government. As evidence of this last grievance the author says that "from the period of the first settlements until the year 1810, out of one hundred and sixty-six viceroys, and five hundred and eighty-eight captains-general, governors, and presidents appointed in Spanish America, only eighteen have been Creoles, and these few only in consequence of their having been educated in Spain."[9] Despite these complaints, he adds, the new continent might have continued in its state of dependency for generations, and even centuries, had not Napoleon "loosened those bonds which united the New to the Old World" (pp. 20–5).

In the second chapter of part I, the author covers the period between July 1808 and the beginning of 1810, that is, from the moment Spanish Americans heard the news of Napoleon's invasion of Spain until they began to abandon their faith in the mother country. The events of Bayonne stunned Spanish Americans, and that moment might have been a favorable one to declare the new continent's independence. But the Spanish Americans were so attached to the mother country and the situation of the royal family was "so lamentable and interesting" that they failed to act. In contrast to the governors, who scarcely hid their affection for Bonaparte, the inhabitants of Spanish America displayed an extraordinary attachment to Ferdinand. As evidence of these feelings the author quotes at length a letter sent by Captain Beaver to Sir Alexander Cochrane, describing an eyewitness account of the events of Caracas of July 15, 1808. Upon hearing the news of Napoleon's ousting of the Bourbons in 1808, Beaver writes, "10,000 inhabitants surrounded the house of the captain-general demanding the proclamation of Ferdinand VII." Beaver then relates the events that led to the persecution of Napoleon's envoys by the inflamed Venezuelan royalists.[10] After the fall of the Bourbons, the inhabitants of Caracas and of the other cities of Spanish America tried to create juntas not unlike those formed in Seville and Asturias. But these attempts were rapidly, and often violently, opposed by the Spaniards living on the new continent. A mood of rebellion began to stir throughout Spanish America. Though the declarations of attachment to the mother country were sincere, the hopes for reform had never been realized, and so Spanish Americans began "to grow weary of their dependence." Everywhere the question was asked: "What will become of us, should Spain be conquered?" And the discussion of this topic led to others of deeper importance. The central junta of Spain tried to lull the colonies into apathy by issuing a pompous statement declaring that the colonies were equal to the mother country, but the junta continued receiving money from Caracas and sending Spanish officials to occupy every public position: "Such was the attention paid to the interest of the new continent!" With that angry phrase the author brings the second chapter to a close (pp. 26–46).

He next discusses the circumstances that led to the dismissal of the Spanish authorities and the formation of juntas in the different regions of Spanish America. The author insists that, even after the news arrived that Bonaparte was the master of Madrid, Spanish Americans continued sending supplies to

Spain. He writes, "If, during this time, there were any distur-
bances or plans for reform in America, they are to be attributed
to the misconduct of the Spanish chiefs, their illiberal views,
and their mysterious proceedings, but not to any motives of
radical disaffection to the mother country." News then arrived
in Caracas that the French had invaded Andalucia, that the
central junta had been dispersed. Immediately afterward, the
Americans received a proclamation signed by a regency that
had been formed illegally on the island of León by the deposed
members of the central junta. The *caraqueños* quickly responded by dismissing the Spanish governors and forming a
junta suprema, which published its acts in the name of Ferdinand. In many proclamations they continued offering assistance to the Spaniards in their war against Napoleon, though
they never recognized the authority of the Regency. Similar
juntas were formed in Buenos Aires, Bogotá, Chile, and Mexico (pp. 47–53).[11]

The second and third chapters of the *Outline*'s general discussion of the Spanish American Revolution thus focus on the facts
and events of July 15, 1808, and April 19, 1810. The fourth
chapter turns to the correspondence between the Regency and
the Caracas junta. The author quotes at length the indignant
letter in which the Regency declared Caracas in a state of blockade. He goes on to describe the letter in which the people of
Caracas refused to acknowledge the authority of the Regency (a
letter, we may recall, that Bello had drafted). This letter, he
says, "had excited great indignation in the members of the
regency and the people of Cadiz, who expected nothing from
the Spanish Americans but a submissive conformity to their
decrees." The author then blames the merchants of Cádiz and
the Cortes for the intransigence they displayed in all their de-
liberations and for igniting the spirit of civil war (pp. 55–60).

Although the author describes the contending parties of this
civil war with some detachment, he cannot hide his partisan
feelings: "The Spaniards are fighting to reconquer their once-
possessed territories, the Spanish Americans to obtain freedom. The first are cruel in the hour of triumph, and with
adversity their enmity increases; the latter are courageous in
attack, and, when defeated, still ready to place confidence in
their leaders, and again to rally under their banners." In the last

forty pages of part I of the *Outline,* the author attempts to summarize the events between 1810 and 1817. He describes in considerable detail the many occasions on which the Spaniards broke treaties or acted with cruelty. He says that the revolutionary spirit "was confined at first to very few persons" but that it soon spread to the whole continent and led to a movement that favored emancipation. The author publishes Venezuela's declaration of independence of July 5, 1811, and notes that similar declarations were made in Mexico, Cartagena, Nueva Granada, Buenos Aires, and other regions of Spanish America. The Spanish Cortes were alarmed by the growing disaffection of the Spanish Americans and tried to listen to the American deputies. But in the end the Cortes rejected or delayed all the attempts at reform presented by these deputies (pp. 61–79).

The author then examines the connection between the Bonaparte family and Spanish America. He quotes at length a document found in the office of the secretary of the Caracas junta (i.e., in Bello's office) in which Joseph Bonaparte gave instructions to his agents to kindle the spirit of insurrection among Spanish Americans. But, the author adds, these agents were poorly received, which convinced the English "that there neither was a party for Joseph Bonaparte, nor even a numerous one for independence in Spanish America."[12] The English government, having pledged assistance to the Spaniards, attempted repeatedly to act as an intermediary between the Cortes and the dissenting provinces. But the Cortes rejected Britain's mediation (pp. 79–94).

While the British were attempting to become mediators in the wars of independence, the revolutionaries had made important advances. But the change in Napoleon's fortune brought the release of Ferdinand, which threatened to undermine the Revolution. Ferdinand was restored under very favorable auspices. The suffering of his youth and the treachery with which his kingdom was taken from him inspired both Spaniards and Americans with an attachment that "nearly bordered on adoration." Spain was then ruined by a desolating war, and Spanish America destroyed by civil contests. The author adds, "What a happy opportunity for Ferdinand to have shown himself the restorer of tranquility, the mediator between his contending subjects, the angel of peace." As Ferdinand's absence had provoked the civil war in Spanish America, his return should have healed dissension. And in fact a sort of stupor pervaded the revolutionary army. If only they had been encouraged to return to peace, "their swords would quickly have been sheathed." But then came Morillo's expedition. "Alarm was now spread among those who had been fighting for the cause of independence. All hopes of reconciliation were abandoned, and a revolt in Spanish America against the authority of Ferdinand the seventh, dates from this period." Part I of the *Outline* closes with a description of Morillo's ruthless reconquest of Venezuela and Nueva Granada (pp. 94–100).

Thus, part I of the *Outline* contains the essence of the author's thoughts about the Revolution. His analyses of the developments of the Revolution in different regions constitute the last three parts of the work. For our purposes, we may concentrate on what he says about two protagonists of the Revolution: Miranda and Bolívar.

The author of the *Outline* consistently praises Miranda. He observes that the general's proposed constitution closely followed the existing traditions of Spanish America, whereas the radical innovations proposed in the constitution of the first republic did not: "One might have been formed better adapted to the customs and characters of the South Americans" (p. 119). Later the author describes Miranda's dictatorship and the difficulties he had in his struggle against Monteverde: "He marched to meet the enemy at the head of 2,000 men, armed with the few guns that had been rescued from the ruins after the earthquake." He then praises Miranda's actions of 1812 and says that his "judicious conduct" began to restore order in Caracas and reinstate discipline in the army before the fateful fall of Puerto Cabello (pp. 127–30).[13]

If the author consistently praises or justifies Miranda, his depiction of Bolívar has more shadows. The Libertador is often presented in a favorable light: the triumphal entry into Caracas in August 1813 is described as a moment of great joy for Venezuelans in which thoughts of peace rather than vengeance predominated: "Notwithstanding [the] state of popular ferment, none of the Spaniards were insulted; an universal feeling of gratitude and satisfaction filled the mind of every individual" (p. 141). Bolívar's repeated offers to exchange prisoners are also praised, and though some of his lieutenants are accused of abusing their power, "Bolívar never improperly availed himself of the power he possessed" (p. 146). But the darker side of Bolívar is also shown. The author first attacks him, though not by name, for the imprisonment of Miranda: "The conduct of some of his countrymen towards Miranda was marked with ingratitude" (p. 132). Later the author adds, "The capitulation concluded by Miranda was not approved by Bolívar" (p. 137) and lets his readers fill in the blanks. Sometimes the criticism is more overt, as when the author declares that "Bolívar's military government had displeased the people" (p. 157).

The author's complex feelings about the man who was becoming the undisputed leader of the war haunt the passage in which Bolívar's darkest hour is described:

The massacre of many of the inhabitants of Ocumare, three of whom were murdered in the church, created much indignation in the mind of Bolívar, who thirsting with revenge, though overpowered with cares, did not know on which side to turn his attention. In one of these agonizing moments, in which his soul was first swayed by fear, then worked up to anger, he gave orders for the execution of the prisoners, and shocking to relate, eight hundred men were killed on this occasion. (p. 152)

In trying to find some justification for the *guerra a muerte*, the author here begins to tell the story from Bolívar's perspective. The language and the imagery are thoroughly Virgilian, from the swaying movement of the emotions to the formulaic expression of shock (a translation of "*horresco referens*" or "*horribile dictu*"). Arístides Rojas, the Venezuelan man of letters who described the peaceful poetic gatherings of the Ustáriz family, wrote that Bello was the Virgil of the epic in which Bolívar played the role of Aeneas. This would be true if we thought of the *Outline* as the epic of the Revolution. For here Bolívar is consciously treated with that mixture of courage and rage that marks the Roman hero.[14]

The arguments of the *Outline* are, in sum, far removed from the ideas of the more intransigent and ideologically secure members of the first republic, such as Palacio Fajardo. They are rather the product of a man who, from the start, has been torn by the Revolution, and if he shows his sympathy for the cause of the patriots, it is only after he has presented his divided feelings and alliances. One might go so far as to say that the *Outline* and Palacio Fajardo's *Rapport* reveal two extremes in the interpretation of the Revolution. In the former, the deliberate presentation of facts is used to give a feeling of impartiality; in the latter, an ardent rhetoric infuses the facts with a single, overarching purpose. The first is the logic of the spectator; the second, that of the actor.

Once we accept the internal evidence of Bello's authorship of the *Outline,* we must reconsider the external evidence. Why did Palacio Fajardo appear as the official author of the *Outline* in the records of Longman's, the publishing house, in the pages of the *Correo del Orinoco,* and in the *Censor Americano?* One compelling hypothesis is suggested by the saliency of a kind of ghost-writing in Bello's career: the letter to the Regency was signed by José de las Llamosas and Martín Tovar Ponte; the diplomatic documents of 1810 and 1811 were signed by Bolívar and López Méndez; and a letter to the Pope in 1820 was signed by Fernando Peñalver and José María Vergara. During his years in Chile the majority of Bello's writings were either unsigned or signed by some government official. For a variety of reasons, we know these works are Bello's: sometimes by his own confession (the letter to the Regency), or by the surviving manuscripts in his handwriting (the letters signed by Bolívar and López Méndez), and sometimes by the confession of the official signatory (the letter to the Pope of 1820). Bello's search for anonymity in part reflects the standards of the time. But Bello also displayed a scrupulous desire not to be identified with works containing historical and political views, such as the *Resumen de la historia de Venezuela.* It is in Bello's circle that Palacio Fajardo is most closely linked to the *Outline* – as if Bello wished to encourage that misdirection.

In 1816 Palacio Fajardo may well have instructed Bello to compose a justification of the Revolution to aid the campaign to enlist foreign legionnaires.[15] Bello was the logical choice: he had already written for Palacio Fajardo the long letter to the government of Cartagena, and he had had contact with the envoys of Argentina, Chile, Nueva Granada, and México and kept an excellent collection of *gazetas.* Furthermore, Bello was a skilled and experienced writer and had been preparing documents since his youth. More importantly, Bello was probably the only Spanish American then living in London who could write fluent English prose. Yet, like all the works Bello wrote for the independence cause, the *Outline* bespeaks a personal vision that deviates sharply from the ardent revolutionary faction.

The *Outline* offers an explanation of the Revolution that gives shape to the ideas scattered in Bello's other works. The main events since 1808 appear connected here. And it is only through the peculiar logic of the *Outline* – peculiar in that it favors the Revolution, but only with great misgivings – that we can make sense of Bello's otherwise fragmentary allusions to the Revolution. Until 1815 or 1816 Bello still hoped for a reconciliation between Spain and America, and his writings show the ambivalence of a man who ideologically stood on the side of enlightened Spaniards like Jovellanos and Blanco White but who knew that his past and future belonged to Spanish America. The *Outline* is one of the most compact and interesting versions of this dilemma, central to Bello's political thought.

The *Outline* also confirms the view of the Revolution presented in the poetry that Bello was writing around 1817. While he was preparing the prose narrative of the Revolution, he also began to write poems celebrating the fallen heroes of the war; these verses were the groundwork for his 1823 poem, "Alocución a la Poesía." The parallels between the *Outline* and Bello's poetry, noted by Pi Sunyer and Grases, are indeed striking. In the second part of the *Outline* and in the *Borradores*, the same events and frequently the same details are chosen:

> Yacen García Toledo,
> Ayos, Granados y Amador y Castillo,
> de Cartagena estirpe generosa.
> (*OC*, 2: 108, ll. 1489–91, first draft)

> yace Cabal de Popayán llorado,
> llorado de las ciencia: mortal bala
> el pecho de Camilo Torres hiere;
> Gutiérrez el postero aliento exhala;
> (ll. 1491–4)

(Here lie García Toledo, Ayos, Granados and Amador and Castillo, the generous progeny of Cartagena.

Here lies Cabal mourned by Popayan, mourned by science; a deadly bullet wounds the chest of

Camilo   Torres;   Gutiérrez   exhales   his   last breath.)

The same names appear in exactly the same order in the *Outline:* "García Toledo, Ayos, M. Granados, M. Amador . . . were executed on the 24th of January" (p. 234) and "Among those executed were . . . Don J. M. Cabal, a distinguished chemist [*sic*]; Don C. Torres, a man distinguished for his learning; Don J. G. Gutiérrez Moreno" (p. 99). Bello's earlier lists of the plants of Spanish America give way to lists of fallen heroes. In his two versions of the Revolution – one written in Spanish verse, the other in English prose – the lamentation of those who have fallen in battle becomes a leading concern.[16]

On the cover page of the *Outline* appears an epigraph taken from book 10 of the *Aeneid:* "Fata viam invenient" (The Fates will find the way), Jupiter's closing words in response to the fierce debate in which Venus has advocated the cause of Aeneas and the Trojans, and Juno that of Turnus and the Latins. I hold this epigraph to be the brand of Bello's thinking about the Revolution until 1817. He has been the man who hesitates, the one who views the independence as a tragic confrontation, a conflict that can be settled only by higher laws – the fatalistic view of history manifest in his poem in Latin hexameters. And he has conceived of the Spanish American Revolution as an event of singular magnitude in the history of humanity. This was no ordinary war; "it had no parallel in the annals of history," he wrote in the *Outline.* At the beginning of his career, Bello saw in Virgil a perfectly patterned and established poet who sang the end of civil disturbance and called for national reconstruction. But now, after years of civil wars, Bello seeks in Virgil not a literary model but a historical perspective, not the equilibrium of a conclusion but the agonizing shifts of the process of creation. Now he seeks in Virgil the *vates,* the interpreter of the fates. In quoting the *Aeneid* – the poem most often used by rulers as the legitimizing voice of imperial rule – to introduce an analysis of the disintegration of the Spanish Empire, Bello is seeking in Virgil not the rhetoric of imperial propaganda but the state of mind that prevails when one is confronting great historical upheavals.

6

The new Augustus

In the *Georgics* and the *Aeneid* Virgil recorded the thoughts and images that emerged from his contemplation of the fall of the Roman republic and the consolidation of the empire under the rule of one man. In the poems Bello wrote between 1810 and 1820 he recorded the thoughts and images that emerged from his contemplation of the fall of the Spanish Empire and from the struggle to fill the vacant seat of power. In the critical years of the Revolution, between 1815 and 1819, the two figures struggling for preeminence were Ferdinand and Bolívar, each of whom proposed his own version of Augustanism. During this time, Bello's thoughts on Augustanism continued to evolve as well.

Ferdinand's model of reconquest entailed returning to the orthodox brand of Augustanism without any of the modern traits that men like Jovellanos and Meléndez Valdés had tried to impose. It was a model intolerant in matters of religion, absolutist in matters of politics, and classicist in matters of art. A Spanish poet like Juan Bautista Arriaza exemplified all the values Ferdinand wished to reestablish. Arriaza was a strong partisan of absolutism and wrote a large number of odes, sonnets, and hymns in honor of Ferdinand and the royal family. He was named the court poet in 1814 and also held the positions of "second majordomo" and "adviser and secretary of decrees." In fluid neoclassic verse – Arriaza had the reputation of being a great improviser, or *repentista* – he glorifies the values of old Spain: one king, one faith. For example, in a hymn composed for the guards of the king on the occasion of the king's saint's day, "*su augusto día*," Arriaza celebrates Ferdinand's restoration:

> Genios tutelares, que en su cautiverio
> Defensores fuisteis de su bella edad,
> Y que en vuestras alas al hispano imperio
> Con su Rey trajisteis paz y libertad.

Prodigad hoy rosas a su augusta frente,
Y con canto hacedle de celeste voz
Olvidar los males que sufrió inocente,
Y aun de su tirano la memoria atroz.[1]

(Tutelary spirits who defended his beautiful
youth during his captivity and who, in your
wings, brought peace and liberty to the Hispanic
empire.

Scatter roses on his august brow, and with a song
of a celestial voice make him forget the evils
which he innocently suffered, and even the atrocious memory of his tyrant.)

The royal epithet *augusto* is a favorite of Arriaza's. As in Bello's
youthful "Oda a la vacuna," the king assumes a superhuman
dimension. In a stanza of another of Arriaza's poems celebrating the return of Ferdinand, the epithet is applied to various
members of the royal family: Charles III is the "*augusto abuelo*,"
Ferdinand has a "*semblante augusto*," and his brother is the "*caro
augusto hermano*" (p. 86).

Indeed, the epithet *augusto* enjoyed great currency during
the reconquest, not only at court but also in the pulpit. In 1816
caraqueños heard the epithet adorning a homily delivered by
Father Salvador García Ortigosa in the spirit of Bishop Viana.
The captain general of Venezuela, Salvador Moxo, with the
approval of Archbishop Coll y Prat, promoted the publication
of Ortigosa's five homilies, the third of which was dedicated "to
the respect owed to the kings" and quoted Saint Peter: "Deum
timete; Regem honorificate," the familiar epigraph used by
Bishop Viana. In another homily, Ortigosa wrote: "The fear of
God must include the honor to the king, as His representative
on earth. His dignity is august and sacred: his power comes
from that of God himself, and depends on none other than
Him alone; his selection and elevation over men are enacted for
the preservation and happiness of empires." Ortigosa then re-
argues Bishop Viana's point that the Savior himself, the king of
kings, offered the most brilliant examples of obedience and
submission to royal authority. Jesus, he explains, did not come
to extinguish the law of obedience but, on the contrary, to give
this law a sublime degree of perfection. If his parents decided
to take a long and arduous trip when Mary was about to give
birth, and if Jesus was born in a manger, these are conse-

quences of the perfect obedience of the Savior to the laws of Augustus, to the imperious edicts of Caesar ("todo son consecuencia de la obediencia exacta del Redentor a las leyes de Augusto, y a los edictos imperiosos del César").

The fifth and last of Ortigosa's homilies, read on Holy Thursday, was dedicated to the love that is owed to the king, to the "work of love, protection, and munificence of our august monarch don Ferdinand VII."[2] The *august* power of the monarch and the exemplary authority of Augustus support the authority of Ferdinand. Not only do Augustus and Ferdinand share the epithet, but both are monarchs to whom all subjects owe complete obedience.

Bishop Viana had not gone that far, but then the crisis of 1797 had not been so serious. And it was in the nature of the royalist rhetoric during the reconquest to sound the full fanfare of Augustan propaganda. In the poems of Arriaza and in Father Ortigosa's homilies, one sees the last stand of the Augustan model in its peculiar orthodox Spanish configuration. The frequency of the epithet and its explicit association with Augustus betray a desperate attempt to recover power, to spell out the meaning of the myth. Bishop Viana's evocative allusions to paradise and hell, to the royal power of the Roman *princeps*, and to the fire of republicanism had been much more effective and terrifying. He had set in motion a chain of associations not easily put to rest.

From the palaces of Madrid to the churches of South American villages the royal epithet still resonated. Bolívar, sensitive to the effects of the royalists' propaganda, decided to counter by appropriating their rhetoric, and in one of his most daring moves, he planned to close the decade on a note of triumph. The patriots had assembled in the town of Angostura, by the banks of the Orinoco River, to await a final engagement with the royalists. The troops of the patriots were now swollen with the *pardos*, who had abandoned the cause of the royalists, and with the Irish and British legionnaires who started to arrive in 1818. New names began to surround Bolívar: Páez, Rourke, O'Leary. Before they set out to vanquish the enemy, Bolívar presented a new constitutional plan in a speech known as the Discurso de Angostura. As he had in 1814, he claimed that it was time to restore the republic. With appropriate solemnity, though still representing but a small portion of northern South America, Bolívar summoned the representatives of the people and opened the second Congress of Venezuela.

He began by saying that he considered himself the happiest of men, "since I have had the honor of bringing together the representatives of the people of Venezuela in the august Congress, the source of legitimate authority, depository of the sovereign will and arbiter of the nation's destiny." His vocabulary of monarchic rule – *augusto, legítima, soberana* – continues throughout the speech, especially in those passages in which Bolívar lays out his constitutional plans. Thus, he tells the legislators, "Your august duty is to dedicate yourselves to the happiness of the republic." Later he evokes the "august temple of Liberty" and tells the legislators that they hold the power to grant honors of the order to the liberators of Venezuela: "It is your duty to exercise this august act of national gratitude." *Augusto* is purposely used in those passages that define the new order; it is applied to the republic, to freedom, to the power of the legislature. In short, Bolívar challenges the royalists' attempt to limit *augusto* to the personages of a divinely sanctioned monarchy.[3]

But Bolívar has not gathered the representatives of Venezuela to subvert the power of monarchy and extol the virtues of republicanism. The federal republic of Venezuela, he says, failed; absolute democracy is the sure road to absolute tyranny. Besides, Venezuela cannot expect to imitate the model of the United States. As Montesquieu has shown, the laws of each country have to be related to its physical conditions, to its climate, to the quality of the soil, to the customs of the people. The political system of Venezuela must be republican, and it must have divisions of power and civil liberty. It must also proscribe slavery and the privileges of monarchy. Bolívar, however, does not wish to define this republic after the two models – France and the United States – on which the first Venezuelan republic was based. Rather, he proposes to look to the Roman and British governments:

Rome and Great Britain are the most outstanding nations among all those ancient and modern. Both were born to lead and to be free, but both were formed with solid foundations, not with brilliant forms of liberty. Therefore, representatives, I recommend to you the study of the British constitution, which appears to be the one destined to work the greatest good on the people who adopt it. Despite its great virtues I am, however, far from proposing to you its slavish imitation. When I speak of the British government I am referring only to its republican traits; and in truth can one label *monarchy* a system that recognizes popular sovereignty, the separation and equilibrium among powers, civil liberties, freedom of conscience, freedom of the press and all that is sublime in politics? Can there be more freedom in any kind of republic?

These, then, are the two models: Rome and Great Britain. But which Rome – the republic or the empire? It is hard to say. Earlier Bolívar described the "monstrosity" of the Roman republic, especially the system of two consuls, and made the point that Rome attained its greatness despite its institutions. So perhaps he is thinking of the empire rather than the republic when he refers to the "solid foundations" of Rome. But the Libertador quickly forsakes the Roman example for the British model, in which even the more ardent patriots could find some merit. At first he defends his choice of the British system by saying that he will preserve only its republican elements, but he changes course and asks if the British monarchy is not indeed a republic. His ostensible defense of republican values thus modulates into a tribute to Britain's constitutional monarchy, the political model that in the aftermath of the French and Spanish American revolutions offered the greatest possible combination of freedom and stability.

Bolívar then describes the legislative branch of his constitutional plan. He proposes a hereditary Senate, modeled after the Roman Senate and the British House of Lords, to be composed of the descendants of the heroes of the Revolution. These future legislators are to receive a special education and form a "race of virtuous, prudent, and determined men." The executive branch is to be headed by a president given greater powers than the British monarch. Bolívar explains that, while in a monarchy the legislature has to have the greatest power since everything conspires in favor of the monarch, in a republic the executive has to have the greatest power since everything conspires against this branch of government. In addition, Bolívar introduces a "Poder Moral," a moral branch of government entrusted with reinvigorating the character and the customs of Spanish Americans.

At the climax of his speech, Bolívar imagines the reunion of Venezuela and Nueva Granada in the distant future. He envisions this new country as the center of the human family, sending gold and silver to all corners of the earth. He continues, "I see her sitting on the throne of Liberty, holding the scepter of Justice, crowned by Glory, showing the Ancient World the majesty of the Modern World." The final vision of Bolívar's new land seals the royalist themes that run throughout the Discurso de Angostura. Not only the language of the new republic but also the forms of government are constituted by an idiosyncratic version of British monarchy.

A comparison of Bolívar's Discurso de Angostura with Augustus's speech to the Senate in 27 B.C. shows both men to be liminal figures, forced by circumstance to propose highly ambiguous forms of government. Just as Augustus appropriated republican rhetoric in the transition from republic to monarchy, so Bolívar appropriates monarchic rhetoric in the transition from monarchy to republic. In Bolívar's speech one hears the original Augustan rhetoric, as he repeatedly announces himself to be the restorer of the republic and promises to return the reins of power to the people. Like Augustus, Bolívar says he is tired, that he can no longer bear the burden of the state, that he will yield all power to the legislators: "Now I can breathe, returning to you this authority that I have managed to keep with great risk, difficulty and hardship, in the midst of the most horrifying tribulations that can afflict a society." And like Augustus, he proposes a form of government that is a monarchy without a monarch, that legitimizes a position only he is called to fill.

At the beginning of the wars of independence two clearly demarcated sides were struggling for power in Spanish America: the Crown was supported by the legitimacy of classical tradition and by the legitimacy of the Vatican; the republican cause, violent and revolutionary, was inspired by Rousseau and the Jacobins. This two-sided struggle survived as long as the patriots pursued truly republican reforms. But when the first Venezuelan republic failed, republicanism became a password in opposition to the Spanish monarchy; not so much a political creed, republicanism signaled a war faction. By 1819 some patriots preserved the fire of the republican rhetoric, but at Angostura Bolívar calls instead for a new version of Augustanism. At this point, then, the two principal antagonists, Ferdinand and Bolívar, are not proposing to implement vastly different political systems, but rather are attempting to impose their own versions of the Augustan model.

Ferdinand's absolutist version insists on the central role of the monarch. All his subjects are to follow the example of Christ and submit to the king's edicts. Bolívar's handling of the model is more complex. His rhetoric still reveals the influence of the French Revolution, but now his republicanism resembles Voltaire's, a republicanism that implies an independent legislative power but tolerates and often requires a strong executive branch. In the ambiguity of his constitutional designs, and in his apparent attempt to restore the republic and to abandon power, Bolívar offers a more faithful version of the original Augustan model than does Ferdinand's imperial Spain.

As the first decade of the wars of independence came to a close, Bello, too, was struggling with the meaning and relevancy of the Augustan model. In his correspondence and in his poetry, he scrutinized both the religious and the cultural legitimacy of the Spanish monarchy.

The religious legitimacy of the Spanish Crown in Spanish America had been reconfirmed by Pius VII in the encyclical "Etsi longissimo," published in 1816. The Pope restated the Vatican's traditional support for the Spanish Crown and urged Spanish Americans to lay down their arms and submit to the power of Ferdinand.[4] The *real patronato*, the three-century-old tradition by which the Church had invested the Spanish monarch with complete control in religious matters in the New World, was thus upheld. The effect of the papal encyclical was not insignificant; priests in Spanish America pressed the message in their homilies: the king of Spain was preeminent in both temporal and spiritual matters.

The *real patronato* was among the principal obstacles to Spanish America's emancipation. For the Church to recognize the sovereignty of the new countries in Spanish America, it would have to disown a long-standing arrangement with the Spanish Crown. In pursuit of a settlement with the Vatican, Bolívar's government sent two envoys to Europe in June 1819. These envoys, Fernando Peñalver and José María Vergara, arrived in

London late that year with instructions to write to Pope Pius VII. Like other Venezuelans who arrived in London, the two envoys soon approached Bello for help. He composed for them a letter in Latin to the Pope, dated March 27, 1820, on the subject of the *real patronato*.

Bello writes that the governments of Nueva Granada and Venezuela had refrained from contacting the Pope at an earlier date out of respect for the pact between His Holiness and the Catholic Majesty. He then says, "It is not hard to estimate how much authority and power [are] vested on the kings as a result of the *patronato*, which is now the unhappy cause of discontent between the people and their pastors and the pernicious fuel of civil war that our enemies have abused" (*OC*, 8: 460). The Spaniards have succeeded in withdrawing the priests and bishops who were sympathetic to the revolutionary cause, thus leaving whole regions in utter spiritual abandonment. Moreover, the sacred ceremonies that are conducted betray the corruption of the pastoral duty and incite civil war. In the name of the citizens of Venezuela and Nueva Granada, Bello emphasizes the need for new bishops, but these must be men who will offer peace and comfort, and not open the wounds of war. He suggests that the nominations be made by the new governments.[5]

Most apologists for Bello's Catholicism have focused on this letter to the Pope as unmistakable evidence of the strength of his faith. But the letter directly attacks the role the Church has played in promoting the civil wars of Spanish America. In one passage, for example, Bello cites priests who have abused their position by provoking violent encounters in which hands were stained with the blood of brothers ("ad homines excitandos ut fraterno sanguine manus imbuant"; *OC*, 8: 461).

The letter also illustrates Bello's tepid acceptance of republican ideas. As in *Interesting Official Documents*, he makes no attempt to justify republicanism, which he again presents, much as he had in 1812, as a measure of last resort: "The republican system that they had to adopt does not conflict with the principles of this holy religion" (*OC*, 8: 461).[6] Yet although Bello does not champion republicanism, the letter marks a significant departure from the orthodox colonial Augustanism, predicated on the close alliance between Church and Crown, that he celebrated in "Oda a la vacuna."

By this time Bello may even have departed from respect for "*la religión de nuestros padres*" (our forefathers' religion), influenced by his close contact with convinced anti-Catholics like William Blair and José Blanco White. Bello's contacts with Blair and the British and Foreign Bible Society do not incriminate him as an enemy of the Roman Church. But they do challenge the traditional portrait of Bello as a man who preserved his solid Catholic orthodoxy in an environment hostile to Catholicism.[7] Bello's collaboration with the Bible Society is but one reflection of persistent anticlerical themes in his poetry and correspondence.

The British and Foreign Bible Society was formed in 1804 for the purpose of distributing the Bible throughout the world, in the vernacular language and without notes. The Bible Society was interdenominational, but the almost complete marginality of Catholicism in England at the beginning of the nineteenth century made the society a point of contact among the different Protestant churches. The desire to preserve the dividing line between Protestants and Catholics was a tenet firmly held by member William Blair. A prolific writer and an ardent Protestant, Blair had written works on venereal disease and the smallpox vaccine, and he frequently published attacks on the Catholic Church. A typical title, published in 1819, was *The Revival of Popery, Its Intolerant Character, Political Tendency, Encroaching Demands, and Unceasing Usurpations, in Letters to William Wilberforce*.

As early as 1805 Blair sought to print a Spanish Bible. In a letter dated December 31, 1805, to one of the secretaries of the Bible Society, he wrote, "I hope great care will be taken not only to have the sheets carefully revised by a Spaniard, if possible, but also by a *Protestant*." In the next ten years, Blair managed to produce, with great difficulty, a Spanish Bible, but he was dissatisfied with the outcome. Besides, the Bible Society's attempt to distribute the Bible in Spanish America had met with the opposition of Church authorities. In 1816, on the recommendation of the Mexican freethinker Francisco Fagoaga, Bello began to assist Blair on a Spanish edition of the New Testament. According to Kathleen Cann, the Bible Society's former archivist, Bello initially edited and proofread a new edition of Sebastián de la Enzina's New Testament, which had been published in Amsterdam in 1708. In 1820 and 1821 Bello worked in conjunction with Blanco White to edit Felipe Scío's translations of the New Testament and the Bible.[8]

A memorandum written by Bello in 1817, in which he refers to himself in the third person, attests to his close working relationship with Blair. Addressing Mr. Tarn, the accountant and assistant secretary of the Bible Society, Bello requests additional remuneration for his work in correcting the Bible and gives precise information about the tasks he has performed. He adds that he has also endeavored to change those parts of the edition that made it unacceptable to the Catholic bishops in Spanish America. In addition, Bello says that he has corrected many ungrammatical passages and tried to sustain a solemn style. He closes his memorandum by emphasizing the cooperation between himself and Blair on the project: "As none of these alterations has been made without Mr. Blair's previous approbation, nobody is better able to judge of the degree of attention and trouble which they required."

On January 19, 1818, the Bible Society decided to comply with Bello's request: "Mr. Blair is of opinion that Mr. Bello is entitled to an extra remuneration for the new edition of the Spanish Testament, and that he has produced a book which will be read without prejudice by the Spaniards, far superior to former editions. Mr. Blair thinks £5.5 should be given to Mr. Bello."

These documents shed some light on Bello's links with an institution that came to play an important role during his stay in London. Had Bello, like Blanco White, abandoned Catholicism? As in much else that concerns Bello at this time, we cannot be certain. Bello did preserve at least some ties to the Catholic Church, where he baptized his three children. And the existing documents suggest that he tried to make the Bible Society translations acceptable to Church authorities in Spanish America. But his letter to the Pope and his relations with Blair and the British and Foreign Bible Society reveal a man who was openly critical of the role played by the Church during the Revolution and who collaborated with an institution whose tenets were fervently anti-Catholic. In the opinion of Blanco White, Bello – like Meléndez Valdés – was a "devout Deist."[9]

As Bello implored the Pope to renounce the religious legitimacy of the Spanish monarch, during his first ten years in London he also continued to question the cultural and historical legitimacy of the Crown. As we have seen, from approximately 1810 to 1814 Bello worked on a modern version of the *Georgics*. He focused on two passages in which Octavian is invoked: the first one hundred lines of book 1 and the praise of the fatherland in book 2. With the exception of the brief periphrasis about Ferdinand in the years of the reconquest, Bello made no attempt to invoke an Octavian or an Augustus. By 1815 the events of the Spanish American Revolution compelled Bello to abandon the georgic genre and take up the epic mode. He again chose a passage in which Augustus figures prominently, the end of book 6 of the *Aeneid,* and he again decided to leave vacant the place occupied by the *princeps.* As Miguel Antonio Caro first observed, Anchises' presentation of Rome's heroes is the model for Bello's list of heroes who sacrificed their lives for the cause of independence.[10] Like Virgil, whose gallery of Roman personalities includes men known for their virtue or for their cruelty, Bello mentions men who have shown great courage, like Ricaurte or Rivas, and those who have revealed a barbaric nature, like Boves. But unlike Virgil, who dedicates twenty lines to Augustus at the end of book 6, Bello offers no salute to monarch, prince, or president.

During his first decade in London, in sum, Bello was examining the cultural underpinnings of the Augustan model and questioning the universal validity of classicism and Catholicism as the legitimizing powers of the monarch. He had begun to elaborate two series of poems that were circumscribing an absence.

The differences between Bello's version of the Augustan model and Ferdinand's version are obvious. The Spanish monarch's superannuated form is one the Venezuelan poet cast aside before he left Caracas. Bolívar's version of Augustanism is another matter, however. There appears to be no conflict between Bolívar's version and Bello's. Indeed, they are potentially complementary: Bello is establishing the cultural framework that signals a void that Bolívar is eager to fill. Over time, their views have become quite compatible. Both believe that the form of the new government must suit the customs and habits of Spanish Americans. Both understand the dangers of republicanism and urge a kind of revised regalism that would centralize spiritual and secular decisions. And by 1819 Bello has come to agree that independence from Spain is inevitable. In all these matters, Bello and Bolívar saw eye to eye. Committed to eliminating the Spanish monarch from the center of the Augustan model, they joined forces in attacking the foundation of royal power in Spanish America, the *real patronato*.

The new Augustus might have been eager to receive praises from friendly poets, but the new Virgil was not willing to sing the name of Bolívar. In fact, as the second decade of the wars of independence began, Bello was not willing to see *any* Spanish American assume the place of Augustus. Instead, he became convinced by San Martín's argument that the only way to put an end to the civil wars of Spanish America was to invite a European prince to the New World. The coronation of a prince from an ancient royal lineage, Bello hoped, would infuse Spanish Americans with respect for authority and encourage European thrones to recognize the independence of the New World.

7

The campaign of the monarchists

Augustus still survives in Maro's strain
And Spenser's verse prolongs Eliza's reign;
Great George's acts let tuneful Cibber sing;
For Nature form'd the Poet for the King.

Samuel Johnson

As the struggle for Spanish American independence entered its tenth year, the patriots could still not agree on the appropriate form of government for the new nations. Some, like Roscio, wished to see republican institutions; others, like Bolívar, urged a monarchy without a crown; still others, like Iturbide in Mexico, wanted to be emperors. Then there was San Martín, the liberator of Argentina and Chile, who maintained that only with a king would peace be restored; only with a king would the European nations acknowledge the independent status of the new nations.

San Martín had a trusted ally, Bernardo O'Higgins, who was named *director supremo* of Chile after the battle of Chacabuco in 1817. At the end of 1818, probably influenced by San Martín, who was then in Santiago, O'Higgins sent Antonio José de Irisarri as envoy to London. Irisarri, a native Guatemalan with family connections in Chile, was charged with three important missions: to gather intelligence on the expedition the Spaniards were preparing in Cádiz, to obtain a loan from British banks, and to coordinate his efforts with the envoy from Buenos Aires, Valentín Gómez, who was at the court of Louis XVIII negotiating the possible transfer of a European prince to the New World. Irisarri knew London from an earlier diplomatic mission, and now he socialized with the British elite, saw Foreign Secretary Castlereagh, and denounced the Spaniards' campaign against Spanish America.[1]

On January 1, 1820, the Spanish troops stationed in Cádiz joined in a rebellion sparked by a young colonel, Riego. The ˌrebellion, fueled by the dire conditions of the military and the grim prospects of crossing the Atlantic to continue the savage war, quickly spread throughout Spain. Ferdinand had no choice but to accept the conditions of the 1812 constitution. The liberals were once again in power in Madrid.

With the imminent danger of a Spanish invasion from Cádiz quelled, Irisarri concentrated his efforts on the financial and political parts of his mission. The monarchic project received the enthusiastic backing of Bello. On April 25, 1820, he wrote to Blanco White consulting his friend about the possibility of establishing a monarchic government in the provinces of Buenos Aires and Chile:

One of the American diplomats in London, a man of talent and good judgment, asks me to make an inquiry of you. The question is this: Supposing that one of the American governments were to establish a monarchy (not like the one of the Spanish Constitution of 1812, but rather a true, though not absolute, monarchy), and this government were to ask the various courts of Europe to send any one of the princes of the reigning families, possibly even a Bourbon. Would this proposal be favorably received, given the present circumstances? It appears to me that no other proposal better reconciles the interests of the [Spanish] Americans (who as you very well know are not fit to be republicans), the antidemocratic principles of the Holy Alliance, the needs of the trading and industrial nations of Europe (which have a strong interest in the peace, if not in the independence, of America) and the interests of Spain herself.

It would be a shame, Bello continued, if the European governments were to forfeit such a good opportunity to reestablish peace. What, he asks Blanco White, would be the best way to propose this project? Which should be the first government to be approached? (*OC*, 25: 94–5).[2]

Blanco White immediately answered Bello's letter: "It seems to me that the only way America can establish a basis for her prosperity and put an end to the barbarous war that is destroying her is by abandoning the republican ideas that have prevailed until now in those countries." He is somewhat skeptical, however, of the plan – how trustworthy is the offer, and how stable are the forces that the deputy represents? Instead of secret negotiations, he suggests a public declaration by a province or a state in favor of a constitutional monarchy. The declaration would offer the throne to a member of the established royal houses. If more than one candidate presents himself, the Congress would make the final selection. The declaration should also include the principles of constitutional monarchy: a bicameral congress, a semi-independent judiciary system, and a free press. Blanco White disregards Bello's suggestion of a Bourbon prince and suggests that the English and Russian royal families be approached (OC, 25: 95–7).

In June 1820 Irisarri invited Bello to participate in publishing a journal that would promote the European recognition of Spanish American sovereignty. In July the first issue of El Censor Americano appeared; the fourth and final issue was published that October. The private letters of Bello and Irisarri show that the political views of the two coeditors were very close. Both were committed to establishing one or more constitutional monarchies in Spanish America. According to Irisarri, Bello was the major contributor to the journal: "Later I published several monthly journals with the title El Censor Americano, in which I was determined to point out the failures and successes of the American governments in their new political journey. This journal became a large volume that draws some of its value from my contributions and much more from the articles with which the very erudite and kind Mr. Bello assisted me."[3]

The style of the articles supports Irisarri's assertion and suggests that most of the contributions to the Censor were written by Bello. In a few articles, for instance "Política" (vol. 3, pp. 195–8), and in a response to an antimonarchist (vol. 4, pp. 281–90), we recognize Irisarri's rich style, his use of metaphors and slight sarcasm, the kind of combative brilliance that led him at times to use the acronym AJI (chili pepper). But Bello's hand is seen throughout the journal. On the first page of the "Prospecto" we read, "It is impossible to abandon the bad road, and to take up the good road, if you do not first know the nature of each one."[4] The "bad road," as the journal sets out to show, is republicanism, while the "good road" is monarchism. The same metaphor appears at the beginning of Bello's letter to Blanco White: "I have no doubt that you will be happy to see that after so many years of nonsense the Americans are beginning to surmise what best suits them and trying to take up the good road."

Primarily a political journal, the *Censor* tells us more about Bello's view of the independence process than the other two journals he coedited in London, the *Biblioteca Americana* and the *Repertorio Americano,* which emphasized literature and science. The first article of the first number, "Estado de la Revolución de América," sets the tone and focus. Ten years have passed, the author writes, since the trumpet of war began to resound in South America. Tyranny and freedom have armed the men who used to be occupied in constructive pursuits: they have replaced the plow with the gun and the sickle with the sword. And the sweet, though violent, peace has been followed by a ferocious and bloody war. Spanish America is not threatened by the expeditions of Spain, but by the "*extravíos*" the new governments must endure before consolidating their independence. The most enlightened men of the New World dazzled the multitudes with doctrines as attractive as they were false, as seductive as they were dangerous. The exaggerated principles of freedom, born in the ardent imagination of Rousseau and Paine, persuaded these men and the people they led that government is a necessary evil, that one should constantly suspect and fear those in power. As a result, authority became worthless, insubordination became a social duty, and government was equated with anarchy. These mistakes were more easily justified among the Spanish Americans than among the Spaniards, who were too close to the French to have forgotten the "evils caused by the false principles of their turbulent and ephemeral republic." While the Spaniards followed the French, Spanish Americans lost their direction by having followed the road of the United States. But both Spaniards and Spanish Americans tried to establish their freedom on foundations of sand.

Later the author defends the monarchic project of the provinces of Río de la Plata: "We are convinced that the South Americans cannot be good republicans, and we believe that this truth is also recognized by the demagogues themselves, who give credence to prejudices that are contrary to this truth in order to favor their ambitious goals." The article ends with a quotation from Alexander Pope:

> Oh stretch thy reign, fair Peace!
> Till conquest cease, and slavery be no more

Till the freed Indians in their native groves
Reap their own fruits, and woo their sable loves;
Peru once more a race of Kings behold,
And other Mexicos be roof'd with Gold.

The poem is translated into Spanish in a footnote; this version has been attributed to Bello by the editorial committee of his complete works. It closes an article that, in my opinion, was also penned by Bello.[5] For a man like Bello, who so closely linked politics and aesthetics, the quotation of these lines from "Windsor Forest" (1714) is a fitting expression of his ardent monarchic phase. In Pope's poem we find both the culmination of the pro-Augustan trend that characterized the reign of Queen Anne and also the beginning of the contemplative and scientific vein that will mark georgic poetry throughout the eighteenth century.

Two other articles in the *Censor* that seem to be Bello's are "Reflexiones sobre la presente constitución de España" (vol. 1, pp. 23–36) and the opening article of the second issue, "Política." These two pieces argue that the Cádiz constitution is not a document that can unite Spaniards and Spanish Americans, despite what many people think, and furthermore that the liberal code is not an extension of the medieval political institutions of Spain. One can trace here Bello's old animosity toward the Spanish Cortes, a feeling he shared with Blanco White. Both articles are characterized by a style that prefers the slow and cautious argument to the brilliant effect, the modulated gradations of thought to the impact of anaphora.[6]

The *Censor Americano* marks a rare moment in Bello's career, his emergence as a political propagandist. Even more than Irisarri, whose opinions about monarchism are often muted, Bello harnesses his full array of linguistic skills to proclaim his ideological allegiances. As in his early London years, he stands close to Blanco White, who in political as well as religious matters continued to be his guide. And through Blanco White – as John R. Dinwiddy has shown – he incorporated the political and cultural baggage of the Whig party, in particular the agenda of Lord Holland and the *Edinburgh Review*. A central tenet of this circle was that government needed an aristocratic higher chamber that controlled a lower chamber which fully represented the people. In philosophical matters Holland's group followed Dugald Stewart and the school of "common sense."

They believed in the preeminence of laws derived from empirical observation, and they distrusted theoretical constructs, particularly in political thought. They opposed the Spanish liberal constitution and the radical democratic principles of Bentham, who in 1820 began to work studiously for the Cortes. And whereas Bentham greatly disliked poetry, Stewart and his disciples at the *Edinburgh Review* held poetry in high esteem. Thus, Bello's political and intellectual affinities were, in 1820, quite distant from those of Bentham and the Spanish liberals but close to those of the Whigs, the group that after 1830 would be called "liberal" in Great Britain.[7]

The *Censor* ceased publication in 1820, but Bello continued to promote the monarchist cause. At the end of 1821, a year in which he lost his wife and suffered a deep religious crisis for which he sought consolation from Blanco White, Bello was in correspondence with Fray Servando Teresa de Mier. The friar had written to Bello in October 1821 and recounted the events since his departure from London in 1816 to accompany the young Spanish liberal, Francisco Javier Mina, in his attempt to liberate Mexico. It had been a disaster. Mina was killed and the friar was once again put in jail: "They buried me in the Inquisition." He remained in jail until 1820, when the liberals outlawed the Inquisition. Mier attacks Iturbide's plans to transform the viceroyalty of New Spain into an independent constitutional monarchy, which could be led by Ferdinand VII or another member of the Bourbon family, and he also lashes out against the United States: "I have written a small work opposing Iturbide's plan with my usual fervor, and it is already printed, but there isn't a damn boat to take it to New Spain. These Anglo-American pigs have been coldly watching as we cut our own throats, and with their promise of nonintervention they have made a deal that trades our blood for Florida." The friar seals his republican convictions by celebrating the Colombian Constitution and its draftsman Roscio, who had died that year (*OC* 25: 111–14).

On November 15, 1821, Bello answered Mier. He reports that Mexican affairs have been followed with much interest in Great Britain, although the British government continues to show its usual reserve. Yet the behavior of Britain has been superior to that of the United States, that "Machiavellian republic," which is, of all nations, ancient or modern, the most hateful to his eyes. Bello then tries to convince his republican friend of the advantages of monarchy:

It is true that England, like the other great European powers, would be happy to see monarchic ideas prevail in our countries. I am not claiming that this movement is the result of their philanthropic views; I know very well the spirit of the cabinets on this side of the sea, and I have never believed that justice and humanity weigh heavily on a statesman's scales. But I will say that on this point the interests of the European cabinets coincide with those of the people of America; that a monarchy (limited, of course) is the only form of government that suits us; and I believe that those countries which due to their circumstances are not allowed to consider this form of rule are most unfortunate. What a shame that Venezuela, after such a glorious struggle, a struggle that in virtue and heroism competes with any of the most famous in history, and that leaves far behind that of the fortunate Americans to the north; what a shame, I say, that for lack of a regular form of government (because republican forms will never be so among us) Venezuela should continue to be the theater of a civil war, especially now that we no longer have anything to fear from the Spaniards.   (OC 25: 114–17)

Bello's letter to Mier was intercepted by the Colombians and wound up in the hands of Pedro Gual, Bolívar's secretary of foreign affairs, who wrote to the Colombian envoy in London, José Rafael Revenga, warning him of Bello's monarchic ideas and urging discretion "in the exchanges with this individual" (OC 25: 118). The letter damaged Bello's reputation among his compatriots, but his cause seemed to gain impetus throughout 1822. The ranks of the monarchists grew with the arrival in England, on August 29, 1822, of San Martín's envoys from Lima, Juan García del Río and James Paroissien, and their secretary, Pedro Creutzer. The mission of these envoys was similar to Irisarri's. They were to negotiate a foreign loan and to make preliminary contacts to establish a European prince in Peru. They had reason to be hopeful: they had come to the European monarchs to offer Lima, the center of wealth, which San Martín had taken pains to avoid damaging in his siege. They were also ready to make substantial concessions to Spain if Peruvian independence was acknowledged.[8]

García del Río and Bello had been friends during the former's earlier stay in London, from 1814 to 1817, as secretary of the mission from Nueva Granada. In September 1822 García del Río was planning to publish a journal, to be called *La Biblio-teca Americana,* and he soon sought Bello's assistance. Mean-while, Irisarri, still in Paris, kept in touch with both Bello and García del Río. But no sooner did the monarchist cause seem to be gathering strength than overwhelming evidence began to arrive from different areas of Europe and America that the forces of history were not on the monarchists' side.

Indeed, as San Martín's envoys crossed the Atlantic, their leader had withdrawn his monarchic plan and yielded to Bolívar's authority. San Martín had liberated the provinces of Río de la Plata, Chile, and Peru – though Spanish troops were still on Peruvian soil. Bolívar had freed Venezuela and Nueva Granada and had formed Colombia, to which he added Quito in 1822. The paths of the two men were converging on the port of Guayaquil. Both could offer reasons to claim that territory, but Bolívar's alacrity ultimately determined the course of events.

Bolívar arrived in Quito on June 16 and soon left for Guaya-quil. He reached the town on July 11 and effectively took con-trol of the port on the thirteenth. Meanwhile, San Martín – ignorant of Bolívar's latest moves – had left for Guayaquil by sea. On July 25 he approached the port and, to his dismay, was greeted by one of Bolívar's assistants.

Bolívar and San Martín had three meetings, the subject of which is veiled by much controversy.[9] For our purposes we shall look at one document, whose authenticity is not questioned, a "confidential note" dictated by Bolívar to his secretary and sent to the Colombian government. It includes an exchange about the political future of Peru and Spanish America in general:

San Martín added that before resigning he would leave the govern-ment's foundations well established, that there should not be a democ-racy in Peru because it was not suitable, and ultimately that a Euro-pean prince should come alone to rule that state. His Excellency responded that it was not suitable to introduce European princes to America or Colombia, because they were foreign to our masses, that he would oppose such a plan if he could, but that he would not be opposed to whatever form of government each state chose for itself, adding on this point all his thoughts with respect to the nature of governments, always referring to his address to the Congress of An-gostura. The Protector replied that the prince would arrive later, and His Excellency responded that the time would never be right for the arrival of such a prince; that he would prefer to offer the crown to General Iturbide, as long as the Bourbons, the Austrians, or other European dynasties did not come.[10]

The document does not say anything new about San Martín's monarchism, but it shows Bolívar's hesitations: he is not against monarchy – he does not object to Iturbide – but opposes a monarchy in the hands of a European. But whatever his hesitations, on one point he is certain: the Spanish American nations will be independent and free only after they have severed all ties to the royal houses of Europe.[11]

San Martín returned to Peru after two days in Guayaquil. His strategy had failed. By avoiding military confrontation in Peru, he may have obtained the goodwill of the Lima aristocracy, but the resolve of his army had been seriously weakened. His greatest obstacle had been communications. Neither he nor La Serna, the Spanish viceroy, could negotiate when the deciding parties were monarchs and princes living an ocean away. Distances had also impeded communication between San Martín and his envoys. It had taken Paroissien and García del Río nine months to travel from Callao to London. Not until February 1823 had they heard of San Martín's decision to step down from power, announced in September of the preceding year.

Further blows to the cause of Bello and García del Río came during the first half of 1823. In April, Spanish Americans, and all of Europe, learned that the royal houses of the Continent were in no mood for constitutional monarchies. French troops carrying the banner of the Holy Alliance invaded Spain and restored Ferdinand VII to absolute power. The Spanish liberals had once again been defeated, this time after three years. They had failed to create a viable constitutional monarchy that could placate the Holy Alliance, on the one hand, or to reach a compromise with Spanish America, on the other. Also during April the principal experiment of a Spanish American constitutional monarchy had reached an end with the fall of Iturbide. Named emperor of Mexico in 1822 after Ferdinand rejected the crown for himself, Iturbide had rapidly revoked the constitutional checks and wielded absolute power until his fall. As Bolívar had predicted in his *Carta de Jamaica*, Mexico had attempted to establish a constitutional monarchy and instead had installed an absolute monarchy. The monarchists' campaign was over. In

June San Martín's envoys received a curt dispatch from the new
Peruvian government, specifically revoking their powers related "to the form of government."[12]

While they were carrying out their political campaign, the
monarchists were also busy contracting loans for the new governments. Irisarri, assisted by Bello, signed in May 1822 a loan
for £1 million, which was placed by Hullet Brothers and Company at 67 percent of the nominal value. Since the Chilean
government had authorized this debt in 1818, Irisarri requested a reconfirmation, but did not wait for the response,
which was negative. The flamboyant envoy was then accused
not only of negotiating a loan without proper authorization but
also of paying himself a 2 percent commission. He later denied
that there was anything immoral about the commission, since it
was customary among other Spanish American envoys. Making
matters worse, he proceeded to spend part of the dwindling
fund (after the discount and commission, little more than
£600,000 was left). He purchased ten tons of copper and other
material to be used for Chilean vessels and a shipment of sugar
that would be sold by the Chilean state. He also acquired at Le
Havre the *Voltaire,* a frigate with twenty cannons on which he
expected to return to Chile.[13] During Irisarri's trip to France to
promote the recognition of the new Spanish American nations,
Bello remained in London, now officially employed at the
Chilean mission.

Another loan for £1.2 million, contracted by García del Río
and Paroissien in October 1822, greatly interested the London
Market. Due to the profits realized on earlier Spanish American loans, the bearer bonds of the Peruvian loan, which were
discounted at 75 percent, soon reached incredible heights.
When García del Río and Paroissien also received a 2 percent
commission, they were virulently attacked by the Peruvians,
and they defended themselves in a pamphlet stating that the
envoys from Colombia, Brazil, Mexico, and Buenos Aires had
received the same commission.[14]

Irisarri's loan contributed to the demise of O'Higgins, and
the junta formed under the direction of Freire sent a new envoy, Mariano Egaña, to investigate thoroughly the Chilean mission in London. García del Río and Paroissien were no longer in
favor in Lima. Their political mission had failed, and their

financial transactions were under scrutiny. Meanwhile, because of his political plans and the intercepted letter to Mier, Bello had become estranged from the Colombian authorities. The position of the monarchists could not have been worse. But these men were determined to have a voice in the affairs of the new nations, and they had enough cash to finance the journal *La Biblioteca Americana,* one of the most splendid monuments of Spanish American culture.

García del Río and Bello had to adjust rapidly to the newest phase of the Revolution. At the moment they prepared to launch the journal, their political formula was no longer viable. The compromise they had sought between freedom and order, of which the British system was the prime example, had vanished. Now the choice was either monarchy or republic – no middle ground existed, no limited or constitutional monarchy. The word "monarchy," never much in favor among the patriots, was by 1823 odious to all. However strong the earlier reasons for favoring a constitutional monarchy, they had all crumbled under the weight of recent events – San Martín's resignation, the Holy Alliance's restitution of Ferdinand, and Iturbide's failed kingdom.

8

Poetry visits America

Besides, a fate attends on all I write,
That when I aim at praise, they say I bite.

Alexander Pope

The first issue of the *Biblioteca Americana*, published in July 1823, was a lavish volume of 470 pages with several color plates of scenes of the New World. Opposite the first page is a lithograph showing a woman in classical attire who is visiting an Indian woman with naked breasts and feathers on her head. The Indian woman is surrounded by palm trees and is sitting on a craggy outcropping at the foot of a mountain. In the background one can see a llama. Between the two women three half-naked children are eagerly playing with gifts that seem to have been presented by the classical woman, who stands with her right arm extended. The gifts include a globe, telescope, lyre, book, bust, palette, and brush. Under the lithograph is the dedication of the journal: "Al Pueblo Americano."

From its very first page, the *Biblioteca Americana* insists on its *americanismo*, its Americanness. It announces that it is underwritten by a Society of Americans ("Por una Sociedad de Americanos"), and the prospectus, signed by García del Río, states, "We shall emphasize throughout everything that is related to America." The editors explain that they will not show a preference for this or that country of the New World; they will address all the inhabitants of the American continent: "We shall not give exclusive consideration to the Colombian, the Argentine, the Peruvian, the Chilean, the Mexican; written for all of them, the *Biblioteca* will be preeminently *American*."

What, we may ask, does the word "América" mean to the editors of the journal? More specifically, what kind of relationship do they envision between Europe and America, between the Old World and the New? The lithograph presents an emblematic answer: Europe, dressed in classical attire, visits America and brings the utensils and objects that mark Western civilization. America's children, in turn, eagerly absorb this culture, as symbolized by their leafing through a printed volume or holding a classical bust. The prospectus of the journal develops this close cultural dependence: the accumulated knowledge of the West must be spread throughout the New World, thus ending three centuries of isolation and ignorance. García del Río, his head filled with the financial transactions that preoccupied him at the time, expresses the relationship between Europe and America as one of creditor and debtor. In the closing paragraph of the prospectus, he elevates the tone of his prose, stating that he foresees a day when rays of truth will shine throughout the New World, when America will traverse with giant steps the roads of the civilized peoples who have advanced before, "until the happy era arrives when America, protected by moderate governments and by enlightened social institutions, rich, flourishing, free, gives back to Europe with interest the wealth of knowledge that she is borrowing today and, fulfilling her lofty destiny, receives the incense of the world."

The *Biblioteca* is divided into three sections: the first is devoted to poetry, literature, and philology; the second, to science and technology; and the third, to politics and history, or – to use the term preferred by the editors – "Ideología," a term borrowed from Destutt de Tracy and the French *idéologues*.[1] Only the first volume of the journal was published in its entirety. Of the second and last volume, only the section devoted to literature was published, in October 1823.

The first piece in the *Biblioteca*'s inaugural issue is a poem by Bello: "Alocución a la Poesía, en que se introducen las alabanzas de los pueblos e individuos americanos, que más se han distinguido en la guerra de la independencia. (Fragmento de un poema inédito, titulado 'América.')" (Discourse to Poetry, which presents the glories of the peoples and individuals of America who have most distinguished themselves in the war of independence. [Fragment of an unpublished poem entitled 'America.']) In the first volume, Bello published the first 447 lines of the poem. The remaining 387 lines opened the second volume of the journal. The manuscripts of the "Alocución" reveal that Bello completed a large portion of the poem between 1821 and 1823, that is, during the years in which he worked as Irisarri's assistant. Sheets 9, 12, and 18 through 25 (containing some three hundred lines of the poem) all show watermarks of those years. Other manuscripts that contain lines of the "Alocución" have no dates, with the exception of sheet 5, which has a watermark of 1814 (see Appendix).

The poem is divided into two sections, which we may term "georgic" (1–206) and "epic" (207–834). In the georgic section the poet invites the goddess Poetry to visit the New World, and to entice her he describes the continent's luscious vegetation and agricultural potential. But on line 207 the poet interrupts his paean to the peaceful beauty of America and asks Poetry if she prefers to sing instead the deeds of war. The rest of the poem is an evocation of the heroes who have perished in the wars of independence. The "Alocución" is thus a reconstruction of the two stages of poetic composition we have noted in Bello's London years. He first focuses on the natural beauty of America, and then – unable to ignore the theme of war – begins to write about the men who gave their lives for independence. The passage that serves as a pivot between these two sections is one that I have dated around 1815 (sheet 5, watermark of 1814), the year that marked a turning point in Bello's reluctant commitment to the patriots. Lines 207–15, in which Bello asks Poetry if she would rather sing about the "impious war" (*la guerra impía*), remind the reader that this poem, which ostensibly celebrates the Revolution, is also a denunciation of those wars.

The poem begins in a mood of rustic serenity, as Bello summons "divine Poetry" to abandon cultivated Europe and to visit the world of Columbus:

> Divina Poesía,
> tú de la soledad habitadora,
> a consultar tus cantos enseñada
> con el silencio de la selva umbría,
> tú a quien la verde gruta fue morada,
> y el eco de los montes compañía;
> tiempo es que dejes ya la culta Europa,
> que tu nativa rustiquez desama,
> y dirijas el vuelo adonde te abre
> el mundo de Colón su grande escena.
>
> (*OC*, 1: 43, ll. 1–10)

(Divine Poetry, you who live in solitude and are taught to learn your songs in the silence of the shady forest; you whose dwelling was the green grotto and whose company was the mountains' echo; it is time that you now abandon Europe, that cultivated land that no longer appreciates your native rusticity, and direct your flight to a place where the world of Columbus opens its great stage to you.)

Ever since Pedro Henríquez Ureña described Bello's poem as a declaration of the spiritual and intellectual independence of Spanish America, these lines have become the cornerstone of *americanismo,* a word that expresses the search for cultural autonomy. Henríquez Ureña was not the first to assign this role to Bello; before him, Juan María Gutiérrez had placed Bello's poem as the front piece of the most famous poetry anthology of mid-nineteenth-century Spanish America, *América Poética,* which was devoted entirely to poetic productions since the Revolution.[2]

To understand what *América* means for Bello and the relationship between the New and the Old World in the "Alocución," we may first look to the context of the published poem. The "Alocución" opens a journal whose guiding hands were two Spanish Americans, Bello and García del Río, who until the eve of publication had advocated inviting a prince of a European royal house to head a monarchy in the New World. The coeditors had earlier embraced Spanish American emancipation in *El Censor Americano* and *La Biblioteca Columbiana,* a journal edited by García del Río in Lima in 1821. But their ideal was an emancipation with close political ties to the monarchies of the European continent. By the time the *Biblioteca Americana* went to press, the monarchic formula was no longer viable, but one still finds testimony to America's dependence on Europe on every page of the journal. The lithograph shows America receiving Europe's gift of accumulated knowledge and glory and America's children promising a new flourishing of the arts and sciences of the West. García del Río's financial metaphor goes even further in suggesting that America is borrowing European culture today and that over the years the New World will repay this loan.

Then comes Bello's "Alocución," whose *americanismo* closely

fits that of the journal. Poetry and America are the two elements that establish the drama of his poem. Bello invites Poetry
to abandon Europe because the Old World can no longer offer
her the natural setting she needs to thrive. But Bello's Poetry is
in every sense a classical construct, a topic of invocation of
Greek, Roman, and British poets. Like the classically attired
woman in the frontispiece lithograph, Poetry is the personifica-
tion of the European spirit in search of a new stage on which to
extend the march of civilization.

If the opening of the "Alocución" is the cry of Spanish America's cultural independence, the cornerstone of its spiritual
emancipation, Bello defines that autonomy not as a break with
Europe, but as an incorporation of the very essence of European culture. America is to be the newest home for a goddess
who has earlier visited the different lands of the European
continent and the British Isles. In "The Progress of Poesy,"
Thomas Gray, a poet praised by Bello in the *Biblioteca*, similarly
shows the route followed by the Muses, who abandon Greece
and Italy – which have been enchained by pomp, power, and
vice – and arrive on the coast of Britain:

> Alike they scorn the pomp of tyrant-Power,
> And coward Vice, that revels in her chains.
> When Latium had her lofty spirit lost,
> They sought, oh Albion! next the sea-encircled
>   coast.[3]

Gray's lines are unmistakably the direct antecedent of the opening of the "Alocución." The theme of wandering Poetry, or
Poesy, who abandons the tyranny and decadence of the European continent in search of a fresh natural setting, is identical
in both poems. The same distance is established between the
new setting of the goddess and the previous places she has
visited. The opening of the "Alocución" may well be the starting
point of *americanismo*, but for Bello this term implied something
essentially akin to Gray's "Englishness," a kind of rhetorical
patriotism, with distinguished classical antecedents, that reas-
serted the centrality and continuing importance of European
civilization.

As in Gray's poem, there is in the "Alocución" a break with
Europe, but it is a break with the decrepitude of the European
continent. At the beginning of his poem, Bello offers to Poetry

a setting that Europe itself can no longer offer her. His strategy will be to entice Poetry to abandon the corrupt courts of continental Europe and settle in the fresh lands across the Atlantic that still preserve the original vigor of Creation ("*el vigor guardan genital primero*"). Bello thus adopts a topos used by enemies of the ancien régime since the eighteenth century, according to which Europe is an old and tired land and America a land of freshness and freedom:

> ¿Qué a ti, silvestre ninfa, con las pompas
> de dorados alcázares reales?
> ¿A tributar también irás en ellos,
> en medio de la turba cortesana,
> el torpe incienso de servil lisonja? (ll. 24–8)[4]

> (What does the pomp of golden royal castles
> have to offer you, sylvan nymph? Will you also
> go there and offer, amidst a crowd of courtiers,
> the dishonest incense of servile flattery?)

The poem proper thus begins with a loud condemnation of the very kind of poetry Bello had practiced in the colonial days, when he set Charles IV amidst clouds of incense. No, he now argues, that is not the setting for Poetry. In the youth of humankind she did not attend luxurious palaces, but simply tried to sing the first laws to the people and their kings. In these lines Bello also calls for "natural" poetry, an aesthetic that will shun the excesses of neoclassicism and return to the models of the Spanish Middle Ages and the Golden Age.[5]

Bello then returns to his attack on the European continent but now he is more specific:

> No te detenga, oh diosa,
> esta región de luz y de miseria,
> en donde tu ambiciosa
> rival Filosofía,
> que la virtud a cálculo somete,
> de los mortales te ha usurpado el culto;
> donde la coronada hidra amenaza
> traer de nuevo al pensamiento esclavo
> la antigua noche de barbarie y crimen;
> donde la libertad vano delirio,
> fe la servilidad, grandeza el fasto,
> la corrupción cultura se apellida. (ll. 33–43)

> (O Goddess, do not linger in this region of light
> and misery where Philosophy, your ambitious

rival who subjects virtue to calculation, has
usurped from you the worship of mortals;
where the crowned hydra threatens to bring to
the enslaved mind the ancient night of barbarity
and crime; where liberty is called vain delirium;
servility, faith; pomp, greatness; and corruption,
culture.)

Arturo Ardao has argued convincingly that the first lines of
this passage are an attack against Bentham's "moral arithmetic"
and his use of "calculation" in ethics.[6] Next, Bello assaults the
"coronada hidra," the tyrannical absolute monarchy, personified
by the Holy Alliance, which threatens to restore the old order.
Bello also criticizes the conditions of Europe, above all those of
Spain and France in 1823; these conditions have distorted the
meaning of words and exacerbated domestic tensions. And Bello censures equally the *liberales* for having transformed the
meaning of freedom into "vain delirium," and the *serviles* for
hiding their political backwardness under the mask of religious
faith. Here for the first time Bello uses *"fe"* (faith) to describe
the reactionary spirit of the Catholic Church and its backing of
the absolutist cause. In Chapter 9 we shall see the significance
of this word in the "Agricultura de la zona tórrida." This entire
passage, in short, is a criticism of the political conditions that
have existed in Europe, and specifically in Spain, during at least
the preceding decade.

Later in the "Alocución" Bello levels a more explicit criticism
at both sides of continental politics – the side of the *liberales* and
that of the *serviles*. In a passage describing the events in Spain
since Ferdinand's reconquest, Bentham's "calculations" again
appear:

¿Puebla la inquisición sus calabozos
de americanos; o españolas cortes
dan a la servidumbre formas nuevas?
. . . .
Colombia vence; libertad los vanos
cálculos de los déspotas engaña.
                    (ll. 546–48, 551–2)

(Does the Inquisition populate its dungeons
with Americans? Do Spanish Cortes give new
forms to servitude? Colombia wins; liberty out-
wits the vain calculations of the despots.)

The two sides of Spanish politics are presented as simply two different versions of despotism. The old version Bello calls the "*inquisición*," his favorite synecdoche for the alliance of Crown and Church; the new version is the liberal Cortes, whose tyranny over the New World is even more absolute.[7] Poetry, therefore, should leave the regions now dominated by the philosophy of Bentham and servitude to the past.

As an alternative Bello presents to Poetry the attractions of America. She could settle near the clear river of Buenos Aires, where the heroes of Albion were defeated; or in the valleys of Chile, where the innocence and candor of the ancient world are combined with valor and patriotism, or in the city of the Aztec, rich with inexhaustible veins that almost satiated the avarice of Europe; or in Quito, Bogotá, or the valleys of Venezuela. Any of these settings would prove hospitable to Poetry, and the day will come when an American Virgil will sing about the agriculture of the New World:

> Tiempo vendrá cuando de ti inspirado
> algún Marón americano, ¡oh diosa!
> también las mieses, los rebaños cante,
> el rico suelo al hombre avasallado,
> y las dádivas mil con que la zona
> de Febo amada al labrador corona;
> donde cándida miel llevan las cañas,
> y animado carmín la tuna cría,
> donde tremola el algodón su nieve,
> y el ananás sazona su ambrosia. (ll. 189–98)

> (A time will come, O Goddess! when some American Maro inspired by you will also sing the fields of grain, the flocks, the rich soil subdued by man, and the thousand gifts with which the zone loved by Phoebus crowns the peasant, where the canes bear white honey and the prickly pear nurtures lively crimson, where cotton waves its snow and the pineapple ripens its ambrosia.)

The "American Maro" is, of course, Bello himself, and these lines are the announcement of his next poem, "Agricultura de la zona tórrida." But Bello has already begun to sing America's beauty in the first part of the "Alocución"; we have already tasted his georgic passion, his gift for describing nature and human transformation of nature.

Thus far, Bello has defined his *americanismo* as a rejection of a specific version of European culture, of which the Spain of the 1820s offers the best example. In the first fourth of the poem he has drawn on the contemporary topos of European corruption and American youth, a ubiquitous theme in the post-Napoleonic era, and he has shown the New World's luscious and pure vegetation. Now the "Alocución" moves from geography to history, and the remaining three-fourths of the poem are devoted to the heroes of the wars of independence.

The names of the greatest heroes – Bolívar, San Martín, O'Higgins – however, do not figure in Bello's catalogue. San Martín is briefly mentioned in a periphrasis. Of O'Higgins, who has just fallen from power, nothing is said. And Bolívar is praised in a roundabout *recusatio* at the end of the poem when Bello says that the deeds of the Libertador will be written by a more skilled pen:

> Mas no a mi débil voz la larga suma
> de sus victorias numerar compete;
> a ingenio más feliz, más docta pluma,
> su grata patria encargo tal comete,
> pues como aquel samán que siglos cuenta,
> de la vecinas gentes venerado,
> que vio en torno a su basa corpulenta
> el bosque muchas veces renovado,
> y vasto espacio cubre con la hojosa
> copa, de mil inviernos victoriosa;
> así tu gloria al cielo se sublima,
> Libertador del pueblo colombiano;
> digna de que la lleven dulce rima
> y culta historia al tiempo más lejano.
>
> (ll. 821–34)

(But my weak voice is not qualified to enumerate the long account of his victories; his grateful fatherland entrusts such a work to a happier talent, to a more learned pen. For just like that *samán* of centuries, venerated by the neighboring peoples, which saw the forest renewed many times around its massive base, covers a vast space with its leafy top, victorious over a thousand winters, thus your glory is sublimated to the sky, Liberator of the Colombian people, worthy to be carried to the most distant future by sweet rhyme and erudite history.)

In the "Alocución" Bolívar's glory is enhanced outside the poem. But we have to go back to the poem in order to realize that the American Virgil declines to praise the new Augustus for reasons that have little to do with the poet's "weak voice." We may then understand why his name is not included in the list of Spanish Americans "who have most distinguished themselves in the wars of independence."

For his list of heroes Bello was inspired, as noted in Chapter 6, by Anchises' catalogue of heroes in book 6 of the *Aeneid*. In a passage devoted to Francisco Javier Ustáriz, Bello names the classical heroes who will accompany the new Spanish American heroes in the Elysian fields:

> De mártires que dieron por la patria
> la vida, el santo coro te rodea:
> Régulo, Trásea, Marco Bruto, Decio,
> cuantos inmortaliza Atenas libre,
> cuantos Esparta y el romano Tibre.
>
> (ll. 653–7)

> (The holy choir of martyrs who gave their lives for their fatherland surrounds you: Regulus, Thrasea, Marcus Brutus, Decius, all those whom free Athens, Sparta and the Roman Tiber immortalize.)

Each of these Roman republicans brings to mind Augustus, who, of course, is not named in the poem. The Decii, for example, were favorite heroes of Virgil praised in both the *Georgics* and the *Aeneid*. The name symbolizes self-sacrifice: with a purple-edged toga, with a veiled head, and invoking the Roman gods, the first Decius ran to meet his death, causing terror among Rome's enemies. Years later, the same act was imitated by the second Decius. The Decii appear in line 169 of book 2 of the *Georgics*, one line before Caesar, and again in line 824 of book 6 of the *Aeneid*, shortly after Anchises has described Augustus to Aeneas (ll. 789–807).

Regulus, the hero immortalized in Horace's Ode 3.5, urged the Roman Senate to reject the unfavorable terms for peace proposed by the Carthaginians, announcing that he would rather be tortured defending the integrity of the Roman republic than yield to its perfidious foes. But Horace praises Regulus in a poem devoted to Augustus – "In honorem Augusti."

In his move from monarchism to republicanism, Bello thus alludes to a poem in which the divinely inspired monarch ("divus Augustus") is set against a background of republican life. But unlike the Augustan poets, Bello refuses to celebrate any monarchs or would-be monarchs.

If Regulus and Decius suggest positive images of the *princeps,* Marcus Brutus and Thrasea are renowned for their opposition to absolute monarchy. Brutus, along with Cassius and other leading Roman senators, assassinated Julius Caesar in 44 B.C. He was later defeated by the forces of Antony and Octavian at Philippi, having failed to restore the republic of the *optimates.* The archenemy of monarchy, Marcus Brutus is placed by Dante in the last circle of hell. Thrasea represents the Stoics who wished to preserve the fortitude of old republican values during a period of imperial oppression. He refused to flatter Nero or to believe in Poppaea's divinity. His unjust death, decreed by that mask of legality that the Senate had become under the Caesars, closes the extant text of the *Annals* of Tacitus, who was, of course, Augustus's classical foe.

Thus, Augustus is absent from the "Alocución" and his foes are celebrated. The same is true of Bolívar, for a large number of the heroes celebrated in the second part of the poem – Ribas, Castillo, Miranda, Piar – were in some important way at odds with the Libertador. Ribas (ll. 490–509) blamed Bolívar for the disaster of Aragua in 1814 and incarcerated him; Castillo (l. 528) was Bolívar's enemy in the civil war that contributed to the fall of Cartagena. Still more incriminating are the long sections on Miranda (ll. 674–702), in whose fall Bolívar was implicated, and Piar (ll. 736–50), who was executed in 1817 for disobeying the Libertador.

Moreover, a veiled but sharp criticism of Bolívar is implied by the overall charge of perfidy that runs throughout the poem. Bello brandishes this charge against the Church (ll. 605–20), but also against the patriots who acted disloyally. After singing the praises of Miranda, Bello defends his capitulation and assails the treachery of those who handed him over to the Spaniards:

> y si, de contratiempos asaltado
> que a humanos medios resistir no es dado,
> te fue el ceder forzoso, y en cadena
> a manos perecer de una perfidia,
> tu espíritu no ha muerto, no; (ll. 694–8)

(and if, assaulted by mishaps that human means
are not able to avoid, you were forced to yield,
and died in chains at the hands of a treacherous
act, your spirit has not died, no;)

Bolívar, as we have seen, played a principal role in the transactions leading to Miranda's imprisonment, and Bello had earlier, in the *Outline*, used a softer word – "ingratitude" – to describe Bolívar's conduct in the matter.

Perfidy also marks the conclusion of the long passage devoted to Morillo (ll. 509–81). The beginning of this passage is straightforward. As in the *Outline*, Morillo is charged with cruelty, particularly in his murderous rampages at Cartagena and Bogotá. The passage continues with what at first appears to be an address to Morillo, who is compared, unfavorably, to Spanish conquerors like Cortés and Pizarro and to the duke of Alba. But the passage ends with accusations that are entirely inappropriate to Morillo:

Quien te pone con Alba en paralelo,
¡oh cuánto yerra! En sangre bañó el suelo
de Batavia el ministro de Felipe;
pero si fue crüel y sanguinario,
bajo no fue; no acomodando al vario
semblante de los tiempos su semblante,
ya desertor del uno,
ya del otro partido,
sólo el de su interés siguió constante;
no alternativamente
fue soldado feroz, patriota falso;
no dio a la inquisición su espada un día,
y por la libertad lidió el siguiente;
ni traficante infame del cadalso,
hizo de los indultos granjería. (ll. 567–81)

(He who draws a parallel between you and Alba,
oh how greatly he errs! Philip's minister soaked
the soil of Batavia with blood, but if he was cruel
and bloody, he was not base; he did not adjust
his appearance to the changing appearance of
the times, a deserter now of this, now of the
other party; he only followed with constancy the
party of his own interest; he was not, alternatively, a ferocious soldier, a false patriot; he
did not give his sword to the Inquisition one day,
and fight for freedom the next, nor as a shameles dealer of the gallows, did he profit from pardon.)

The subject of these lines cannot possibly be Morillo, who defended the royalist cause with persistence and intransigence. No one could say that he had ever surrendered his sword to the Inquisition. This would imply that at some point Morillo was the enemy of Spain. Nor had Morillo ever struggled for freedom. Until 1820, the year he left Venezuela after being forced to sign an armistice with the patriots, Morillo was a relentless foe of the patriots' cause.

Who, then, is Bello talking about in this passage? Who is this man who one day surrendered to the Spaniards and the next day fought for the cause of freedom? The details suggest episodes in the life of Bolívar, particularly the events surrounding the fall of Miranda. It would seem that Bello has veiled his acute censure of Bolívar in the guise of an attack on Morillo. As we shall see in Chapter 10, Bello's criticism did not escape the sharp eye of Bolívar, who offered a fascinating reading of the "Alocución" in his conversations with Perú de Lacroix.

Bello's feelings toward Bolívar covered the spectrum of human emotion, from admiration to anger. In 1820 Bello still expressed even to close friends his admiration for the Libertador. In one of his letters Irisarri refers to Bello's constant friendship with Bolívar, and Alamiro de Avila has suggested that a very favorable biography of Bolívar, which appeared as an appendix to Irisarri's *Carta al Observador de Londres,* was written by Bello.[8] Other documents, especially a letter of November 1826, bear out similar feelings. But in Bello's poetry one detects an undercurrent of sharp criticism of Bolívar, a kind of verbal sneering. In the "Alocución" this criticism is veiled; in other poems – especially the "Carta" to Olmedo of 1827 – it becomes explicit.

The reasons for Bello's anger are understandable. By October 1823 details about the Guayaquil negotiations had probably reached London, and it became clear that the real enemy of the monarchists' cause was Bolívar. Bello had little choice but again to redefine his political outlook. Bolívar's continued ascendancy dashed Bello's hopes for establishing in America political and cultural systems modeled on eighteenth-century Britain: in politics, a controlled or limited monarchy; in literature, an emulation of the Roman Augustan aesthetic reshaped by the absence of Augustus.[9] Like the British Augustans, Bello and the monarchists hoped to fill the center of power with a figure who would preserve the legacy of monarchic institutions and at the same time revoke the absolutist and tyrannical elements those institutions had acquired since the sixteenth century.

In the eyes of the monarchists, the throne could not be entrusted to a Spanish American. The luster of lineage, the almost immemorial ascent to power, gave the royal houses of Europe a privilege and respect that could not be emulated by any upstart. Iturbide was proof of the dangers of any *"monarquía criolla."* First the pretense of freedom, then tyranny. The one experiment with a Spanish American monarchy had devolved into absolute power or, as Bello put it, the "yoke of Iturbide" (*la coyunda de Iturbide,* "Alocución," l. 286). Now that Bolívar had barred any hope of establishing a European royal house in America, Bello creates a poem that extols Bolívar's enemies and declares that Bolívar will have to look elsewhere for his poet. The closing allusions to the future glory of the Libertador and the closing *recusatio* are an elegant form of political attack.

Though Bello has broken with Augustus, he preserves a certain nostalgia for the Augustan order, for its pomp and solemnity. The Augustan model of power never became completely distasteful to Bello:

> ¿Dó está la torre bulliciosa
> que pregonar solía,
> de antorchas coronadas,
> la pompa augusta del solemne día?
> Entre las rotas cúpulas que oyeron
> sacros ritos ayer, torpes reptiles
> anidan, y en la sala que gozosos
> banquetes vio y amores, hoy sacude
> la grama del erial su infausta espiga.
>   (ll. 423–31)

(Where is the boisterous tower crowned with torches which used to proclaim the august pomp of the solemn day? Among the shattered domes that only yesterday witnessed sacred rites ugly reptiles make their nests, and in the hall that saw happy banquets and loves, now wild grass shakes its ill-fated spike.)

But the political model of colonial Caracas could no longer survive. Bello was forced, as were the philosophers and poets of the Enlightenment, to find a political model that could replace absolute monarchy. His next choice, a British-style monarchy, was not to be. He then was willing to settle for the model on which limited or constitutional monarchies were often based, that of republican Rome. Like Voltaire, Bello – though probably still believing in the advantages of monarchy – could call himself a republican. Like Montesquieu, he could easily shift his allegiances between British limited monarchy and Roman republicanism. Like Horace and Virgil, he could hail republican heroes.

By 1823 Bello was convinced that the future of Spanish America would be linked to republicanism. His task would be to give shape to this political formula, to adapt it as closely as possible to a model of constitutional monarchy. As for the luster of kingdoms, the glory of empires – these, like Rome, were fallen. To close the literary section of the second volume of the *Biblioteca Americana*, Bello chose Quevedo's famous poem on what remains of Roman glory. Bello's initials follow the poem, as a signature at the end of his journal, to be sure, but almost as though he has taken an oath of allegiance to Quevedo's theme:

> Buscas en Roma a Roma, oh peregrino,
> y en Roma misma a Roma no la hallas;
> Cadáver son las que ostentó murallas,
> Y tumba de sí propio el Aventino.
>
> Yace, donde reinaba, el Palatino,
> Y limadas del tiempo las medallas
> Mas se muestran destrozo a las batallas
> De las edades, que blasón latino.
>
> Sólo el Tibre quedó, cuya corriente
> Si ciudad la regó, ya sepultura
> La llora con funesto son doliente.
>
> ¡Oh Roma! en tu grandeza, en tu hermosura
> Huyó lo que era firme, y solamente
> Lo fugitivo permanece y dura.
>
> (You look for Rome in Rome, O pilgrim! and in Rome itself you do not find Rome. The walls she once flaunted are now a corpse, and the Aventine is its own tomb.
>
> The Palatine lies where it once reigned, and the medals filed down by time resemble more the destruction of the battle of the ages than a Latin coat of arms.

Only the Tiber was left; and if its current irrigated her as a city, as a grave it now mourns her with a sad, aching sound.

O Rome! from your greatness, from your beauty all firmness escaped, and only what is fugitive remains and endures.)

9

"Agricultura"

Dans les pays Despotiques, où l'esclave n'ose parler à son maître, la langue prendra un ton allégorique et mystérieux: et c'est là que naîtront les apologues et le style figuré.

Jacques Delille

In 1823 the Revolution was coming to an end, and Spanish Americans were beginning to enjoy peace and international support. While Castlereagh had persisted in a policy of neutrality, Canning was decisively in favor of independence, viewing it as inevitable in the long run and also desirable for British commercial interests. In October Canning obtained from Polignac, the French ambassador to London, a memorandum stating that French troops would not invade Spanish America. The same month Canning sent consuls to Buenos Aires, Montevideo, Santiago, and Lima, paving the way for full recognition of Spanish American independence. In December President Monroe announced that the United States would oppose any European power that launched an invasion anywhere on the American continent.[1]

Despite these unmistakable signs of support, there was the unresolved problem of Peru. As Bello had said in the "Alocución": "la ciudad que dio a los Incas cuna / Aún gime esclava" (the city that gave birth to the Incas still groans as a slave). The Spaniards still occupied large zones of the Peruvian *altiplano*, and the patriots were resolved to expel them. There was to be no vestige of imperialism in the New World. On August 9, 1824, cavalry troops from Colombia, Peru, Ireland, and England, under Bolívar's command, defeated the Spaniards in the battle of Junín. Not a shot was fired, and the Spaniards fled after an hour. As Bolívar wrote to Peñalver in one of his rare references to this event: "So great is the reputation of our army that the Spaniards have not dared to fight us. We have made marvelous progress in this country without firing a single rifle shot."[2] Sucre sealed the struggle for independence in December when some five thousand patriots, mostly Colombians, defeated the troops of Viceroy La Serna in Ayacucho.

Meanwhile, Bello had lost his position as secretary of the Chilean mission. After O'Higgins's fall, Freire's new government had sent Mariano Egaña to London, primarily to settle the matter of the Irisarri loan. Egaña did not dismiss Bello from the Chilean mission; not knowing any English, he badly needed his help. But since Bello insisted on defending Irisarri, the tensions between the two men rapidly increased. Bello had already written to Pedro Gual, the secretary of foreign affairs, in August 1824, seeking a position in the Colombian mission. It seems that Bello had first considered the possibility of moving to Chile, but soon dismissed the idea: "The idea of moving to the Antarctic pole and abandoning forever my homeland is unbearable to me" (OC, 25: 133).

Bello wrote to Gual again in January 1825 and renewed his petition. He begins the letter by evoking their happy youth as university students and then asks for news of the university: "And how is our ancient and venerable nurse? Has she already discarded the hoop skirt of the Aristotelian–Thomistic doctrine, and agreed to dress herself for the times? I have no doubt that she has, because the impetus given by the Revolution to new opinions cannot have been favorable to the outmoded fashions that fed pabulum to the imagination rather than the understanding of the Americans" (OC, 25: 142). Again Bello tells Gual that he does not want to end up at the Antarctic pole, and paraphrasing Virgil's first eclogue, he says that he does not wish to die among the Chileans, who are so distant from the rest of the world: "It is painful for me to abandon the country of my birth, and to face death sooner or later at the Antarctic pole among the *toto divisos orbe chilenos* who will no doubt consider me an intruder." In both letters Bello expresses the hope that he can still count on Bolívar's support.

Late in 1824 Pedro Gual wrote to Bello naming him secretary to Manuel José Hurtado, the Colombian envoy in London. In January of the following year the British government announced to Spain its intention to recognize Buenos Aires, Mexico, and Colombia. Bello, who assumed his new position on February 7, participated in the negotiations that led to Britain's full diplomatic recognition of Colombia.[3] British recognition was the long-awaited sign that marked the end of the wars of independence; but Spanish America's problems were far from over. The Revolution had left the new states bankrupt. Several countries were borrowing heavily from Great Britain, but only a small fraction of the £21 million in loans was invested in the new countries. For one thing, the loans were discounted by huge margins: Buenos Aires, for example, received £600,000 for a loan of £1,000,000. For another, a large portion of the funds received had been used to finance the wars, against Brazil in the case of Buenos Aires, against Spain in the campaigns of Junín and Ayacucho in the case of Colombia. Finally, a large outflow of capital from Spanish America resulted from consumer purchases. Nor were the new countries capitalized with direct foreign investment. The investments that poured into Spanish America in 1824 and 1825 went mainly into speculative mining ventures that soon became insolvent. In 1825 Chile, Colombia, and Peru stopped payments on their debt, causing the bankruptcy of seven financial institutions in England and a crisis that had repercussions throughout Europe.[4]

In addition to the economic crisis, Spanish America was suffering from the sordid manipulations of the defeated Ferdinand, who in 1824 used his influence with Pope Leo XII to stage a last attempt to recover the colonies. The Pope's encyclical, which urged the Spanish American nations to recognize the Spanish monarch as their legitimate leader, contributed to the instability of the new republics, though it met with solid opposition. Servando Teresa de Mier wrote an impassioned *Discurso sobre la encíclica del Papa León XII*. His language was scathing: "It is a mere letter of formality written in mystical gibberish, or more exactly: it is an Italian swindle typical of those the Roman court uses to dismiss the straits and bonds in which the crowned heads place her." He charges the Spaniards with creating divisions among Spanish Americans by means of "a Gothic-ultramontane parchment." He even dares the Holy Alliance to attack the New World. Let the Holy Alliance come to our coasts, he says. And if the Pope wishes to form part of the expedition, as temporal prince, war will also be waged against him, as in the times of Charles V and Philip II. The friar concludes his diatribe by warning all Mexicans not to be seduced by the maneuvers of Ferdinand VII and Leo XII.[5]

The Vatican soon accepted the fact that Spain had lost the Indies, and diplomatic relations were established. As the threat of a new invasion from Spain became less likely, the new nations started to exhibit a frail domestic political equilibrium. Bolívar had once said that he was more afraid of peace than of war, and events would bear out his premonition.

A large part of the postwar debate in Colombia concerned the role of the Church. Government representatives, on the one hand, wished to preserve the regalist primacy of state over church and to encourage religious toleration. The Constitution of Cúcuta allowed foreigners to settle in Colombia and also allowed Masonic and Protestant organizations to publish material in opposition to the supremacy of Rome. The leading figures of the Colombian government, furthermore, took a personal interest in promoting a new air of tolerance. Santander, the vice-president of Colombia, and Restrepo, the minister of the interior, encouraged Masonic organizations and anticlericalism. And Pedro Gual became the first president of the Colombia chapter of the British Bible Society, a chapter founded by James Thompson during his extensive travels throughout Spanish America.

The ultramontane clergy, who saw the rise of government-sponsored anticlericalism as a direct threat to the monopoly they had enjoyed, were not ready to yield. It was not, however, in the center of Colombian power, in Bogotá, that the confrontation between the clergy and the state was felt most strongly, but in Caracas. Here the Church opposed the distribution of Spanish Bibles and resorted to the familiar tactics of inciting slaves to rebellion. In 1824 the slaves of Petare, a Caracas suburb, rose in defense of Ferdinand; a priest was accused of promoting the insurrection. Other similar incidents followed, and it was suspected that the Church was coordinating the efforts of rebellion with the forces of Spain and France.[6]

Buoyed by the diplomatic progress with Great Britain, but disheartened by the religious, economic, and political crises,

Bello and García del Río decided to resume publishing a journal. This time, however, they would be more realistic and design a shorter and less expensive format. The title of the new journal was *El Repertorio Americano,* of which four volumes appeared in 1826 and 1827. Guillermo Guitarte is probably right to argue that García del Río played the leading role in the *Biblioteca,* but he is incorrect to extend this observation to the *Repertorio.* As a perusal of the index of the facsimile edition of the *Repertorio* reveals, Bello signed twenty-nine poems, translations, and articles. In contrast, García del Río signed only thirteen articles.[7]

In the *Repertorio* Bello finally seems comfortable with the radical breach brought about by the Revolution, but he continues emphasizing the need to preserve links with Europe, including Spain, and with classical culture and the Enlightenment. His *americanismo* is in the tradition of Miranda, marked by a complex weaving of Western tradition and the energy of the emerging nations. In an article on Columbus, Miranda's tutelary figure, Bello tries to settle the issue of the animosity between Spain and Spanish America, which is perhaps the thorniest topic in any discussion of *americanismo.* Bello says: "We do not have the slightest inclination to vituperate the Conquest. Whether it was atrocious or not, we owe the origin of our rights and our existence to it, and through the Conquest our soil received that part of European civilization that could sift through the prejudice and tyranny of Spain" (*OC,* 23: 452).

Religious tolerance is another topic often raised in the *Repertorio.* In the first volume there is a review of Mier's *Discurso* and one of a favorite work among regalists, Tamburini's *Verdadera idea de la Santa Sede,* both of which emphasize the division of church and state and the limited power of the papacy. In the second volume an article by James Thompson informs the British Bible Society of the progress of Lancaster's educational reform in Spanish America despite orthodox resistance. An attack on innate ideas and a reliance on experience, origins, and clear language run throughout the journal, especially in the articles on philosophy, orthographic reform, and education. Bello uses inductive reasoning in all his scientific articles and expounds on this method in some detail in the "Introducción a los elementos de física del dr. N. Arnott." This article, a translation of Arnott's *Elements of Physics,* originally published in 1825, is a recapitulation of all the advantages of the British Enlightenment and a declaration of faith in scientific progress, economic growth, and free trade.

Many pages of the journal were written by Spanish liberals exiled in London. Vicente Salvá, a philologist and politician, wrote bibliographical notes on classic Spanish texts; Pablo Mendibil, a Basque recommended to Bello by Blanco White, wrote ten articles for the *Repertorio,* including a review of the British legislative and judiciary bodies, based on a book translated into Spanish by Blanco White. In addition, publications by liberal Spaniards – Mora, Canga Argüelles, and Urcullu – were often reviewed in the journal. The Spanish *liberales,* who had been the object of Bello's attack since the beginning of the Revolution, are now his friends, denoting the first sign of reconciliation between Spaniards and Spanish Americans after the wars of independence.

As had *La Biblioteca Americana, El Repertorio Americano* opens with a poem by Bello. The title lines read:

SILVAS AMERICANAS
SILVA I. – LA AGRICULTURA DE LA ZONA TORRIDA

In a footnote, Bello writes: "The fragments published in the *Biblioteca Americana* under the title 'América' belong with these silvas. The author thought of recasting them all in a single poem; convinced that this was impossible, he will publish them in their original form, with certain corrections and additions. In this first part, one will find only two or three lines from those fragments." This explanatory note, the cause of much misunderstanding among Bello scholars, is clarified by an examination of Bello's manuscripts. Shortly before the publication of the "Agricultura" in the *Repertorio* in October 1826, Bello attempted to merge this poem with the "Alocución" in another text, titled "El campo americano."[8]

So as not to confuse readers who were expecting a continuation of the poem *América,* Bello announces his new project, a series of "Silvas americanas," the first one being the "Agricultura." The fragments published in the *Biblioteca* now also belong to this collection of silvas. But this new project, like *América* and "El campo americano," was never completed. Of

the "Silvas americanas" Bello published only the "Agricultura."
The "Alocución" was not republished under the new series title,
though Bello's footnote has led most readers to include it with
the "Agricultura" as one of the "Silvas americanas."

In the "Agricultura" Bello abandons entirely the epic mode
and returns to the georgic tone and theme that had been his
first inspiration upon arriving in London. After Junín and
Ayacucho, the threats of Spanish reconquest had diminished,
and thus the focus of the *Repertorio* shifts from war and independence to the future organization of the Spanish American
republics. Like Virgil after Actium, like Pope after Utrecht,
Bello turns his attention to a plan for peace. But more significantly, in the "Agricultura" Bello offers a recapitulation of the
transformations that the wars of independence have brought
about. It is his most profound meditation on the shift from
colonial servitude to freedom.

In the first two sections of the poem (ll. 1–63) Bello invokes
the natural fecundity of the torrid zone. The first line – "Salve,
fecunda zona" – is drawn, as many critics have observed, from
line 173 of book 2 of the *Georgics* – "Salve, magna parens
frugum, Saturnia tellus" (Hail, land of Saturn, great giver of
fruits) – which immediately follows the three lines devoted to
Octavian in book 2 (ll. 170–2). Bello's opening lines are also
inspired by the opening lines of Lucretius's *De rerum natura*.
The Venezuelan poet recalls nostalgically the fertility of the
torrid zone, where jasmine and cotton, wheat and grapes grow
in abundance. The second section closes with a description of
the banana tree, which Bello associates with *both* slavery and
happiness:

> y para ti el banano
> desmaya al peso de su dulce carga;
> el banano, primero
> de cuantos concedió bellos presentes
> Providencia *a las gentes*
> *del ecuador feliz con mano larga.*
> No ya de humanas artes obligado
> el premio rinde opimo;
> no es a la podadera, no al arado
> deudor de su racimo;
> *escasa industria bástale, cual puede*
> *hurtar a sus fatigas mano esclava;*

crece veloz, y cuando exhausto acaba,
adulta prole en torno le sucede.
                    (*OC*, 1: 66–7, ll. 50–63;
                              my emphasis)
(for you [torrid zone] the banana tree faints under the weight of its sweet burden; the banana
tree, the first of all the beautiful gifts offered
generously by Providence *to the people of the happy
equatorial region.* Unforced by the skill of man, it
yields a rich reward; it owes its bunch neither to
the pruning knife nor to the plow; *it requires only
a small amount of effort, such that an enslaved hand
can steal from its labors;* it grows quickly, and when
it dies of exhaustion, a grown progeny succeeds
it all around.)

Bello also remarks on the relationship between slavery and a
carefree, if not happy, existence in one of his footnotes to the
poem. He says that from the banana tree, and with minimal
effort, the slaves in the haciendas and plantations derive their
nourishment and everything that makes their life tolerable.[9]

In Chapter 1 we observed that Bello frequently drew analogies between the colonial period and the golden age. The first
two sections of the "Agricultura" elaborate on these similarities.
As in the golden age, there is here an abundance of fruits; and
almost no labor, no special technique, no "agricultura" is
needed for the satisfaction of basic human needs. The inhabitants of the torrid zone live in carefree servitude, in a kind of
passable but unenlightened existence. Theirs is a prolongation
of life, as Humboldt put it, and not a full exploration of its
secrets. It is the New World before the Fall.

In the third section of the poem (ll. 64–132), Bello describes
the tensions that underlay the wars of independence. Slavery,
the infancy of colonialism, cannot be prolonged forever. Minimal effort is no longer a blessing for an undeveloped mass of
slaves; rather, indolence hinders the Americans from developing a simple, yet rich life, and Bello launches a tirade against
the *"indolente labrador"* (indolent peasant), who is no longer
identified with the slaves but with the privileged few.

Servitude is sweet and happy – provided that no one challenges it. As soon as prospects for growth and development
arise, the equilibrium of dependency is destroyed. Each of the
two sides of the struggle is an object of Bello's criticism: the

Creole aristocracy has abandoned its fields, and the Church, in representing the Crown, has taken over the fields of the elite and promoted civil disorder:

> ¿Por qué ilusión funesta
> aquellos que fortuna hizo señores
> de tan dichosa tierra y pingüe y varia,
> al cuidado abandonan
> y a la fe mercenaria
> las patrias heredades,
> y en el ciego tumulto se aprisionan
> de míseras ciudades,
> do la ambición proterva
> sopla la llama de civiles bandos,
> o al patriotismo la desidia enerva;
> do el lujo las costumbres atosiga,
> y combaten los vicios
> la incauta edad en poderosa liga? (ll. 75–88)

> (By what ill-fated illusion those fortunate own-
> ers of such a happy, rich, and variegated land
> abandon their ancestral properties to the merce-
> nary faith, to its care, and trap themselves in the
> blind tumult of miserable cities, where perverse
> ambition fans the flame of civil factions, or pa-
> triotism is enervated by laziness; where luxury
> poisons customs, and the vices, assembled in a
> powerful league, attack those of unwary age.)

"*Fe mercenaria*" (mercenary faith) alludes to the Church's role during both the colonial period and the Revolution. During the colonial period, the Church had a virtual monopoly on official credit in the colonies through the system of *censos,* or mortgage loans. One kind of *censo* could be redeemed after the capital had been paid in full, while a second type – sometimes called *censo perpetuo* (mortgage in perpetuity) – was nonredeemable and served a spiritual rather than a temporal function. Under a *censo perpetuo* the Church would dispense favors (e.g., say a mass on a given date, year after year) in return for interest payments representing 5 percent of the value of the property, which was mortgaged in favor of some parish, chaplaincy, or convent. Established in perpetuity, the *censo* created an obligation that was passed from generation to generation.[10]

A contemporary source illustrates the kind of animosity toward the Church that these mortgages generated during the last years of the war. In a pamphlet published in 1823, José Tomás Sanauria explains that almost all the mortgage loans in Venezuela had been extended by the Church. The holders of these loans, or *censualistas*, Sanauria charges, have seized and liquidated agricultural property at a time when the disasters of the war have prevented normal repayment. The author blames the Church for the pitiful state of postwar Venezuelan agriculture: "The valleys of Tuy, Caucagua, Guatire, Aragüita, Río Chico, Mamporal, Santa Lucía, and others present the most dreary and horrible effects of the arbitrary foreclosures performed upon the request of the chaplains, trustees, and administrators of churches, for the sake of a miserable sum of past-due interest owed to them."[11] Throughout Spanish America during the years of the Revolution, the Church became a mortgage bank that made loans to landowners. Though the rate of interest was low, the clergy gained considerable influence over its clients.[12]

Bello's specific charge in this section of the "Agricultura" is that the landowners lost their property to the Church and flocked to the city, where they became slaves to the allure of new luxuries. In the city the Church fanned the fires of civil war – a charge Bello made in the letter to the Pope. Similarly, in the "Alocución" Bello accused the clergy of serving as an accomplice of Spanish tyranny. It is possible that in the "Agricultura" Bello is defending the Colombian government's strong stance against orthodox intolerance, a debate that reached its peak in Caracas in March 1826, some seven months before the poem's publication.[13]

Bello's criticism of city life continues as he shows the landowners becoming experts in seduction and gambling. His attack on urban life is drawn in part from the closing of book 3 of Virgil's *Georgics* but more significantly from Tibullus and Jovellanos.[14] Against the image of contemporary city life, Bello evokes the strong government of the ancient Roman republic, when citizens were called from the fields to run the state, long before Rome had tasted the luxuries of empire. Bello is now ready to specify the political ideal of the "Agricultura." He has had to give up his ideal of a constitutional monarchy, but the powerful executive arm of the first centuries of the Roman republic, the consuls who inherited in part the majesty of kings, is a close substitute. Addressing America's idle urban dwellers, he argues:

> No así trató la triunfadora Roma
> las artes de la paz y de la guerra;
> antes fió las riendas del estado
> a la mano robusta
> que tostó el sol y encalleció el arado;
> y bajo el techo luminoso campesino
> los hijos educó, que el conjurado
> mundo allanaron al valor latino. (ll. 125–32)

> (Triumphant Rome did not handle the skills of war and peace in this way. Instead, she entrusted the reins of the state to the strong hand which the sun tanned and the plow hardened; and under the luminous ceiling of the countryside she educated her children, who subjected the conspiring world to Latin valor.)

In the fourth section of the "Agricultura" (ll. 133–201) Bello again recalls republican Rome and the virtues of a simple life. This section is based almost entirely on the famous passage of book 2 of the *Georgics:* "O fortunatos nimium, sua si bona norint / agricolas . . ." (How exceedingly happy are the farmers, if they only knew their blessings). In the preceding section of the "Agricultura" Bello associated city life with civil war. He now focuses on a passage in which Virgil associates the countryside with a particular kind of peacefulness. The countryside is distant from civil factions (the *"discordibus armis"* of Virgil's passage), and Bello tells the landowners, the *"afortunados poseedores,"* to return to the countryside; there, freedom can be found. In the countryside, Bello says, they will find pure feelings and honest love, and will be free from the machinations of the *"ajena mano y fe"* (foreign hand and faith) that marries people *"por nombre o plata"* (for renown or for money) – another attack on the Church's financial ambitions.

The countryside in the aftermath of the Revolution is the setting for the beginning of the poem's fifth section (ll. 202–68). The lands have been abandoned by the war. The jungles are again to be laid low, so that coffee and fruit trees can be planted. Now, for the first time, the word *"agricultura"* appears in the poem:

> Ya dócil a tu voz, agricultura,
> nodriza de las gentes, la caterva
> servil armada va de corvas hoces. (ll. 224–6)

> (Agriculture, nurse of the people, the servile throng armed with curved sickles now advances obeying your voice.)

The wars of independence have completely altered the terms of existence described at the beginning of the poem, when colonial servitude was associated with the easy sustenance provided by the banana tree. The natural fecundity is now replaced by the toil of agriculture; the happy slaves are now a servile throng. But the Revolution has also created an opportunity for transforming this situation, which is what Bello does in this extraordinary section of the poem. Each member of the servile throng, as he first destroys the jungle and then cultivates the land, is transformed into a *"fatigado agricultor"* (tired farmer, l. 261).

In the fifth section (ll. 269–350) Bello speaks of "la gente agricultora / del ecuador" (the agricultural people of the equatorial region). This expression concludes the series of transformations from the colonial period to the postwar era, from happy servitude to a new freedom that allows people to change their lives, till their lands, and, as Bello says later in the poem, trade their goods:

lines 54–5:   *"las gentes del ecuador feliz"* (the people of the happy equatorial region) – colonial slavery

lines 224–5:   *"agricultura, nodriza de las gentes"* (agriculture, nurse of the people) – the aftermath of war

lines 271–2:   *"la gente agricultora del ecuador"* (the agricultural people of the equatorial region) – the future period of freedom

On almost all counts the model of Augustan Caracas is now crumbling and the institutions that shaped that order have also fallen, despite the attempt of the Crown and its ecclesiastical branch to regain power. The golden age of peace and easy sustenance is never to be regained. Instead, the sacrifice and the higher challenge of *"agricultura"* and freedom are the new alternatives.

What is extraordinary about the "Agricultura" is that Bello chose to inscribe the fall of the old order within a Virgilian framework, the very framework that had given legitimacy to that order. And Bello organized the *Repertorio Americano* in a way that emphasized this framework: immediately after his poem is the article "Estudio sobre Virgilio, por P. F. Tissot," a translation signed by Bello of a review article originally published in 1826 in the *Révue Encyclopédique* of Tissot's Virgil studies. The article begins with a condemnation of the eighteenth century for not having paid close attention to the sacred language of the ancients. But the political turmoil of the last decades, it continues, has opened the eyes and expanded the minds of many authors, who have realized that the best way to surpass the moderns is to be as good as the ancients. Tissot, who had been chosen by Jacques Delille – *"el primer poeta del siglo"* – to take over the chair of classical studies at the Sorbonne, is praised for revealing in this study of Virgil the ancient mysteries of the Muses. After an extensive quotation of Tissot that surveys the whole gallery of Western authors, the article pays tribute to Delille:

And you, illustrious translator of the Georgics, whose friendship honors me, whose selection [of me] caused me such lively restlessness! If from the day of your death I have not let pass a single day without paying homage to your memory; if faithful to the duties of the heart, I have directed all my work to the one who imposed them on me in an adoption that was so dear to me – condescend to accept these studies as the religious offering of a disciple to his master.

Bello surely chose to publish Tissot's tribute to Delille as a way of making his own tribute. Delille, born in 1738, was a proponent of the seemingly contradictory alliance between neoclassical poetry and antiabsolutist politics that surfaced in eighteenth-century Britain and that seemed to have reached a climax in prerevolutionary France. He was a fairly active member of the intellectual opposition, yet at the same time he was almost entirely dedicated to the revival of the Virgilian tradition, both in his original poems – such as "L'homme des champs" – and in his translations of the *Aeneid* and the *Georgics*.

While in London, Bello had translated two of Delille's long poems under the titles "La luz" and "Los jardines." But it is in Delille's most famous work, his translation of the *Georgics,* that we find the most fruitful connection between the two poets and an explanation of the secret meaning of *"agricultura."*

In Delille's preface to his translation of the *Georgics* one can see the coexistence of the georgic vogue and the virulent anti-Augustan tradition that had been brooding throughout the eighteenth century. The preface was both a defense of the Roman republic and an attack on Augustus. Written in 1756, it exemplifies the savage feelings against the *princeps* in the years that preceded the French Revolution. This is, for instance, Delille's comment on the proem to the *Georgics:*

> There is nothing more pompous and more base than this invocation to Caesar. Two poets after Virgil degraded themselves with less poetic and more base invocations; Lucan lavished the vilest adulations on Nero, and Statius on Domitian. The latter is the guiltiest of the three. Augustus succeeded at the end of his reign, and Nero at the beginning of his; Domitian was always a monster. At any rate, one should not accuse these poets of deifying human beings – the customs of their country allowed such a practice – but of placing assassins who barely deserved to be called human in the ranks of the gods.[15]

Delille also tells us that one can easily recognize in the *Georgics* the influence of Maecenas, to whom the ideas and intention of the proem can be attributed. The lamentation at the end of book 1, Delille says, is caused by the decay of agriculture (*"la décadence de l'Agriculture"*). At the end of book 2, he adds, in his beautiful praise of country life Virgil seems to have assembled all the power and grace of poetry to excite among Romans their ancient love for agriculture. Delille always capitalizes *agriculture* in the preface, and its figurative meaning becomes clearer in the following sentence: "L'Agriculture a exercé non seulement les plus grand héros, mais encore les plus grands écrivains de l'antiquité" (Agriculture fostered not only the greatest heroes of antiquity but also the greatest writers, p. 4), an echo of the opening of the *Histories,* where Tacitus says that the best Roman minds vanished after Actium. It is not just the tilling of fields Delille is praising. Rather, "Agriculture" is a code word for the Roman republic. Elsewhere in the preface Delille explains that figurative language arises when writers cannot speak freely.

Whereas Delille views Augustus and Agriculture as enemies, Bello instead organizes his "Agricultura" so as to describe the transformation from a servile model to an order in which freedom prevails. Although Bello sometimes referred to the colonial period as a time of chains and despotism, more often he thought of the colonial era as a stage of civilization in its infancy, dominated, or, as he said in the "Alocución," "lulled," by superstition. It was not a world of unbearable oppression, but one deprived of freedom. In the last section of the "Agricultura," when Bello compares the two orders, he says, "La libertad más dulce que el imperio" (Liberty, sweeter than empire). The liberal model is justified as a higher good.

In the eighteenth century European culture was torn between two world views – in one, power was centralized, symbolized by the figure of Augustus; in the other, freedom predominated and individuals sought to restore the values of republican Rome and to develop the arts and sciences under freedom. Virgil's *Georgics* became the battleground for these conflicting world views. Depending on which aspects of Virgil one chose or omitted – whether Octavian's apotheosis in book 1 or the simple life in book 2 – one was choosing monarchy or republic, obedience to established rules or free inquiry. In his final version of the *Georgics* Bello has suppressed Augustus and tipped the balance on the side of freedom, the higher challenge – *agricultura*.

10

Bolívar's poetics

Más vale un desengaño que mil ilusiones.

Simón Bolívar

If Bello attempted to express the new revolutionary order by evoking the Augustan poets and omitting any mention of Augustus, the Ecuadoran poet José Joaquín Olmedo took on the task of evoking Horace and placing Bolívar in the place of the *princeps*. Born in 1784 in Guayaquil, Olmedo was educated in Lima, where he composed panegyrics to the Spanish imperial family characteristic of the late colonial style. He was a deputy to the Cortes and left Spain once Ferdinand returned to power. In 1822 he presided over the Guayaquil junta and fled to Peru after Bolívar seized that city, but once San Martín stepped down Olmedo's relations with the Libertador improved. In December 1824, after the battle of Junín but before he had news of the triumph of Ayacucho, the battle that sealed Spanish American independence, he was already corresponding with Bolívar and announcing a poem to him. The correspondence intensified in January. On January 6 Olmedo addressed his letter "To the Libertador, to the ever-victorious, Simón Bolívar"; on January 31: "To Simón Gótico." In this last letter Olmedo tells Bolívar that he has already written fifty lines and proclaims that both of them will attain immortality: "If inspiration comes to me and I can fulfill the magnificent and daring plan I have conceived, the two of us will be immortal together."[1]

Before seeing the finished poem, Bolívar had already decided to send Olmedo as an envoy to London. This caught the poet by surprise: "Only you could be able to find a connection between a poet who plays his flute on the banks of his river and an ambassador who represents a nation in the courts of kings."[2] In the same letter Olmedo says that the 50 lines have increased to 520, but that the poem is still not finished. On April 30 Olmedo sent his completed poem, followed by a letter on May 11 in which he describes the poem and apologizes for its faults.

Olmedo's *Victoria de Junín: Canto a Bolívar* opens with these lines:

> El trueno horrendo que en fragor revienta,
> y sordo retumbando se dilata
> por la inflamada esfera,
> al Dios anuncia que en el cielo impera.
> Y el rayo que en Junín rompe y ahuyenta
> la hispana muchedumbre,
> que más feroz que nunca amenazaba
> a sangre y fuego eterna servidumbre;
> y el canto de victoria
> que en ecos mil discurre ensordeciendo
> el hondo valle y enriscada cumbre,
> proclaman a Bolívar en la tierra
> árbitro de la paz y de la guerra.[3]

> (The horrifying thunder that bursts and roars, and rumbling with a faint sound extends through the inflamed globe, proclaims the God who rules in heaven. And the lightning at Junín that shatters and disperses the Spanish multitude which was wielding the threat of eternal servitude more fiercely than ever, and the song of victory which roams about in a thousand echoes deafening the deep valley and the craggy summit, proclaim Bolívar the arbiter of peace and war on earth.)

Olmedo then describes the battle of Junín and, through the apparition of the Inca Huaina Capac, announces the victory of Ayacucho. A chorus of the "*vírgenes del Sol*" (virgins of the Sun) celebrates Spanish American freedom and welcomes Bolívar in his triumphant entry to Lima. He is acclaimed as the angel of peace, as the genius of peace and glory, who advances "*en inefable majestad*" (in ineffable majesty). And from a hundred vases of alabaster a transparent cloud of incense sheds its fragrance and rises to the sky.

The first criticism of the *Victoria de Junín* came, at Olmedo's request, from Bolívar himself. The hero censures the poet for turning the leaders of Junín and Ayacucho into gods or demigods: "You turn me into Jupiter, Sucre into Mars, La Mar into Agamemnon, Necochea into a Patroclus and an Ajax, Miller into a Diomedes, and Lara into a Ulysses. . . . You have elevated us to such heights that you have flung us headlong into the abyss of nothingness." Bolívar then asks whether Olmedo might have written the poem in jest, that Olmedo perhaps was trying to parody the *Iliad* in depicting the heroes of the poor farce played out at Junín ("*con los héroes de nuestra pobre farsa*"). But this thought cannot be sustained. At any rate, Olmedo should know that there is a fine line between the heroic and the ridiculous. Spanish Americans will read his poem as a Homeric song, while Spaniards will think it is a lectern song by Boileau.[4]

In a second letter, dated July 12, Bolívar continues his review. He invokes classic and neoclassic criticism, Horace and Boileau, and playfully fulfills his role of enlightened ruler. He tells Olmedo that he does not mind being the king in this comedy, giving his opinion on poetic matters. Bolívar then invokes Horace's *Ars poetica*, which he uses as his guide throughout the letter. He tells Olmedo that he should have let his song sit for some time, as if it were fermenting wine. He then censures the Inca Huaina Capac's speech and also the opening of the poem, which he finds "*rimbombante*" (bombastic), unlike the opening of Homer's *Iliad*, which was celebrated for its modesty by Horace and Boileau.

Bolívar also counsels Olmedo to use his stay in London as an occasion to perfect his poetry:

Pope, the poet you so admire, can give you lessons to correct certain lapses that even Homer himself could not avoid. You will forgive me for using Horace to pronounce my oracle; this nit-picker was enraged that Homer should ever fall asleep. And you know very well that Virgil, after nine or ten years begetting his divine daughter, the *Aeneid*, was disappointed by his creation. Thus, my friend, more and more buffing is needed to polish the work of men.

With that, Bolívar, king and critic, concludes his playful criticism of the poem. But the praise that follows is serious in tone. He says that Olmedo, for the most part, preserves a continuous and lively fervor throughout his song. The thoughts are noble and beautiful. At one point he can identify Achilles, and in the presentation of himself in Junín, Bolívar recognizes Aeneas before his battle with Turnus.[5]

Bolívar had read broadly and especially enjoyed history and poetry. Defending himself against charges of ignorance, he reminded Santander in May 1825 that he had studied geography and belles lettres with "our famous Bello." In the same letter he pointed out that he had read all the classical authors of antiquity and all the modern classics of Spain, France, and Italy, and even the great majority of the British classics. This was probably an exaggeration, though a study by Manuel Pérez Vila reveals that the Libertador carried in his campaigns a portable library that included Plutarch's *Vie des hommes illustres*, Fergusson's *Décadence de la République romaine*, several books on Napoleon, including Constant's *Lettres sur les cent jours*, French translations of the *Iliad* and the *Odyssey*, a Spanish translation of the *Aeneid*, and two copies of Caesar's *Commentaries*. Among modern authors he had nine volumes of Frederick the Great, Humboldt's *Voyage*, Adam Smith's *The Wealth of Nations* (in a French translation), and *The Federalist* (in the original).[6]

The *Victoria de Junín* was reviewed by Bello in the first issue of the *Repertorio Americano* (October 1826). His criticism is almost entirely the opposite of Bolívar's. Unlike the Libertador, he praises Olmedo's use of the Inca Huaina Capac as a device to unify the battles of Junín and Ayacucho in one poem. Bello is especially fond of the section of the poem that describes Bolívar *before* the battle and of the chorus of the "*vírgenes del Sol.*" This last section, he explains "forms a subtle contrast with the description of combats, deaths and horrors that precedes it," and is quoted at length; it is interrupted just before Bolívar's triumphant entry into Lima. Bello ends his review by praising, among other things, Olmedo's refined diction and his solid knowledge of Latin authors, particularly of Horace (*OC*, 9: 225–32).[7]

Olmedo's poem also received the attention of two of Bello's favorite disciples, the brothers Miguel Luis and Gregorio Victor Amunátegui, who traced some of the Horatian sources of the poem. Of particular interest is the parallel they draw between the opening of the *Victoria de Junín* and Horace's ode to Regulus. As they noticed, the first lines of Olmedo's poem are taken directly from the beginning of Horace's poem:

> Caelo tonantem credidimus Jovem
> Regnare: praesens divus habebitur
> Augustus, adjectis Britannis
> Imperio gravibusque Persis.

(We have come to believe that thundering Jove
reigns in heaven; Augustus will be held as a god
on earth, once the British and the powerful Per-
sians are added to the empire.)

Olmedo preserves the thunder and the division of power: God
in heaven, Bolívar on earth.[8] The hero of Olmedo's poem does
not have any divine attributes, though his triumph at the end of
the poem certainly has a majestic and religious dimension.

Later, Miguel Luis Amunátegui mistakenly wrote that
Bolívar named Olmedo envoy to London as a compensation for
the *Victoria de Junín*. Bello's biographer, however, displays his
usual slyness by bringing out a barbed parallel: "To compensate
him for such magnificent and well-constructed verses, and in
recognition of his indisputable merits and public service, the
Augustus of that Horace named him plenipotentiary of Peru in
London." Bello, of course, refused to play Horace or Virgil to
Bolívar's Augustus, but Olmedo filled the role so well that
Bolívar himself asked the poet in the mocking tone of the letter
of July 12: "Why have you made me king?"[9]

After Bolívar liberated Peru, he was summoned by the
people of Alto Peru, who were ready to give him full powers
and to honor him further with the name of the country:
Bolivia. In 1826 Bolívar could still maintain the illusion that a
great federation would extend from Panama to Bolivia, a
federation that could even include Mexico, Chile, and Argentina. To carry out his plan he needed faithful and efficient
lieutenants. He had Sucre in Bolivia, Santa Cruz in Peru, Santander in Bogotá, and Páez in Venezuela. He was alert to any
news from the south that might present opportunities to expand his power. While he was in La Paz, he had promising
meetings with Alvear, who fired the imagination of the Libertador with plans to extend the new republic of Bolivia to the
south. In the calls for the return of O'Higgins, Bolívar saw a
hopeful sign that a man whom he trusted could hold power in
Chile.[10]

Bolívar prepared for Bolivia a constitution that was essentially an implementation of the plan he had devised at Angostura. In the document, published in 1826, the executive
body is headed by a president-for-life who has limited powers;
unlike a kingship, the title is not hereditary. The legislative

body is composed of a lower chamber of tribunes and a higher chamber of senators. In addition there is a chamber of censors: "The censors exercise a political and moral power that somewhat resembles the authority of the Aeropagus of Athens and the censors of Rome." The judiciary branch is completely independent of the executive branch; its candidates are selected by the people, and the final choices are made by the legislature. Finally, the fourth branch is an electoral body that rotates every four years; there is to be one elector for every ten citizens. But the strangest of all stipulations of this constitution is Bolívar's plan for a hereditary vice-presidency.[11]

In a letter to Sucre dated May 12, 1826, Bolívar provides more details about his political plans:

The Libertador, as commander in chief, will go out each year to visit the districts of each state. The capital will be in a central point, such as Quito or Guayaquil. Colombia should be divided into three states: Venezuela, Cundinamarca and Quito. One, probably Cundinamarca, shall be called Colombia; the federation will name itself as it sees fit, but the name is likely to be the Bolivian Federation.

In the letter Bolívar invites his lieutenant to consider the possibility of establishing, someday, a monarchy: "They have offered me a crown that cannot rest on my head and which, in the darkness of future permutations, I can see lightly falling over the temples of the hero of Ayacucho."[12] The Bolivian Constitution, like all constitutions, was a mirror of the political setting that surrounded its framer. Bolívar justified it as the middle ground between monarchy and federalism. It was in fact a political extravaganza.

Bolívar sent his constitution everywhere – to Santander in Bogotá, to Páez in Caracas. He had it printed on fine paper and sent it to Olmedo, who had moved to Paris as the envoy of Peru, asking him to have it translated into English and French.[13] But the growing tensions in all parts of Colombia soon dashed Bolívar's grand plans. In April 1826 the central government had ordered Páez's removal and had summoned him to Bogotá. In the town of Valencia, Venezuelans rose in his defense. Bolívar believed that his presence could calm the animosity between Santander and Páez and that this crisis might provide just the occasion to institute his constitutional plans. But he lingered in Peru, where he had been named president-for-life after his constitution had been adopted by that country. Bolívar did not want to leave without some assurance that his government would be long-lasting. Peruvians begged him to stay – they feared that in his absence the whole political edifice would crumble. When a commission of women asked him to defer his departure, he gave a heartfelt chivalric reply: "Ladies, silence is the only response I can give to those charming words, which shackle not only my heart but my sense of duty as well." But he excused himself; his fatherland called him.[14]

Bolívar arrived in Bogotá in November and took over the presidency. He stayed for only a few days, making budgetary reductions, and then proceeded to establish his authority in Venezuela. Meanwhile, he had named a new envoy to London. The choice did not fall on Bello, who had taken the position of financial attaché and was second in command at the Colombian embassy, but on another poet, José Fernández Madrid. The new envoy was alarmed that he, and not Bello, had been selected, but Bello took the news well. In March 1827 he wrote Bolívar a letter expressing his full support. "Mi Amado y Respetado Libertador" (My Dear and Respected Libertador), the letter begins. Bello says he is happy to hear that Venezuelans have expressed their backing for Bolívar and for a system that combines individual freedom and public order. He then writes:

The difficulties of Colombia are great, and consequently much is expected of the most illustrious of her sons. Among the benefits that only he can give his country, the most urgent and essential is that of a solid and strong government. Experience has shown us that institutional stability in circumstances such as ours does not depend so much on intrinsic goodwill as on external support, which comes from the personal traits of those individuals in power. The victories of Your Excellency, your talents and virtues, have gained for you that luster, that influence, or better still that command over public opinion, which alone can replace the venerable varnish that the centuries usually give to the works of legislators.

Bello concludes with the hope that Bolívar will continue to establish public order on the basis of firm foundations, which, inspiring trust, will cause the tilled fields of Spanish America to flourish.

For the first time since 1810 Bello was opening an avenue of communication with Bolívar. They had been apart. Yet their political ideas were not totally dissimilar. Both saw the need for strong leadership and a political framework not distant in spirit from the British model. Bello may have realized his mistake. Could not Bolívar become the new leader, a king without a crown, the strongman of a new constitutional order?

There were also other, more personal considerations. Bello was an underpaid, aging subordinate of Colombia and thought that, without succumbing to flattery, he might be able to strike a relationship of mutual benefit with an old friend. These hopes could only have been encouraged by a letter he received from Bolívar in which he addresses Bello and Fernández Madrid as close friends and tells them that the fire of civil war has been extinguished and that he has resigned from the presidency. Bello wrote back on April 18. Europe sees in Bolívar, he says, the most glorious personage of the times, one destined to influence a large family of nations for many centuries. He urges the Libertador that, "imitating another great man, he should believe he had accomplished nothing as long as there was something left for him to accomplish" (*OC*, 25: 287–9). The allusion to Julius Caesar was not trivial, for Bolívar's plan, if not monarchist, was Caesarist. Like the Roman leader, Bolívar faced the dangers of republican institutions and the difficulties of embracing monarchic forms.

But all of Bello's hopes for an understanding with Bolívar were in vain. Even as Bello was writing his admiring letter to Bolívar, the mail was carrying a decree signed by Bolívar in November of the preceding year in Bogotá. By this decree Bello was effectively demoted from financial attaché to secretary of the new Colombian envoy, Fernández Madrid. This was a big blow. Bello's letter to Bolívar, written on April 21, barely hides his indignation: "I regret very much this decree . . . not for the financial damage it imposes upon me, although in my circumstances this is serious, but for the kind of rebuff that accompanies it." In the letter Bello assures Bolívar that such a demotion is illegal (*OC*, 25: 296).

A few days later, on May 3, Bello sat down, lit a cigar, and began to answer a letter he had received from Olmedo. The two poets had struck up a close friendship and kept a frequent correspondence devoted mostly to poetic topics. Bello was busy obtaining material for the *Repertorio* and kept pressing his friend to send him the translation of Pope's *Essay on Man*. But in a recent letter Olmedo had raised the topic of religion:

> In every sense there has been a noticeable backward trend in this place, but we can hope that all will be reestablished and will prosper with the firm protection that is granted here to our holy religion and her clergy.
> All roads are bristling with + + + instead of trees, with chapels instead of farmhouses and cottages, with friars who beg and loot from travelers, and who recite rosaries and responsories for money, instead of shepherds who give cream and fruit to their guests and who then help them fall asleep with happy songs to the tune of the melodious flute. This is how the people will achieve true happiness, which does not consist in the ownership of goods and other temporal pleasures, but in spiritual and eternal ones. (*OC*, 25: 257)

Bello's response to Olmedo, the extraordinary "Carta escrita de Londres a París por un americano a otro," is a long meditation on the failure of Spanish American independence to bring about the promised freedom and a sharp attack on Bolívar, who, with the Church's support, was trying to reinstate the old order.[15]

At the beginning of the poem Bello calls on Olmedo to abandon the frivolity of Paris and come to England, where a faithful, truthful, constant soul (*un alma fiel, veraz, constante*) will greet him. He then describes, as in a dream, the return of the golden age and contrasts it with the order Bolívar has begun to establish in Colombia in 1827. In Bello's ideal society, peaceful people live happily, wearing shepherds' attire. And they reject all attempts to reinstate the imperial order:

> Ni halló jamás cabida la perjura
> fe, la codicia o la ambición tirana,
> que nacida al imperio se figura.
>
> Ni a la plebe deslumbra, insulsa y vana,
> de la extranjera seda el atavío,*
> con que tal vez el crimen se engalana.
>
> Ni se obedece intruso poderío,
> que, ora promulga leyes, y ora anula
> siendo la ley suprema su albedrío.
>
> Ni al patriotismo el interés simula,
> que hoy a la libertad himnos entona
> y mañana al poder, sumiso, adula;

Ni victorioso capitán pregona**
lides que por la patria ha sustentado,
y en galardón le pide la corona.
                    (OC, 1: 96–7, ll. 88–102)[16]

[Alternative readings: *de púrpura soberbia el
atavío; **ni victorioso general pregona]

(Nor did perjured faith, greed and tyrannical
ambition – which, once born, resemble the empire – ever find a place there.

Nor does the garment made of foreign silk,*
with which crime perhaps adorns itself, dazzle
the dull and vain rabble.

Nor does [this ideal region] obey an intruding
power, which now proclaims laws and now an-
nuls them, and [the intruding power] respects
only its own freedom as the supreme law.

Nor does self-interest pass for patriotism, [self-
interest] which today sings hymns for liberty,
and tomorrow meekly flatters power.

Nor does a victorious captain boast** about the
struggle he has fought for his homeland, and
seek a crown as his reward.)

[Alternative readings: *the garment of magnificent purple; **Nor does a victorious general
boast]

Bello thus answers Olmedo's attack on the Church with his
own censure of that institution. Once again Bello repeats the
old charges of perfidy, ambition, and greed, except that here
for the first time they are brought together. Again the Church
is portrayed as a foreign power, *"intruso poderío,"* an accusation
made in the "Agricultura" and in Mier's response to the encyclical of Leo XII. More importantly, Bello sets his attack
against the Church side by side with an attack against Bolívar
that echoes the "Morillo" passage of the "Alocución" (see p.
107). Like other opponents of the new regime, Bello condemns
the configuration of power that began to emerge in 1827, as
Bolívar tried to reestablish his rule. Similar charges were made
by many of the partisans of Santander: Bolívar, triumphant
from Junín and Ayacucho, shifted to conservatism as a pream-
ble to monarchy. In a variant of the last quoted line Bello sub-
stitutes *"general"* for *"capitán,"* thereby identifying Bolívar more
precisely.

Throughout the "Carta" Bello maintains the sharp division between an ideal world of freedom and the real world of total power. The quest of the past twenty years, Bello says, can be compared to a boy who sees a rainbow and pursues it; but just as he believes he has reached his goal, the image disappears, *"huye el prestigio aéreo"* (the airy illusion vanishes), and with shame he is forced to admit his mistake. This passage is followed by a section that Bello completely crossed out but that the editorial committee of his complete works took great pains to decipher:

> Sí; la bella apariencia nos engaña
> de libertad, que asegurar pensamos,
> y con fuga veloz se nos extraña.

> Al yugo aborrecido sometamos
> dormida la cerviz, y el fruto sea
> de tanto sacrificio hornada de amos.

> De la razón extíngase la lumbre
> y embravecido el pensamiento humano
> haga otra vez la sujeción costumbre.

> Tales los bienes son con que tu mano,
> vencedor de Junín y de Ayacucho,
> brinda al pueblo feliz americano. (*OC*, 2: 99)

> (Yes, we are deceived by the beautiful appearance of freedom, which we thought to establish, and it escapes in swift flight.

> Let us humble ourselves under the hated yoke, and may the masters receive the rewards of so much sacrifice.

> May the light of reason be extinguished and may brave human thought be once again accustomed to servitude.

> Victor of Junín and Ayacucho, such are the gifts which your hand offers to the happy American people.)

Bello's attack on Bolívar was fierce; whatever the virtues of strong leadership, Bello could not easily bear the effects of the illegal decree that demoted him. He delivers a final blow to Bolívar in a variant of the last tercet:

> Tales los bienes son con que tu mano
> ¡oh de libertadores jefe augusto!
> brinda al pueblo feliz americano.

(August leader of the liberators! Such are the
gifts which you offer to the happy American
people.)

Here Bello finally grants Bolívar the Augustan epithet, but
only in bitter denunciation. The former flatterer of the "Oda a
la vacuna" has recovered the epithet *augusto* and the language
of adulation and turned them on their heads. Moreover, Bello
no longer holds out the liberal order as an improvement on a
somewhat benign imperial order, as he had done in the "Agricultura" ("*la libertad más dulce que el imperio*"); rather, he focuses
on the evils of the imperial order. Bello openly takes the side of
liberty, but only now that he believes that liberty is the stuff of
utopia. The "Carta" has the clarity of a great disappointment.

After April 1827 Bello was indeed a disappointed man, and
not just because of his demotion. He saw the cause of freedom
threatened on all sides – by anarchy as the town of Valencia had
shattered the integrity of Colombia with the uprising of April
1826; by despotism, as Bolívar placed himself above the law;
and by isolation, as the foreign debt crisis continued to worsen.
In the *Repertorio* Bello and García del Río had tried to inspire
optimism and, above all, a general consensus on the virtues of
the Enlightenment. But the fourth and last volume, published
in August 1827, bespeaks its editors' discouragement. A portrait of Miranda appears in the volume, and documents related
to his fall in 1813 and death in 1816 are published on pages
264–77, followed by Santander's message to the Congress of
Colombia on January 1, 1827, which deals with the events of
Valencia. One reads of civil tensions, of the war between Argentina and Brazil, of the imminent dismemberment of Colombia.
Alert readers could not but think of Miranda's failed dream.

During 1827 and 1828 Bolívar kept in touch with Bello and
Fernández Madrid, whom he entrusted with the sale of his only
remaining asset, the mines of Aroa. He repeatedly assured his
diplomats that his only ambition was to abandon power and
Colombia, and asked them to deposit the proceeds of the sale of
the mines in a British bank. He expected to receive £40,000 and
to live on the annuity of that capital. In his varied correspondence at this time, Bello's attitude toward Bolívar gives mixed
signals. In some letters, he still places some hope in Bolívar's

ability to unify Colombia, but other letters reveal scattered traces of growing bitterness. For example, the envoy of Colombia at the Vatican, Ignacio Tejada, had requested that Bello translate an Italian poem in which, apparently, the Libertador was praised as a republican. But Bello responded saying that he could not translate such a work without violently damaging his own feelings. Bolívar, he points out, is generally believed to have chosen models somewhat different from Brutus or Washington. Besides, Bello would not like to have the public think of him as a flatterer. He adds that he believes that his two poet friends, Fernández Madrid and Olmedo, will also be unable to comply with this duty (OC, 25: 372).

Bello speaks more directly in a letter to Restrepo announcing that the publication of the *Repertorio* must stop. He explains that it has become increasingly difficult to avoid politics, an adventurous endeavor in times of factions, when truth has a bitter taste and when freedom is precarious. And nothing is more insipid, he adds, than political discussions written by those who cannot speak freely (*OC*, 25: 386).

Seeing that his future in Colombia was uncertain, and fearing old age and destitution, Bello started making plans to move to either Argentina or Chile. Mariano Egaña, the Chilean envoy, had forgotten his earlier rift with Bello and had actually become a friend and a *compadre*. When Bello mentioned that he would consider moving to Chile, Egaña seized the opportunity and wrote to Chile's minister of foreign affairs on November 10, 1827, recommending that Bello be named to a suitable post: "Don Andrés Bello, ex-secretary of the Chilean legation in London, and the current secretary of the Colombian legation to the same court, is willing to go to Chile and to settle there with his family, if he is given the suggested post of undersecretary, or an equivalent one, appropriate to his career and his superior knowledge."[17]

But Bello was still hoping that Bolívar would offer him a better position, one that would allow him to cancel his trip to Chile. Bolívar did in fact ask him to become the envoy to Portugal and also requested that he go to France and expedite the full recognition of Colombia. But Bello took these offers as personal insults. As he explained to Amunátegui, there was little substance in such overtures, since the emperor of Portugal was highly intolerant of the new Spanish American republics and had no desire to establish diplomatic links with Colombia, and, moreover, there were no funds for Bello to go to France.[18]

We do not know Bolívar's motives for making diplomatic decisions that humiliated Bello. But an episode in Perú de Lacroix's *Diario de Bucaramanga* provides a rare glimpse of Bolívar's reaction to one of Bello's poems, and this incident perhaps sheds some light on Bolívar's thinking. The entry for May 25, 1828, describes Bolívar and his assistants going to mass. As on other occasions, they sat in the choir loft of the church. During the consecration a woman fainted, and the people surrounding her created such a stir that the parishioners started shouting and running toward the gate of the church, believing that an earthquake was the cause of the uproar. Perú de Lacroix and Bolívar's assistants witnessed all this from the choir loft and, also believing there had been an earthquake, ran toward the stairs. Throughout the commotion, however, Bolívar himself remained fixed in his seat reading a volume of *La Biblioteca Americana*.

After mass, Bolívar went home and began to discuss with his assistants and Perú de Lacroix the events of 1817. Until that year, he said, the patriots had displayed their heroism on many occasions, but there had been no unity, no single act that turned the general opinion in their favor. His name was already well known, his reputation was established, but more was needed in order to win the country's independence and to establish a central government. Given these circumstances, he said, his decision to eliminate Piar was a political necessity that saved the country. Piar's death prevented a racial war, a war that would have ended with the extermination of the patriots and the triumph of the Spaniards. His death was a political masterstroke that terrified the rebels and precluded further sedition; it ensured his own authority, thwarted civil war, and allowed him to prepare his campaign of Nueva Granada and to form the Republic of Colombia.

Later in the conversation, Bolívar returned to the subject of Piar, adding, "In the history of Colombia my name should not stand next to that of Monteverde, Boves, and Morillo. What? They were the executioners of their king's enemies and I would be the executioner of my compatriots."[19] The mention of Piar,

Monteverde, Boves, and Morillo and the talk of "executioner" suggest that Bolívar's mind was focused on the closing section of the "Alocución," which appeared in the second volume of *La Biblioteca Americana;* for in that section Bello praises the virtue of Piar and discredits "the bloodthirsty Boves" (*el sangriento Boves*, l. 497), Morillo and his "vile satellites" (*tus viles satélites, Morillo*, l. 511), and the perfidy of the "arrogant canary" (*canario soez*, l. 728), a periphrasis for Monteverde elucidated by Bello in a note. Until the moment Bolívar read *La Biblioteca Americana* in early 1828, he rarely reminisced about the wars of independence.[20] Indeed, Monteverde, Boves, and Morillo are names Bolívar almost never mentioned after 1822. But these are precisely the men excoriated as criminals in the second part of the "Alocución."

Bolívar, we may surmise, had read the "Alocución" and saw it as an indictment of the bloodshed during the Revolution and of measures he had taken, actions that led to the death of some of his compatriots. In his conversation with Perú de Lacroix, the defensiveness, the furor, and the passion are those of a man justifying himself against the accusations implicit in Bello's poem. Bolívar had read the "Alocución"; and instead of finding praises to his name, he had found a sharp rebuke.

For it was all a question of imposing a name, and the name was Bolívar. He did not want a crown; he was not about to repeat Napoleon's mistake. His ambition, and his challenge, were greater than a throne surrounded by incense. He wished to create a new order, a new political system that would be neither republic nor monarchy, but an association of nations – Bolivia – under the aegis of a president-for-life whose title was Libertador. So when he had finished talking about Piar, the group sat down for lunch and Bolívar began to invoke the name that Bello had so tenaciously avoided in his poems: "He later began to compare the names of 'Bolivia' and 'Colombia' and maintained that although the latter is very sonorous and harmonious, the former is even more so. He then began to take them apart, separating their syllables and comparing them. '*Bo*, he said, sounds better, than *Co*, *li* is sweeter than *lom*, and *via* is more harmonious than *bia*.'"[21]

Such was the state of affairs between the warrior and the poet. Bolívar had answered Bello's covert attacks with diplomatic assignments that implied, at best, a second demotion and, at worst, a taunting insult. Bello was torn with uncertainty and could not decide whether to go to Chile or Colombia. He finally resolved to go to Chile and on the day of his departure he wrote a letter to his dear friend Fernández Madrid, the last letter he would ever write in London, a city "for many reasons hateful to me and for many others worthy of my love." He warmly thanks his fellow poet for having provided him consolation "among so many humiliating circumstances" (*OC*, 25: 408–9). On February 13 he boarded the *Grecian* and left for Valparaíso.

Fernández Madrid had written to Bolívar about Bello's imminent departure. Bolívar came too late to the rescue, though his response remains a thoughtful tribute to a difficult friendship:

Three thousand pesos were recently sent to Bello so that he might go to France, and I beg you earnestly not to allow this illustrious friend to be lost in the country of anarchy. Persuade Bello that Colombia is the least of all evils in America, and that if he wishes to be employed here let him say so and he will have a good career. His fatherland should be placed before everything else, and he is worthy to hold an important position here. I am aware of the preeminence of this *caraqueño*, who is my contemporary. He was my tutor when we were the same age, and I loved him with respect. His indirectness has separated us somewhat, and therefore I want to be reconciled with him, that is, to gain him for Colombia.[22]

As Bolívar dictated these words, Bello was crossing the Atlantic. A form of friendship survived the series of muted insults they had exchanged, but they were never to be reunited. Like Ovid, Bello offended the ruler and was forced to go to the end of the world, an exile.

PART III

Santiago (1829–1865)

11

The liberal poets

Chile, país inventado por Andrés Bello.

Roberto Matta

The country Bello had chosen for his return to South America was at the farthest corner of the continent, a narrow piece of land stretching from the mines of Copiapó to the Bío-Bío River, between the Andes and the Pacific Ocean. It was a time of heated political confrontation in Chile. The liberals, or *pipiolos*, were in power but their political base was fragile. The president of the new republic was an old friend of Bello's from his early London years, Francisco Antonio Pinto; the ideologist of the group was the Spaniard José Joaquín de Mora, who had come to Chile after Rivadavia's fall from power in Argentina in 1827. Mora had drafted the Chilean Constitution of 1828. A skillful propagandist, he promoted the liberal cause through the pages of *El Mercurio Chileno*. The political opposition, the *pelucones*, were associated with the clergy and the party that favored O'Higgins, still in exile in Lima. Their leader was the entrepreneur Diego Portales.

Bello arrived on June 25, and his first impressions of Chile were recorded in a letter to Fernández Madrid:

My dear benefactor and friend: At last we have arrived in Santiago, after a long but generally happy and pleasant voyage. The country pleases me so far, although I find it does not quite live up to its reputation, above all in terms of its natural beauty. I notice the absence of our lush and picturesque vegetation, our diverse crops, and even in some respects the intellectual climate of Caracas during the blissful period before the Revolution; and I would like to notice the absence of our poor roads and domestic discomfort, a graver matter here than in our countries, because the weather in winter is harsh indeed. In compensation, one enjoys here true freedom for the time being: the country prospers; although immoral, the common people are docile; the youth of the upper class demonstrate a strong desire to learn; everyone is pleasant; dealings are easy; there are few priests to be found; the friars are rapidly dwindling and in fact one enjoys all the tolerance one could wish for.

The first paragraph of this letter sets out two themes that dominate Bello's Chilean period. One is his liberal, indeed anticlerical, streak. The other is his longing for the lush natural setting and high cultural level of colonial Caracas. As a liberal, he became the most talented member of the only Spanish American nation that was able to institute civil liberties in the aftermath of the Revolution. As an exile among the *toto divisos orbe chilenos,* he longed for a world and a culture that had vanished forever.

In his letter Bello goes on to say that in order to avoid criticism from Colombians, he anxiously awaits Bolívar's approval of his move to Chile. He also thinks that he has brought too many copies of Fernández Madrid's book of poetry and regrets that there are few admirers of belles lettres in Chile. Still, he has made announcements of the book in several newspapers, and a review will appear in Mora's *El Mercurio Chileno,* an excellent paper that, however, scarcely has sixty subscribers. Bello also tells his friend that he has doubts about the viability of Chile's liberal government, a thought that prompts him to reiterate his old assault on the imitation of the United States model on Spanish American soil: "What a predicament our countries are in! And we still have not come to disabuse ourselves and realize that the slavish imitation of the institutions of the United States can only bring us ruin, unrest, anarchy falsely called freedom, and sooner or later military demoralization!" (*OC,* 26: 6–8). Throughout his letter, Bello sounds like a liberal who is happy to enjoy the present freedoms, but who is fearful and even despondent about the calamities that are sure to come.

"Poesías de D. José Fernández Madrid," the review announced in the letter, is a passionate defense of liberalism. Fernández Madrid is called a "liberal poet" and linked to the Spanish exiles who escaped the tyranny of Ferdinand and produced great works in England, where they were "without the hindrances of the double despotism, political and religious." The reviewer then describes the range of topics to be found in the works of Fernández Madrid and his Spanish counterparts:

The inexhaustible theme of the modern liberal poets, that is to say, the love of liberty, the hatred of despotism, the bitter censure of the infamous alliance of tyranny and fanaticism that oppresses and humiliates Europe, has supplied the author with a subject matter worthy of his inspiration. . . . In all times liberal ideas have lent themselves admirably to poetic expression, and if there have been Horaces and Virgils who have achieved immortality, paying a deplorable tribute to the times they lived in, an extraordinary combination of highly distinguished gifts has been required in order to save them from the oblivion that usually falls upon those who embrace that party.

Bello scholars disagree about who wrote this review. The Amunátegui brothers attributed it to Mora, while Grases believes it was Bello's.[1] The passionate rhetoric of the piece suggests Mora. In his Chilean years Bello was to embrace liberal ideas, but his was always a qualified liberalism, one marked by caution and even skepticism. The review, in contrast, still breathes the fire of the Cádiz liberals; it is the rhetoric of a man who sees himself as among the heralds of a new age in which monarchic absolutism and classical aesthetics have no claims. It is a rhetoric that had gained considerable ground among the continental liberals of the 1820s. The distinction between the classical-monarchist and the romantic-liberal parties was in the air, and the following year Hugo would draw the battleground along the same lines in his preface to *Hernani*.

The rhetoric of the liberals had considerable appeal for Bello, and the article in the *Mercurio Chileno* touches on many of his own aesthetic creeds. After his arrival in Chile, Bello stopped writing imitations of Virgil and Horace, and began instead to look for poetic inspiration among romantic poets such as Byron and Hugo. But Bello always kept an eye on the past; far from rejecting the Augustan poets, he tried to find a place for them in the new republic. Though he often assailed the old orthodoxies of Crown and Church, he never rejected the guiding hand of Horace and, especially, of Virgil. The sharp dividing line between the Augustan party and the liberal party drawn in the article on Fernández Madrid is almost certainly Mora's, for nothing like it appears elsewhere in Bello's works. Furthermore, the list of "immortal" liberal poets the article invokes is much more characteristic of Mora's taste than of Bello's. This list includes Byron, Moore, Béranger, Monti, and Lavigne. Of these, only Byron had any significance for Bello, while Mora had shown considerable interest in all these poets before 1829.[2]

Like Fernández Madrid and Mora, Bello was a "liberal poet," but his was an aristocratic liberalism, reminiscent of the British Whigs and perhaps of Benjamin Constant, a liberalism that deeply mistrusted egalitarian democracy. Bello's doubts only grew as the crisis of Chile's liberal government accelerated. Scarcely a month after Bello's arrival, President Pinto resigned, leaving a power vacuum among the *pipiolos*. By October political chaos was so generalized that Bello reported a bleak picture to Fernández Madrid. In this letter all of Bello's established political beliefs return to the surface. He speaks of "factions full of animosity, a wavering constitution, a weak government, disorder in all branches of the administration." Then, in a part of the letter unfortunately torn in a critical place, Bello expresses openly his antidemocratic feelings: "Fortunately, democratic institutions have lost here [. . .] everywhere their pernicious prestige; and those who advocate them do so principally because they do not know what to replace them with, not because they sincerely believe in them."[3]

The confrontation between the *pipiolos* and the *pelucones* was now inevitable, and in April 1830 their armies met at Lircay. The *pelucones* won the day and the conservative forces assumed power. The reins of the country were in the hands of Diego Portales, who set out to restore the power of the executive and the principle of authority. A freethinker from the Creole aristocracy, Portales had no faith in the "obscure" politicians who had risen since the Revolution. He also strongly disliked the emerging cult of personality in Spanish American politics and strenuously fought against many of his own partisans who longed for the return of O'Higgins. When the elections of 1831 gave General Joaquín Prieto the presidency of the country and Portales the vice-presidency, Portales declined the position and moved to Valparaíso. Nevertheless, he maintained a determining influence on the executive. In 1835 he returned to the limelight and established a virtual dictatorship until his assassination in 1837.

From the beginning, Bello collaborated with the Portales regime. He became the head of the Colegio de Santiago, a school designed as an alternative to the Liceo de Chile, directed by Mora. When the Colegio de Santiago hired several French professors, Mora attacked the move, saying that Chileans would be poorly served by men who could not even speak the native tongue. The issue developed into a debate on Spanish usage, and the ensuing articles that Bello and Mora wrote offer an arid discussion about the appropriate forms of different Spanish expressions. But behind the rhetoric, one perceives an essential political cleavage between the two men. In his speeches and in his acts, Mora wished to question and test the limits of the Portales regime, while Bello became its literary spokesman.[4]

Bello soon became the target of the more vocal opponents of the Portales regime. One such opponent was José Miguel Infante, an old Chilean patriot who published *El Valdiviano Federal* and wished to eliminate from the Chilean curriculum the study of Latin and Roman law, the vestiges of imperial Spain. Bello replied by asking Infante whether, in his eyes, reading Virgil or Cicero in the original had no value; or if he knew of any translation that approximated the beauty of style and feeling exhibited by these and other Latin authors. Then Bello presented one of his most audacious arguments, a revisionist proposition intended to find a place for Virgil in the era of liberalism. With the renaissance of Greek and Roman letters, Bello explains, a new era began. Philosophy shook off the chains that had until then burdened human reason, and "the scholastic filth" (*la mugre del escolasticismo*) disappeared from scientific language. The love for that recovered classical literature encouraged the love for freedom. And just as ancient letters inspired enormous change at that time, so will they now (*OC*, 8: 487–94).

Thus, Bello places Virgil at the head of a historical chain that leads to liberalism. In contrast, Mora's argument in the 1829 article on Fernández Madrid holds Virgil and Horace as the principal opponents, not the founders, of liberalism. Bello's defense of the curriculum invoked other reasons for learning Latin, one of which was the study of Roman law, the basis of the imperial civil laws of Spain, which were still in effect in Spanish America, though in a state of utter confusion. The debate between Bello and Infante, as we shall see, soon extended into the arena of politics.

As he made himself at home in Santiago, Bello also resumed the activities he had mastered in his happy days in Caracas. His opinions on foreign affairs were greatly esteemed by the

Chilean government. Soon after his arrival in Santiago, he was quick to show his expertise in international law and in 1832 he published *Principios de derecho internacional,* which he signed "A. B." He never occupied the cabinet seat of foreign affairs, but he was consulted on every issue and drafted most of the documents of that ministry; in the opinion of most historians, he directed Chile's foreign affairs between 1830 and 1853.

Bello became the editor of the literary and foreign affairs sections of the official government newspaper, *El Araucano,* but he eventually expanded his scope and used the newspaper to publish most of his writings, including his *Civil Code,* a work that gave him an international reputation as a jurist. He was also a teacher: he first gave a course on legislation based on Dumont's translations of Bentham and then gave private lessons at home.[5] Bello drafted many of the official documents of the executive branch, including the presidential addresses from 1832 to 1860, and of Congress, including the Senate's official response to the presidential address. It is not quite clear what role he played in drafting the central text of this period, the Chilean Constitution of 1833, though Portales – who was a godfather of one of Bello's sons – attributed to Bello the final form of the draft of the constitution.[6]

But it would be misleading to suggest that between 1830 and 1865, the year of his death, only Bello gave policy directions in Chile. If he did draft the constitution, this document was hardly the result of his thinking alone, but the product of extended negotiations in a well-publicized constitutional assembly. There were in essence two forces in the assembly. The first was led by Mariano Egaña, who presented a constitutional project that gave preeminence to the executive branch. His plan allowed the president to be reelected for an indefinite number of five-year periods; it also gave the president power to dissolve the lower chamber and immunity from prosecution. A second group, led by Manual José Gandarillas, strenuously objected to the monarchic disposition of Egaña's proposal. The result was a compromise: the president could serve two terms, but he was not granted immunity and did not have the power to dissolve the chamber. In addition, the president could select all the *intendentes* of the provinces, thus eliminating all vestiges of decentralization and federalism. Bello stood behind the constitution and even wrote a poem, "La cometa" (1833), attacking unbridled liberalism and defending the law.[7]

As the new regime gained ground, Bello continued to be a target of criticism by conservatives as well as liberals. A large sector of the conservative aristocracy charged him with introducing liberal ideas to Chile, principally through his influence on the Committee on Censorship. Bello was opposed to any censorship, but more orthodox views were represented in the committee by Ventura Marín. Bello's influence, however, proved decisive, and by the 1840s Chileans could read Lammenais and see a Rossini opera or a play by Hugo.[8] Meanwhile, José Miguel Infante continued to criticize Bello, whom he viewed as a symbol of the restoration of old values. Infante charged that Bello had long opposed Spanish American independence and that he was determined to establish a monarchy in the New World. One of their many exchanges started when Bello wrote an article commenting on Santa Anna's expected coronation in 1834. Bello says that the news was not well received by those who wished to see the establishment of order and liberal institutions, but he himself could not condemn monarchy on theoretical grounds. One can judge the merits of a political system only by its results, he says, and even in a monarchy the people may enjoy civil liberty. But it may take many generations for the hereditary power of a monarchy to become firmly established. He then says, "The era of monarchies in America has passed" and reminds his readers that Mexico has already seen the failure of this experiment. Iturbide failed despite the very favorable circumstances of his coronation. Would Santa Anna have any more luck?

In his reply, Infante noted that, for all the nice things Bello said about monarchy, he said nothing at all about republicanism. Was this the way to reinforce the political institutions of a young nation? The opposition to the Portales regime also made much use of the book *Historia de la Revolución Hispano-Americana* by Mariano Torrente, in which Bello was accused of betraying the patriots' cause in the thwarted revolution of April 2, 1810. The rumor became quite nasty in Santiago. Infante even charged that Bello was a "wretched adventurer" who was not allowed to live in his homeland and, worse, that if he had found a *"patria"* in Chile, he owed that to men like those he had had the audacity to attack (*OC,* 26: 114, 439).[9]

Despite these and many other unpleasant events, Bello remained in Chile. Shortly after his arrival, he had received letters from friends in the Colombian government urging him to go to Bogotá or Caracas. Fernández Madrid said that his own wife, Pachita, who had recently joined him in London, had heard the Libertador praise Bello, saying that every Colombian loved him. He also assured Bello that Bolívar had no ill feelings toward him. But between 1829 and 1831, the political foundations of Colombia continued to deteriorate. Monarchic propaganda gained ground, and the conservative men who surrounded the ailing Bolívar tried in vain to lure a European prince to take over after his death. Bolívar died in 1830 in complete desperation, convinced that the disintegration of Colombia was inevitable. And so it was. García del Río, a close adviser of Bolívar during his last years and a monarchic propagandist, wrote to Bello, "Colombia was buried in his tomb" (*OC,* 26: 16). The three separate regions of colonial days became three new countries: Venezuela, Nueva Granada (later Colombia), and Ecuador.

Opinions about Bolívar's achievement differed. Olmedo, in a letter written one month before his own death in 1846, compared Bolívar to Christ. Olmedo says that Christ carried out an incomplete redemption of humankind; he freed us from sin but not from the effects of sin. Any commonplace liberator could do the same (*"lo mismo hace cualquier libertador vulgar"*). Bolívar, for example, freed Spanish America from the Spanish yoke, but left behind all the disasters of the Revolution (*OC,* 26: 149). Bello felt that Bolívar had been driven by noble instincts, but that his colossal plans had in the end undermined his legacy. In an article of 1847 Bello described a set of engravings that show the Libertador with a sword in one hand and the constitution in the other. Of Bolívar's features, Bello says: "The resolute air of that intrepid and nobly disdainful face corresponds admirably to the valiant movement of the entire person. Such is his expression that anyone can read in his brow the thoughts directed to one single object: the liberty and the glory of the fatherland." He also thought, however, that Bolívar's ardent soul, driven by grandiose ideals, had led him to execute political plans that could not be sustained for long. He observed that Bolívar's most peculiar creation, Colombia, did not outlast its creator's life. He also criticized the Bolivian Constitution and was skeptical of the different attempts to revive Bolívar's legacy of a general congress of Spanish American nations that would promote the region's integration. Though Bello admired such an ideal, he thought that progress could best be achieved through bilateral negotiations.[10]

Bello became a senator in 1837, the same year Portales was assassinated. It was also the year in which Chilean troops, aligned with Peruvian exiles who opposed General Santa Cruz, dissolved the Confederation of Peru and Bolivia. Once the war had ended, the Chilean government removed the extraordinary powers of the executive and a moderate spirit began to replace the iron hand of Portales. Trying to keep a balance between his new *patria* and his broader commitments to the whole of Spanish America, Bello again tried to stretch his allegiances. He wrote patriotic hymns that celebrated the Chilean victory, but he was also in correspondence with the new foreign secretary of Peru, Felipe Pardo, who had been exiled in Santiago during the Santa Cruz years.

The ensuing peace also allowed for discussions about poetry, and in 1840 Bello published a review of Mora's *Leyendas españolas,* a work that transfers to Spanish the humor and rapid transitions of Byron's *Don Juan* and *Beppo.* Bello welcomed this work with unusual enthusiasm: "It would be misleading to think that there is only a small wealth of poetic beauties in this natural, calm, and simple language which avoids anything that reeks of epic heights, and descends without degrading itself to the tone of familiar conversation." Bello appreciated Mora's light sarcasm in poems such as *Don Opas,* and he enjoyed introducing and quoting some passages about the Spanish prelate who was in some accounts responsible for the events that led to the conquest of Spain by the Arabs:

> Desvelábase este perverso prelado en tramar una
> rebelión para precipitar del trono a Rodrigo, y
> colocar en él la raza de Witiza.
>   Viendo cuán vanos eran sus conatos,
>   dijo don Opas entre sí: "Paciencia;

ya que lo quieren estos insensatos,
consúmanse en brutal indiferencia.
Cubran mi mesa suculentos platos;
brillen en casa el lujo y la opulencia;
manténganse los sacos de oro llenos,
y haya buena salud; del mal el menos."

(*OC*, 9: 345)

(This perverse prelate did everything he could
to plot a rebellion that would dethrone Rodrigo
and replace him with the race of Witiza: "Seeing
the vanity of his attempts, don Opas muttered to
himself: 'Patience. Since these senseless people
want it so, let them be consumed by my brutal
indifference. May succulent dishes fill my table;
may luxury and opulence shine in my house;
may my sacks be always filled with gold, and
may I preserve my health. This is the lesser
evil.'")

The topos of a powerful and greedy clergy, a theme that
Bello had treated in the "Agricultura" with bitterness, appears
in Mora's poem in a new guise, a guise that Bello now adopted,
as we shall see, in his own poetry. After all the vicissitudes of the
past, the destinies of Mora and Bello had begun to converge.
Bello had stayed in Chile and supported the Portales regime.
Mora had gone to Peru and supported Santa Cruz. However
different the sides they took in 1830, by 1840 their deep convictions were almost identical. The Spanish liberal had been so-
bered by the continued defeats of the orthodox liberal experiments. Besides, the liberalism that traced its roots to the French
Revolution and the Cádiz constitution was in decline, and even
Mora could be found criticizing the excesses of the sovereignty
of the people.[11] Meanwhile, Bello was listening with increasing
attention to a poetry that was new in the Spanish language. In
1840, no doubt inspired by Mora, he announced: "A new era is
dawning for Spanish letters. Writers of great talent, humaniz-
ing poetry, bringing her down from the stilts that she was fond
of using to lift herself up, are working to restore her primitive
candor and her ingenuous graces, the lack of which has no
compensation" (*OC*, 9: 362).

Chile's stability was reaffirmed after the presidential elections
of 1841, when General Manuel Bulnes, the hero of the recent
war and head of the moderate party, replaced General Prieto.

Liberals protested that the transfer of power was dynastic (Bulnes was the nephew of Prieto), while conservatives objected to the growing power of the military. But an alliance was established between the moderate and liberal parties, and their combined forces were able to defeat the conservative candidate, Joaquín Tocornal. This alliance was cemented by the marriage of Enriqueta Pinto, the daughter of the liberal leader, to General Bulnes.

After 1841 Bello began to enjoy an extraordinary reputation in Chile and abroad. Through his personal influence in the government and, perhaps more importantly, through the pages of *El Araucano,* he moderated public opinion and left his personal imprint on the direction favored by the country's growing oligarchy. In 1842 Bello published "La acción del Gobierno," an article that established the guiding political framework of the Bulnes government. Bello begins by reminiscing about the constant ideological vicissitudes of the revolutionary years, when no progress was made to establish "the desired well-being of a regular and stable order, or of a conservative and beneficial government." As he had done in the *Censor,* he criticizes the double influence of the French Revolution and the Spanish Constitution of 1812, which had almost abolished the power of the executive. Among Spanish American countries, Chile was the first to establish "a regular state of affairs and one adapted to its circumstances, with a government that preserves order, promotes progress and yet is limited in the exercise of power by healthy restraints."

The progress achieved by Chile was, according to Bello, the combined effect of freedom and a powerful executive, which he defines with the epithet "regular." The influence of the executive should, he urges, apply not only to politics but to economics. Bello had always been a partisan of trade liberalization, and in his book list for the University of Colombia he had recommended the works of Smith, Say, and Ricardo. But he always rejected doctrinaire economic freedom. In "Acción del Gobierno" he specifically condemns the classic maxim of pure liberalism – "dejad hacer y dejad pasar" (laissez faire; laissez passer). The examples of France and even more clearly of the United States, he says, have shown the need for government assistance in large investments of infrastructure, such as irrigation and railroads. Bello, however, believed that citizens must actively participate in their government: "Our republican system requires this cooperation of all citizens who love their country." He concludes by recommending what he calls a mixed system, a *"sistema mixto."*[12]

The *"gobierno regular"* also had an aesthetic that was midway between extremes – neither absolutism nor unfettered liberalism, neither classicism nor romanticism. That was Bello's cultural creed in the first years of the moderate Bulnes regime. He began to lay out the basis of his creed in a series of articles that reviewed the work of the Spanish grammarian Gómez Hermosilla. Classical and romantic writers, Bello says, closely resemble monarchists and liberals, respectively. For classical writers and monarchists alike, the authority of the doctrines and the practices that have the seal of antiquity can never be repealed, and any step taken off the well-trodden path is considered a rebellion. By contrast, romantic writers and liberals, in their attempt to emancipate creativity, sometimes confuse liberty with unbridled licentiousness. Developing this political–aesthetic parallel, Bello observes that the classical sect divides genres with the same care that the monarchists divide social classes, while the romantic school tries to bring together the buffoon and the king, the prostitute and the princess.

Gómez Hermosilla, whom Bello labeled an ultramonarchist and an ultraclassicist, becomes the object of Bello's censure. In all four articles devoted to this author Bello surveys Hermosilla's evaluation of the poems of Moratín. Avoiding stock arguments against neoclassicists, Bello attempts instead to defeat Hermosilla on his own terms. The appropriateness of an epithet and the mistranslation of a verse by Horace are often the topics of discussion. At the same time Bello is reinforcing his old conviction that the basis for the new poetry is the natural style, devoid of neoclassical and romantic rhetoric. He closes his articles on Gómez Hermosilla by inviting young poets to be daring but without affectation (*OC*, 9: 373–413).

Around 1840 many Argentine liberals fleeing the dictatorship of Rosas began to settle in Santiago and Valparaíso. One of them was Domingo Faustino Sarmiento, a schoolteacher born in the interior provinces who was eager to show his talent and rouse the spirits of all Chileans. In a series of articles written in 1842 Sarmiento accused Bello of imposing a rigid formalism that stymied the creativity of young Chileans. There was no literature in Chile, Sarmiento concluded, and he called (in jest, of course) for Bello's ostracism. In the oversimplified version of most literary histories, this became the origin of the debate between Bello and Sarmiento, between classicism and romanticism, between the old and the new. But in reality there was no such debate. Bello published one rather innocuous article, denouncing Sarmiento's idea that all authority in matters of language rests with the people. Sarmiento's articles, however, had two profound effects on Chilean culture. In the first place, they provoked young Chilean writers, many of them students of Bello, to prove the Argentine wrong, and thus Sarmiento may be credited with inspiring the development of postindependence Chilean literature. Second, Sarmiento's views forced Bello to probe deeper into his own political and aesthetic thinking, and even stimulated him to resume writing poems.

First came five imitations of long poems by Victor Hugo. In the *Museo de Ambas Américas,* the journal García del Río edited in Valparaíso in 1842, Bello published "Las fantasmas" and "A Olimpio." In the latter poem Bello returns to the accusation of treason that was launched against him in 1810. The poem shows Olimpio dismissing all the accusations with the composure and indifference of a Stoic. The next year Bello published "Los duendes," a poem that explores the possibilities of different Spanish meters, and "La oración por todos," in which he probes the intimate tone of prayer. There is nothing public in these imitations of Hugo. These are often private outpourings of intense emotion, provoked by events in Bello's own life.

Bello also brought up the issue of romanticism and liberalism in his inaugural speech at the University of Chile in 1843. Here he finally endorsed the principle of sovereignty of the people, an old right, he says, that should be restored and purged of the stains it acquired under despotism and of the contradictions it has generated through the ages. The speech closes with Bello's definition of the university's mission:

Liberty, set as a bulwark against the servile docility that accepts everything without question, but also against the disorderly license that threatens the authority of reason and the noblest and purest instincts of the human heart, will constitute no doubt the theme of all the sections of this university. (*OC,* 21: 21)

As rector of the University of Chile until his death in 1865, Bello planned a radical transformation of the country's educational establishment. This transformation first entailed the de-Latinization of Spanish American culture. Despite his admiration for Cicero and Virgil, Bello recognized that he had to put an end to the supremacy of Latin in secondary and higher education. Latin had a place, a very important place, but it was not to be the founding block of all knowledge. Instead, Spanish became the language of schools at all levels. In order to encourage proper usage, Bello published in 1847 the *Gramática de la lengua castellana destinada al uso de los americanos*, a work that followed his earlier monograph, *Análisis ideológica de los tiempos de la conjugación castellana* (1841), in its attempt to remove the strict servility to Latin grammar displayed in the grammar of Nebrija, the text of colonial education. The *Gramática* also followed in spirit Bello's earlier study, *Principios de la ortología y métrica de la lengua castellana* (1835), which foreswore the analysis of Spanish meter using the long–short vocalic distinction of Latin verse still prevalent among neoclassic critics.

In his new position of influence Bello continued to favor the campaign for popular education begun in the 1830s in the pages of *El Araucano*. Indeed, his first task as rector was to embrace Sarmiento's proposal to simplify the alphabet. In truth, Sarmiento was only echoing an article written in 1823 by Bello and García del Río, in which they proposed that the number of letters in the Spanish alphabet equal the number of sounds in the spoken language. The main result of this reform was the replacement of Latinate spelling by one that was more logical and intended for intensive use in popular education.[13]

In 1845 the Argentine Juan María Gutiérrez began to compile a large anthology of Spanish American writers – *La América Poética* – which was published as a series in Valparaíso. Gutiérrez kept up an active correspondence with Bello. In a letter of that October, Bello complains to Gutiérrez about his enormous work load and adds that he has almost lost contact with the Muses: "I cannot recall any first-rate poet who has been anything but a poet. High society, the hubbub of the world of affairs, especially of political affairs, which are so favorable to oratory, are not so for poetry, which enjoys the contemplative mood even in the heart of society." He then suggests to Gutiérrez that he abandon the alphabetical order of his anthology, that he juxtapose serious pieces and comic ones, and set philosophical and religious themes between erotic themes. In a characteristic note of moderation, however, he advises him to avoid strong contrasts. Bello also tells Gutiérrez that among his papers he has a translation of *L'Orlando Innamorato*, but adds that it is a very free translation, with original introductions to the cantos and adapted to modern taste (*OC*, 26: 108–11).

Bello had begun the translation of Berni's version of Boiardo's *Orlando* in London. And this work was his major attempt to explore the fantastic, irregular, and variegated strains of romanticism. The version is also influenced by Byron, and some of its frequent digressions remind the reader that the poem was written in the nineteenth century. But in the year that he wrote his letter to Gutiérrez, Bello was still writing a work that was known only after his death. It is a long narrative poem about the Revolution called "El proscrito" (The proscribed man). This is the opening stanza:

> Ante la reja está de un locutorio
> de monjas, a la hora de completas,
> (no digo la ciudad ni el territorio
> por evitar hablillas indiscretas),
> la mujer del anciano don Gregorio
> de Azagra, caballero de pesetas
> pocas, pero de alcurnia rancia, ilustre,
> a quien ni aun la pobreza empaña el lustre.
> (*OC*, 1: 577)
> (In front of the locutory parlor of a nunnery, during compline – I will omit the city and the region so as to avoid indiscreet gossip – stood the wife of old don Gregorio de Azagra, a gentleman of few pesetas, but of old, distinguished lineage, whose luster not even poverty can tarnish.)

The conflict, and the tone of the story, are suggested in the first two lines. The poem's title and the line "Ante la reja está de un locutorio" suggest the image of a prisoner's locutory parlor. But this image is immediately altered with a daring run-on line – "de monjas, a la hora de completas" – that clarifies that this is the locutory parlor of a convent. The intentional ambiguity of the word "*locutorio*" thus points toward the drama's double plot, one that will join Captain Araya, a Chilean hero proscribed by the Spanish forces during the reconquest, and Isabel Azagra, a beautiful young woman who has been confined to a nunnery.

The action begins when Isabel is about to enter the convent. From her early childhood Isabel has been studying at the convent, and now the time has come for her to decide whether to take permanent vows. She has some hesitations, but these are quickly dispelled by her mother and especially by Fray Facundo, her mother's confessor. Two thousand pesos are needed for her dowry, and Isabel's mother and Fray Facundo pressure Gregorio de Azagra, Isabel's father, to raise this amount. Azagra says that he does not have that kind of money, but maybe with the money from the mines. . . . At this point, his wife breaks in. She is furious with her husband because she knows full well that the mines are a net expense to the family. Just when she is about to burst, the friar intervenes and suggests that, if the mines cannot yield some profit, there may be other ways to raise the money, for example, a mortgage, or *censo*, on some property:

> "Mi don Gregorio, en esto está el busilis
>
> (Dice con una flema, una cachaza
> admirable), en que den. Pero yo pienso
> que podemos hallar alguna traza . . .
> algún arbitrio . . . verbigracia, un censo
> sobre la hacienda." Doña Elvira abraza
> la indicación con un placer inmenso:
> "Ya se ve; ¿por qué no?" "Si acaso el fundo
> no está gravado (agrega fray Facundo;
>
> Y una mirada exploratoria lanza,
> como que algún obstáculo presuma);
> y si lo está, con una buena fianza
> podemos a interés buscar la suma.
> Mi compadre don Alvaro Carranza . . ."
> "Al que en sus garras pilla lo despluma,
> (responde Azagra). No se piense en eso;
> un dos por ciento, padre, es un exceso."
>
> (*OC*, 1: 581, ll. 160–76)

("My dear don Gregorio, this is the point [he says with admirable phlegm and calm], that they should yield. But I think that we can find some scheme . . . some special procedure . . . for example, a mortgage on the farm." Doña Elvira

embraces this suggestion with great pleasure:
"There you go, why not?" "If by chance the
farm is not encumbered [adds Fray Facundo,
casting an exploratory gaze, as if he presumed
an obstacle], and if it is, with a good guarantee
we can obtain a loan. My *compadre* don Alvaro
Carranza . . ." "He skins whomever he clutches
in his claws," Azagra answers. "Don't even think
about that; a two percent interest, father, is excessive.")

The friar then suggests a third alternative; the money might
be procured from a friend of Azagra, don Agapito. Though
don Agapito is accused of being a Freemason and a democrat,
he has money, and since there seems to be no other alternative,
everyone agrees that he will be the one asked to provide the
funds for Isabel's dowry. As the friar leaves, Azagra experi-
ences a great crisis: he likes neither the new financial bind nor
his daughter's future in the convent. He then resolves to ask his
friend don Agapito to deny the loan for the dowry. But by the
time he arrives, Fray Facundo has already visited don Agapito
and closed the deal. Azagra is deeply disturbed and contem-
plates his daughter's future.

> "La que renuncia al mundo en esa verde
> edad primera, ¿podrá ser que estime
> lo que le aguarda, o sepa lo que pierde?
> Y cuando, vuelta en sí, ve que la oprime
> cadena eterna, y despechada muerde
> el duro hierro, ¿a quién acusa, dime?
> Al que su juicio leve, antojadizo,
> debió haber alumbrado, y no lo hizo."
>   (*OC*, 1: 591, ll. 577–84)

("Could the girl who abandons the world in her
green, young age ever fathom what awaits her
or know what she is losing? And when, having
regained consciousness, she sees that an eternal
chain oppresses her, and in despair she bites the
hard iron, tell me, whom does she accuse? The
one who should have illuminated her slight, ca-
pricious judgment, and didn't.")

Such thoughts cause Azagra to become ill. After a meeting of
several doctors, who display the full range of colonial medical
knowledge, don Agapito and a young enlightened man are able

to convince the others that Azagra is suffering from an emotional crisis. He is sent to the farm of don Agapito to recover, and Isabel takes leave of the convent to care for her father.

Isabel starts feeling free in the countryside, and she starts thinking about love. One night, a bleeding man enters her room. She is terrified and cries for help, but he convinces her to stop and is able to escape from the farm. The next day a peasant tells Isabel that a nephew of don Agapito has been found, and that he is badly hurt. She goes to see the man, and as she suspects, he is the man she had seen the night before. He is Captain Araya of the Chilean army. She ministers to him, and as he begins to regain consciousness they exchange glances that fill Isabel with new feelings. The interaction between the hero and the heroine is now interrupted as the author takes us back to the battle of Rancagua (October 1814), which is the theme of the fifth and last canto. The poem ends as the captain rides his horse across the Andes in order to join other patriots in Mendoza.

Like so many other poems that Bello wrote, "El proscrito" was never finished. Enough is said, however, for the reader to imagine that both the hero and heroine have escaped from their confinement, thus challenging the political and religious forces that had proscribed them. "El proscrito" is the domestic equivalent to the central sections of the "Agricultura." The same anticlerical bent, the same allegorizing complete Bello's view of the Revolution. The action of the poem takes place during 1816, the year in which Bello became convinced that the decided revolution was inevitable. In Captain Araya and Isabel, Bello presents his symbols of the new era, Spanish Americans who are able to break away – to use Mora's liberal terminology – from the double despotism of Crown and Church.

The tone, the theme, the versification, and the lexicon of "El proscrito" are drawn from Mora's *Leyendas españolas*. But standing behind both poets is the example of Byron, the poet who exerted the greatest influence on Spanish American romanticism. It is here, in this final, half-jocular version of the Spanish American Revolution, that Bello finds the new tone that best expresses the profound cultural transformation of the past forty years. The poetry he has begun to write at age sixty-five is a poetry of daring transitions, one in which lofty ideals are set next to popular language. "El proscrito" offers the best counter-balance to the high-minded language of Bello's official prose. In this poem he leaves behind the Ciceronian periods that filled the pages of *El Araucano* and government documents and begins a more intimate kind of address. He condenses his thoughts in the Byronian epigraph that opens the work: "Keep thy smooth words and juggling homilies for those that know thee not."

"El proscrito" was Bello's most ambitious attempt to write a romantic poem. But Bello's approach to romanticism, as with liberalism, was one of restrained admiration. He does embrace romanticism, but with great nostalgia for the classical model. The romantics he follows are those who share his deep longing for the classics. He admires Byron because he preserves Pope's wit and imagination and Horace's free urbanity; he imitates Hugo because of all romantic poets he most consistently speaks with a Virgilian voice. Bello was a liberal poet, but one who always revered the Augustan poets far above all others. In 1856 he advised a young Peruvian poet against the "autopsy of the feelings" and psychological analysis, common in Lamartine, and called instead for actions, gestures, and words that reveal the passion of the character. Virgil remained for him the consummate poet: "I summarize my ideas regarding this method of the great artists with a single word: *Dido*. There is nothing more noble or elevated in art" (*OC*, 26: 327). As Grases has so aptly observed, Bello's liberalism was firmly grounded in the classical tradition; it was a "*liberalismo humanista.*"

12

The exile

Virgil is Rome, and all of us Westerners of today are
exiled Romans.

Jorge Luis Borges

During his Chile years Bello was ready to embrace the politics
and aesthetics of the new age, but he stubbornly refused to
devalue or dismiss the past. Young Chilean liberals who were
also his students – Lastarria, Bilbao, his own son Juan – were
calling for a complete break with colonial servitude, but Bello
was always ready to temper their claims. The most serious confrontation between Bello and the young liberals was provoked
by Lastarria's study of Chile's colonial years. Bello responded
with a series of historical articles that comprise his last and best
exposition in prose of the transformation brought about by the
Spanish American Revolution. Here he finally endorsed liberalism, but only after he had made a balanced assessment of the
old order.

José Victorino Lastarria's *Investigaciones sobre la influencia social de la conquista y del sistema colonial de los españoles en Chile* was
submitted in September 1844 as a thesis at the University of
Chile. In this work, Bello's disciple states that history is the
oracle through which God reveals his wisdom to the world.
Rejecting the narrow definition of history, the "simple testimony of past events," Lastarria wishes to consider the science or
philosophy of history. In this structural approach that pays little
attention to the individualized segments of the historical map,
the conquest appears as a ferocious and shameful act and the
colonial era as a period of utter darkness during which Spanish
Americans suffered in abject servitude under Spain's theocratic
despotism. Lastarria attributes Chileans' desire for independence to the Araucanian element of their mixed heritage, while

the Spanish element was responsible for the intolerance and fanaticism present among Chileans even after the Revolution. The wars against Spain sealed the political independence of the New World and marked the beginning of the "war against the powerful spirit the colonial system infused in our society."

The work took the educational establishment by storm, and in November Bello wrote an article in *El Araucano* in response. While he agrees with his student that the Spanish conquest of America was atrocious, he objects to the assertion that it was "impudent." The Spaniards of the sixteenth century displayed the same disrespect for international law and the same barbarism toward the weak that powerful countries of all times have displayed. It is an illusion, Bello warns, to believe that in the nineteenth century there is greater respect for humanity. If one sees fewer horrors in the present, that is simply a result of improved calculations of material self-interest and the perfection of the art of destruction.

Bello also objects to Lastarria's portrayal of the colonial past as an era of utter darkness. "We must be fair: that was not a *ferocious* tyranny. It shackled the arts, clipped the wings of thought, blocked even the sources of agricultural fertility; but its policy was one of hindrances and privations, not of torture and blood." To understand the colonial period, he explains, one must understand the profound influence of Rome on the old order. Spanish despotism in the New World was just like the despotism of the Roman emperors: the same inefficient benignity of the supreme authority, the same praetorian rashness, the same divine rights of the throne. But in addition to these and other odious parallels, Bello urges his reader to consider the positive ones. Spain played the same civilizing role in the modern era that Rome had in antiquity. The Spanish Empire, in fact, was the extension of the Roman Empire:

Perhaps we deceive ourselves, but it certainly appears to us that none of the nations that sprang from the ruins of the Empire preserved a more pronounced stamp of the Roman genius: the very language of Spain is the one that best preserves the character of that spoken by the rulers of the world. Even the material objects of the Spanish colonial administrations display something that is imperial and Roman. America still owes to the Spanish government all that is splendid and grand in its public buildings.

Bello then discounts Lastarria's discussion of the role that Indian traditions played in the independence movement. That movement, Bello insists, resulted from the spontaneous confrontation of the peninsular Iberian spirit and the colonial Iberian spirit. Bello also expresses great repugnance for Lastarria's assertions that the colonial peoples of Chile and the rest of Spanish America were in a state of complete social and moral destitution. With much anger in his voice, he instructs Lastarria that the acts of the patriots contradict such allegations. The colonial virtues that propelled the revolutionary movement were the product of the Iberian element that Lastarria so much despises: "Anyone who observes the history of our struggle against the metropolis with philosophical eyes will easily recognize that the Iberian element is precisely the one that has allowed us to prevail. The native Spanish steadfastness clashed against the innate steadfastness of the sons of Spain."

Bello stresses the existence of two parallel movements at the time of the Revolution. One was this native, Iberian, sturdy element, which was ready to carry out the mission. The other was a foreign element, which had participated as an ally in the wars of independence. And this foreign element – liberalism – was new and fragile. The problem of the Revolution, he concludes, was the conflict between patriotism and liberalism. The patriotic (Roman, Iberian) element gave way to strong executive leadership, the liberal element to civil liberties. These two elements were not in harmony. One was mature, the other young and inexperienced. This was the state of affairs in which Bolívar found himself. No one loved freedom more than Bolívar, Bello tells us, but he inevitably turned into a dictator.

Up to this point in his article Bello has been concerned with the old order and has attempted to give an explanation for the difficulties of the Spanish American independence movement. He now begins to examine the aftermath of the Revolution, and he takes sides not with the conservative establishment but with the liberals, declaring that the vestiges of the old Spain are the real enemy of the present. Americans snatched away the scepter of the monarch, but not the scepter of Spanish despotism. The old laws, the old military customs still have a resounding voice in Congress. And he warmly agrees with his disciple's description of the nature of the enemy. When the war against Spain ended, Bello echoes, another war began: "the war against the powerful spirit the colonial system infused in our society." Bello also affirms Lastarria's arguments against the accusation of those who challenge the timing of the Spanish American Revolution. The *"extravíos,"* the errors made by the inexperienced patriots, were the result of colonial backwardness. No other time would have been better for independence; to have delayed the struggle would have been to invite the same and even greater dangers. Spanish Americans had to take advantage of the first opportunity for independence or else prolong their servitude for centuries. One could not wait for Spain to educate the colonies in the ways of freedom: "We had to educate ourselves, no matter how dearly we paid for the attempt."

The article ends with long quotations from Sismonde de Sismondi's *Etude sur les constitutions des peuples libres* that describe the passage from the servile to the liberal model. The serviles are wrong, says Sismondi, to censure the inexperience of the liberals. One cannot argue that the disasters that inevitably accompany the independence of young nations are worse than the degradations suffered under an absolutist state. The liberals made mistakes, but these were the result of their justice and generosity. And they destroyed a shameful system that fostered slavery, the greatest degradation of all. But Sismondi does not wish to excuse the faults of the liberals. Though they perceived the evil they wished to destroy, they had false ideas about the future they wished to establish. They believed they had found principles when they had discovered only paradoxes (*OC,* 23: 153–73).

This was the first article. Bello was then at the height of his power. He was a senator, the president of the University of Chile, the editor of *El Araucano,* the spokesman of the Bulnes government. The young liberals wished to provoke a political confrontation, but Bello's article left them, for a while, dumbfounded. He had willingly incorporated the liberal rhetoric at the end of his article and quoted passages of Sismondi that Lastarria himself had quoted, but Bello also emphasized the need to examine the past with precision, to know the facts. As in his London years, he had very little patience with the liberals' theoretical constructs. According to the young liberals, historians should not reduce their work to the mere gathering of facts, but should invoke instead the ideas that govern the course of humanity. History and its methods became the subject of four articles Bello published in *El Araucano* in January and February 1848. The first of these articles was a review of a second work by Lastarria, *Bosquejo histórico de la constitución del gobierno de Chile durante el primer período de la revolución*. Bello countered the philosophy of history, the notion invoked by the young liberals, with what he termed the philosophical study of history. He explained this difference in a passage that develops Gibbon's dictum about Tacitus, "the first of historians who applied the science of philosophy to the study of facts."[1] Bello wished to describe a continuity with the historians of the old order:

To write history is to clarify the facts and the name of this discipline should be granted only to history that is written in the light of philosophy, that is, with an adequate knowledge of man and society, and this philosophy has existed, has sparkled in historical writings long before the nineteenth century. One cannot clarify the facts as Thucydides and Tacitus did, without a profound knowledge of the human heart; and allow us to say (even at the risk of appearing old-fashioned) that one learns more about man and social evolution from the great political historians of antiquity and of modern times than from the general and abstract theories that are called the philosophy of history. (*OC*, 23: 223)

In this and other articles addressed to the young liberals, Bello places himself on their side, but only to warn them against a new kind of servility. He tells his young friends that they must be careful to avoid excessive dependence on civilized Europe. As if following fate, he says, new nations are subdued by those that preceded them. Greece overwhelmed Rome, and Rome overwhelmed the modern peoples of Europe. Greece and Rome together dominated Europe after the Renaissance, and Spanish America is now imitating Europe beyond tolerable levels. We should imitate European independence of thought, Bello tells the young liberals, and examine firsthand the sources of knowledge. What will a Michelet or a Guizot say when he looks at Spanish America and sees only the servile copy of European civilization? He will say, "America has not yet broken her chains; she drags herself across our footprints with her eyes blindfolded; no independent thought breathes in her work –

there is nothing original, nothing characteristic; she mimics the forms of our philosophy, but she does not absorb its spirit; her civilization is like an exotic plant that has not yet drawn its sustenance from the ground around it" (*OC*, 23: 251).

In his articles on history written in the 1840s we find Bello's fondness for the old regime, for vast empires. But at the same time he was aware that, inexorably, centuries of tradition were perishing and well-calibrated hierarchies were foundering. There was no way around it. The power of the old order was waning. The Latin tongue would no longer be the vehicle of learning; monarchs would no longer be surrounded by incense and celebrated by the songs of poets. From the far ends of the world Bello would look back at the old order, as an exile who tries to adjust to his new surroundings but refuses or is unable to disentangle himself from the past.

Bello indeed never felt at home in the Chilean republic. In 1842 he thanked his brother Carlos, by now a rich landowner in Venezuela, for sending him the *Historia de Venezuela* by Baralt and Díaz, an atlas, and some maps. "You have given me one of the greatest pleasures of my long exile," were the first words of his letter. He tells Carlos that, when he opens and surveys the map, memories and images rush through his mind. His eyes cannot stop looking at Caracas, and though in vain he searches for sights that the engraving could not have portrayed, at least he enjoys moments of pleasant illusion. The map of Caracas was to hang in front of his bed and perhaps be the last object his eyes ever saw (*OC*, 26: 75–6).

In other letters Bello begins to remember the natural beauty of the torrid zone. He remembers the rivers, the creeks, and even the trees that he used to see "in that happy period of my life." As he looks at the plan of Caracas, he imagines himself walking again through the streets, in search of familiar buildings, in order to ask after his friends that are no more. He remembers the church and the neighborhood of his youth, and the fistfights he had with Carlos. While tasting the coffee sent to him from El Helechal, the hacienda he had owned in his youth, he remembers his happy formative years (*OC*, 26: 116–17, 346, 449).

In his literary work and in his correspondence, especially during the last twenty years of his life, Bello often engaged in similar nostalgic reveries. In one of his most touching letters to Manuel Ancízar, a liberal Colombian writer, Bello expresses a longing for the idyllic simplicity of the past, now threatened by economic expansionism. Inspired by Ancízar's *Alpha,* a book that describes the rural villages and churches of Colombia, Bello reflects on the world he has lost. He thinks about the misery that is the result of industrialism. Instead of independent weavers, he tells Ancízar, there will be several large-scale manufacturing companies that will turn those weavers into paupers, or at best will allow them to receive a meager salary from a capitalist, usually a foreigner. The country will gain, but what is the country without its inhabitants? When he imagines those honest weavers turned into humble workers, or perhaps into worse, his economic theories waver (*"mis teorías económicas vacilan"*; *OC,* 26: 295–6).

Bello was an exile from the lush nature of colonial Caracas; but as the letter to Ancízar shows, he was also an exile from a world to which he could never return because that world itself was vanishing. This may explain the depth of his nostalgia. In his last years he called himself a Spaniard, and the Amunátegui brothers tell us that in 1861 he allowed them to publish his sonnet on the victory of Bailén, which he recited with jubilation. He did not want to recover all of his past, however. When his brother Carlos wrote him that Bishop Talavera had published in Caracas large segments of the "Oda a la vacuna," which the bishop had learned by heart before the Revolution, Bello wrote back, "It must be very poor since I do not even remember it."[2]

Bello had long ago left the land of his youth, the luscious Edenic valleys that surrounded Caracas, but he treasured the culture that had marked his early days. He may have forgotten his youthful poem, but not the cultural life that had shaped that poem, the culture shared at the meetings with Bolívar and Ustáriz, which he recalled with so much emotion when he began to tell the story of his life to his biographers, the Amunátegui brothers. For Bello the years in Caracas had been the best years of his life (*OC,* 26: 30). He never stopped recalling with emotion the last years of the old order. He liked to call himself "a poet of the previous century" (*poeta del siglo pasado*), and he always felt some scorn for the nineteenth century, which he labeled "the century of centuries" (*el siglo de los siglos*) (*OC*, 1:277, 309).

The cultural and even the political models of Rome and Spain continued to have a strong appeal for Bello. In the 1840s he prepared a detailed study of Horace, an expanded version of one of his London literary articles occasioned by Javier de Burgos's translations of the *Odes*. He also edited Ovid's *Tristes*, the work in which Ovid, having been exiled by Augustus, longs for his return to Rome, and the *Cid* – another book about exile. In politics, he made no references to his monarchic past and espoused republican principles. Yet despite his avowed liberal principles, in one of his letters he expressed his admiration for Juan Manuel de Rosas, the nemesis of Argentine liberals.

Bello now attempted to give a coherent version of the culture he had absorbed in his youth – Roman culture, a culture increasingly threatened or displaced by the advent of romanticism. In 1850 he published the first two parts of a vast project, the *Compendio de la historia de la literatura,* a text of literary history prepared for the high school students of the Instituto Nacional. A third part of the *Compendio,* a history of Latin literature, was published the same year, with some comments by Vandel-Heyl, who held the chair of classics at the University of Chile. But Vandel-Heyl published only the first two parts of the manuscript, those that discussed the first two eras of Roman history, from the foundation of Rome to Catullus. Of the third part, which Bello labeled "*el siglo de Augusto,*" or "Augustan Age," Vandel-Heyl published but a short fragment. Not until Amunátegui's edition of Bello's complete works appeared was Bello's extended exposition of the Augustan Age known.

We have seen how closely Bello followed the Augustan poets when he expressed his political thoughts. It is therefore enticing to think that in the unpublished portion of his history of Latin literature he tried once again to record the profound aesthetic and political transformation that he and Spanish America had undergone since the early days of the nineteenth century. Not that we should read these pages as an allegory of the Revolution or find in every allusion to Virgil or Augustus a hidden reference to Bello and Bolívar. In fact, Bello expressly warns against this kind of reading. When he discusses Virgil's *Eclogues* he says that forcing allegorical interpretations on all the details of the poems, by means of remote analogies, is a puerility that no poet of the Roman golden age would have suffered. Still, we find in Bello's description of the Augustan poets passages that inevitably bring to mind his own political and cultural role during the vicissitudes of the Revolution.

Bello discusses the *Eclogues* and describes how Virgil – through the voice of the shepherd – alludes to the court of Augustus in order to thank the tyrant of Rome and to pay tribute in the form of servile adoration. And then we read Bello's praise of the *Georgics*. Lucretius may surpass Virgil in sublime ideas and poetic courage, but in all other virtues the *Georgics* is superior to *De rerum natura*. Bello objects to Tissot's call for greater order and regularity, since the poem would lose the air of spontaneity that is one of its most excellent attributes. But he does agree with Tissot that the proem of the *Georgics* is an "undignified and absurd piece of flattery" contrary to all rules of common sense and art. He goes on to note that Virgil not only deifies a mortal at the beginning of a work that is dedicated to the idealization of agriculture, but goes as far as devoting more lines to him than to all the deities of the countryside combined. He immediately says, however, that the charm of Virgil's poetry is such that one cannot stop to consider its defects. Bello then spends two pages listing the various beauties of this poem, which he terms, in agreement with the "unanimous vote of all intelligent men," the most perfect poem of the greatest Roman poet.

In his discussion of the *Aeneid*, Bello, following Fenelon, writes that the kingdom of Priam is accessory to the poem, while Rome and Augustus are always present in the poet's mind. But whereas in his reading of the *Georgics* Bello accuses Virgil of endorsing Augustan despotism, Bello's strategy in reading the *Aeneid* is first to emphasize the link between Virgil and Augustus and then to show their differences:

Virgil had first conceived the plan to celebrate the deeds of Augustus. To link the birth of Rome to the fall of Troy, adopting the Romans' national traditions; to give a legitimate appearance to Augustus's usurpation by passing on to him the tradition of Aeneas, the father of the royal race that, it was believed, had founded the eternal city; to reconcile the Roman people with a prince who, after copiously shedding the blood of the people, wished to grant them the gift of peace and hide the features of the executioner behind a mask of clemency;

to advocate a limited monarchy in a country torn by civil factions, and perhaps to soften the iron soul of the tyrant, made callous by the proscriptions, by inclining it toward pardon, religious piety, and moderation in supreme power – such are the intentions of Virgil in the *Aeneid,* and the very selection of his hero proves it. The traits he grants Aeneas, the pious Trojan prince, the model of filial love and of human feelings even toward his enemies, prevents us from refusing Virgil a tribute of recognition. By praising Octavian, Virgil has sought to cooperate in the metamorphosis that was taking place within this illustrious criminal and to teach him to be worthy of the name Augustus. (*OC,* 9: 150–9)

In this remarkable passage Bello wishes to inscribe the *Aeneid* within the two traditions that surround the name of Augustus: the pro-Augustan tradition, which emphasizes the transformation of the *princeps,* and the anti-Augustan tradition, which denies that such a transformation ever took place. Bello wishes to relegate the pro-Augustan tradition to the *intentions* of Virgil: the poet created a sublime model for Octavian in order to promote his transformation. But Bello's language undermines the effect Virgil's words could have had on Augustus. The features of the executioner behind the mask of clemency, the iron soul of the tyrant, the illustrious criminal – with such expressions Bello evokes the harsh, severe anti-Augustan tradition of Gibbon, Voltaire, and Montesquieu – the tradition of Tacitus.

In the last line Bello alludes to the pagan and old republican meaning of "augustus," the one given to the word by Ennius, expressing the highest conceivable level of spirituality and a sense of awe that constantly tends to increase. The final negotiation is between "augustus" and "Augustus," between the epithet and the man who was being taught by Virgil to deserve the attributes of the epithet. The *Aeneid,* in Bello's interpretation, shows Virgil as a moral voice who tried in vain to transform Octavian. The *princeps* was too stained with blood ever to achieve the high level of spirituality signified by his new name. Virgil's effort ended in failure: he tried to create a limited monarchy, but Rome yielded to despotism. Augustus did not listen. He failed Virgil. And now he had fallen – for Augustus could only fall from the very center of the myth, from the poem in which his name had survived through the centuries.

In his studies of Augustan poets, Bello tries both to condemn Augustus and to save the culture that was created around him.

He constantly turns to poems in which Augustus figures prominently but downplays his role in those poems. When Bello talks about Horace, he does not deny that the poet was an accomplice in the apotheosis of Augustus but points out that in one of his best odes, the so-called Regulus ode (3.5), Horace quickly abandons Augustus and dedicates his attention to Regulus, the prototype of republican Rome, the martyr of ancient discipline. Bello also wanted high school students to hear the story that surrounded the epistle to Augustus. When the despot complained to Horace that he never wrote poems for him in fear of accusations by posterity, the poet finally wrote the poem that opens his second book of epistles, *Cum tot sostineas,* in which, again, after a few lines of praise he turns to an entirely different subject, Roman literature, and produces one of the most instructive of his epistles. We see how Bello tries to disentangle Horace from his patron, to minimize the poet's involvement in the monarchic settlement. Bello, as a prominent republican, had to reshape the culture of his youth. Adjustments were needed, rectifications of old pieties. The high school students of Chile had to be given a version of antiquity that did not offend the incipient civil liberties.

Bello's thoughts on the Augustan Age after the deaths of Virgil and Horace appear in his detailed account of the events that led to Ovid's exile. At age forty-two, Ovid published the *Ars amandi.* This poem can be seen as a portrait of Rome in that age of corruption and tyranny: "There we see the magnificence and the luxury of a people that has been enriched by the spoils of the three parts of the world; lords of the universe but subjugated by sensual delights and slaves to one man." But, he adds, Ovid did nothing to contribute to the depravity around him; on the contrary, his language was more restrained than that of Catullus and Horace and even of Augustus himself, who composed "shameful odes." Ten years passed, and Ovid's work enjoyed extraordinary success. But his good fortune ended. Following Villenave, Bello explains that Tiberius and Livia were determined to banish from Rome a man who had witnessed secrets that affected the fate of Augustus's grandchildren. At their request, Augustus exiled the poet to Sarmatia, to the last frontiers of the empire.

The exiled poet lived for eight years in Tomos, near the

shores of Pontus Euxius, suffering freezing weather and the alarms of war, surrounded by savage and hostile tribes and relying for his safety on Cotis, the king of the Tomitans. At times he had to pick up a helmet and sword and run to protect the gates against an attack of the barbarians who swarmed the valley. Poetry was his only consolation. In Tomos he wrote the *Tristes* and the *Pontics;* he also concluded the *Fasti,* and even wrote an apotheosis of Augustus in the language of the Tomitans. In the elegies written in exile Ovid speaks with the overpowering language of misfortune, of misfortune without measure, without end, without hope (*OC,* 9: 139–45).

As an exile of fallen Rome and of fallen Spain – an exile of the "Imperio," a word used by Bello to describe Rome and the Iberian extension of the Roman Empire – Bello tried to rework the classical tradition, to adjust that extraordinary legacy to the new order of freedom. He was ready to admit the newness of romanticism, the mythology of irregularity, but he was not ready to give up the consummate works of antiquity, the poets in whose footsteps he had labored throughout his long career. He therefore endeavored to add an ancient luster to the poor mythology of liberalism.

In his poetry and essays Bello views the Spanish American Revolution as a radical expression of a movement of the West that called for the dismantling of a culture based on authority and hierarchy – a system supported by the institutions of Church and Crown – and the construction of a network of shared signs and meanings in which this foreign ingredient, freedom, yet unknown in Spanish America, could flourish. The new culture would aim at establishing the principles of "*libertad,*" a new word in our culture, addressed by both Bello and Olmedo as a "kind stranger" (*amable peregrina*), a concept that for Bello in his old age stood midway between servility and unbridled freedom (*libertinaje*). The center of power would be filled by a strong and impersonal state that would gradually accommodate civil liberties.

In the new republics there would be no *princeps* at the center of power. The Spanish American Revolution had shattered the image of a distant superhuman king, and though many of Spanish America's strong men secretly wished to emulate Augustus, and attempted to prolong their power in the name of freedom, republican principles and ideals – the principles and ideals that triumphed in the Spanish American Revolution – signaled a course of action that no strong man could reverse.

Bello – much like Montesquieu, Voltaire, and Gibbon – saw Augustus as the centerpiece of an era that was coming to a close in the West. But we read Bello, as we should read authors of the eighteenth century, not for his programmatic rejection of the *princeps,* but for the energy he invested in understanding the Augustan phenomenon. The principate, and the culture it generated, had become an obsession in the eighteenth century – everyone had to study it; everyone had to write about it. One's opinion of Augustus was the concise, civilized way of expressing one's political stance. And though he lived in the nineteenth century, Bello experienced a cultural evolution that was not untypical of the Enlightenment. Like Pope and Voltaire, Bello showed an early devotion to the classical model, followed by a final and often angry rejection of the Augustan principate.

But no other poet experienced as profoundly as Bello did the clash between the old and the new orders. Pope and Voltaire may have criticized Augustus, may even have been at war with classical political or poetic principles, but they lived in a world that was still in harmony with the past. Theirs was a world in which classical culture could still find room for new ideas, new discoveries, new principles. Bello lived in a world that, in Shelley's words, was weary of the past. By the time Bello wrote the last fragments of *América* it had become increasingly difficult to rework Virgil's *Aeneid* and *Georgics* in order to accommodate the claims of liberalism. The West had reached a point at which the main texts of its culture were at odds with the kinds of political institutions it was seeking to establish.

Bello's poetic and political pronouncements show us the itinerary of a man who assimilated the claims of liberalism but who also contemplated with great misgivings the gradual collapse of Augustanism. Bello wanted to leave the old order but not to break with it. He wished, so to speak, to preserve diplomatic relations with that order. We therefore read his works for their adumbrations of freedom, but also for the almost desperate attempt to seize a piece of the past, some remnant of Europe's monarchic institutions. His logic provides a unified narrative to a radical shift in the West; it is a logic marked by contrasts and antitheses that could not occur to poets or thinkers who had witnessed only one stage of this transition. What makes Bello's works so interesting and challenging is that here – in one man's life and works – one can witness the disintegration of the classical model of empire and culture.

As the wars of independence came to a close, Spanish America began to emerge from the Augustan model of empire and culture. The attractions of that model – its clear-cut hierarchies, its awesome antiquity – made it difficult for men like Bello and Bolívar to replace it with the liberal model. And once the wars against Spain had been won, almost at the cost of self-destruction, the removal of Augustus left a void in the institutions and culture of Spanish America, a void that invited nostalgia for the lost order.

Until the very end Bello meditated on the meaning of Virgil; until his last hour he tried to salvage the culture of the old order and to frame his own thoughts within that tradition. As Amunátegui tells us:

Having experienced a peaceful delirium, this ailing illustrious man imagined that he saw the verses of the *Iliad* and the *Aeneid* on the walls of the room and on the draperies of the bed. He was mortified because frequently they appeared to be blurred and he could not make them out. From time to time he murmured fragments of his own works.

Appendix: dating the manuscript sheets of *América*

The manuscripts of Bello's *América* are kept in thirty-five folders in the Casa de Bello in Caracas. Each folder contains a single or double sheet, except for the first folder, which contains only a ribbon. Of these sheets, twenty-one have watermarks, many of which show the date of manufacture of the paper, sometimes next to a seal and the name of the manufacturer.

An examination of the correspondence between Bello and his closest associates during his London years shows consistently a lag of approximately two years between the date of the watermark and the date of the letter. Of the thirteen letters I examined in the Caracas archives (Archivo de la Casa de Bello and Archivo del Libertador), only one letter was written on paper whose watermark predated the letter by more than two years.

Letters written by Bello

Addressee	Date of letter	Watermark (manufacturer)
Gobierno de Cundinamarca	February 7, 1815	1813 (Jellyman)
J. R. Revenga	March 8, 1826	1824 (J. Whatman)
J. R. Revenga	April 12, 1826	1824 (Gater)
S. Bolívar	March 21, 1827	1826 (J. Green & Son)
S. Bolívar[a]	April 18, 1827	[1826] (J. Green & Son)

[a]This letter does not show the year of manufacture, but the paper and the seal of the watermark are identical to those of the letter of March 21, 1827.

Letters received by Bello

Sender	Date of letter	Watermark (manufacturer)
López Méndez	February 14, 1814	1810
Blanco White	December 30, 1815	1814
Blanco White	January 5, 1816	1814
Blanco White	July 8, 1821	1820 (W. Thomas)
Blanco White	October 4, 1822	1821 (J. Whatman)
Blanco White	June 7, 1824	1822 (John Hall)
Irisarri	June 1, 1822	1821 (H. Smith & Son)
López Méndez	January 14, 1825	1824 (John Hall)

On the basis of this strong correlation, it is possible to offer an approximate date of composition for those sheets of the *América* manuscript that show the year of manufacture in the watermark:

Folder	Lines[a]	Watermark (manufacturer)	Approximate date of composition
2	1–20	1810	1811–12
	183–232		
3	21–38	1813	1814
	62–109		
	362–73		
	395–419		
	501–13		
	634–63		
4	110–82	1812 (Joseph Colles)	1814
	664–718		
5	233–52	1811	1813
6			[1813]
7	296–362	1811 (Harris)	1813
14	775–897	1825 (Huxham Mill)	1826
15	898–1024	1825 (Huxham Mill)	1826
16	1025–60	1825 (Huxham Mill)	1826
	1135–1304		
17	1061–1139	1824 (J. Whatman)	1826
18	1306–12	181[4][b]	1815
20	1339–79	1821 (R. Barnard)	1823
21	1380–1409	1821 (R. Barnard)	1823
23	1426–88	1814 (R. Barnard)	1815–17
27	1553–75	1821 (R. Barnard)	1823
28	1576–1621	1823 (Brocklesby & Morbey)	1823

Folder	Lines[a]	Watermark (manufacturer)	Approximate date of composition
29	1622–51	1823 (Brocklesby & Morbey)	1823
30	1652–84	1821 (R. Barnard)	1823
31	1685–99	1822 (J. Whatman)	1823
32	1700–52	1821 (R. Barnard)	1823
34	1779–88	1821 (R. Barnard)	1823

[a]Numbering given in the second volume of the *Obras completas* (Caracas, 1957).

[b]The paper of this sheet is identical to the one contained in folder 23. One can clearly see the first three numbers of the date – 181 – and a trace of the last number, from which a 4 can be made out.

Notes

1 Augustan Caracas

1 Alfredo Boulton, *El solar caraqueño de Andrés Bello* (Caracas, 1978); David W. Fernández, *Los antepasados de Bello* (Caracas, 1978); Oscar Sambrano Urdaneta, *Cronología de Andrés Bello, 1781–1865* (Caracas, 1986).
2 Miguel Luis Amunátegui, *Vida de don Andrés Bello* (Santiago, 1882), 6–18; Ildefonso Leal, "Andrés Bello y la Universidad de Caracas," in *Bello y Caracas* (Caracas, 1979), 171.
3 José Gil Fortoul, *Historia constitucional de Venezuela* (México, 1978), 1: 335; Augusto Mijares, *El Libertador* (México, 1978), 1: 61; Amunátegui, *Vida*, 27; Felipe Larrazábal, *Bolívar* (Caracas, 1975), 53.
4 Pedro Grases, "La conspiración de Gual y España y el ideario de la independencia," *Obras* (Caracas, 1981), vol. 3; Richard Herr, *The Eighteenth-Century Revolution in Spain* (Princeton, N.J., 1958), 239–68; Raymond Carr, *Spain, 1808–1975*, 2d ed. (Oxford, 1982), 72.
5 *El grado de bachiller en artes de Andrés Bello*, preface by Ildefonso Leal (Caracas, 1978); Arístides Rojas, "El poeta virgiliano," *Humboldtianas* (Buenos Aires, 1942), 2: 126; Leal, "Andrés Bello y la Universidad de Caracas," 174–5.
6 Alexander von Humboldt, *Personal Narrative of Travels to the Equinoctial Regions of the New Continent, During the Years 1799–1804* (London, 1822), 480.
7 Ibid., chap. 12; Amunátegui, *Vida*, 24–6.
8 Rojas, "El poeta virgiliano," 119–21; Amunátegui, *Vida*, 14–16, 32.
9 Pedro Pablo Barnola, S.J., *Apropósitos* (Caracas, 1965), 9–16; Amunátegui, *Vida*, 28–34.
10 Luis Alberto Sucre, *Gobernadores y capitanes generales de Venezuela*, 2d ed. (Caracas, 1964), 306.
11 Ricardo Archila, "La Junta Central de Vacuna," in *Bello y Caracas*, 197–209.
12 Andrés Bello, *Obras completas*, 2d ed. (Caracas, 1981), 1: 8, ll. 1–12. All references to Bello's works, unless otherwise noted, are to this edition, abbreviated *OC*, followed by the volume and page number.
13 See *Diccionario de la lengua castellana* (Madrid, 1726–39); J. Cor-

ominas, *Diccionario crítico etimológico de la lengua castellana* (Berne, 1954).

14 Many European poets serve as examples; for the coronation of Charles II Dryden published "Astrea Redux," a poem in the same vein that celebrates the restoration of monarchy. He was not alone; legions of British writers, including Locke, followed the classical formula. See Howard Erskine-Hall, *The Augustan Idea in English Literature* (London, 1983), chap. 7.

15 "El Obispo de Caracas, Ilustrísimo señor Viana y la revolución de Gual y España," *Boletín de la Academia Nacional de la Historia,* 42 (Caracas, 1959), 533–43; "Pastoral del Obispo de Caracas Illmo Sr. Juan Antonio Viana, con motivo de la revolución de Gual y España," *Boletín de la Academia Nacional de la Historia,* 43 (Caracas, 1959), 159–69.

16 *Biblioteca de autores españoles* (henceforth *BAE*) (Madrid, 1875), 63: 200. Meléndez Valdés's epistles were first published in 1797.

17 Herr, *The Eighteenth-Century Revolution,* 408.

18 Howard D. Weinbrot, *Augustus Caesar in "Augustan" England: The Decline of a Classical Norm* (Princeton, N.J., 1978), 51.

2 Revolt

1 Pedro Grases, "Una nota del Doctor Lecuna relativa a Bello," *Obras,* 2: 50.

2 Amunátegui, *Vida,* 32–51.

3 Federico Álvarez O., *El periodista Andrés Bello* (Caracas, 1981), 19–46; Manuel Pérez Vila, "Andrés Bello y los comienzos de la Imprenta en Venezuela," in *Bello y Caracas,* 265–303.

4 Domingo Amunátegui Solar, *Archivo epistolar de don Miguel Luis Amunátegui* (Santiago, 1942), 1: 10–11; Manuel Salvat Monguillot, "Vida de Bello," in *Estudios sobre la vida y obra de Andrés Bello* (Santiago, 1973), 20.

5 Manuel Josef Quintana, *Obras completas* (Madrid, 1897), 1: 15.

6 The letter to the Regency was signed by José Llamozas and Martín Tovar Ponte, but later in life Bello called it his own, making it one of the few documents not signed by Bello that he later chose to acknowledge. The reason may be that it showed a strong commitment to the cause of the Creoles, if not to the minority position of the young *mantuanos,* and it therefore helped to dispel the rumor of betrayal of the cause of the Revolution that pursued Bello throughout his life (*OC,* 26: 114, 439).

7 Gil Fortoul, *Historia constitucional,* 1: 217.

8 Humboldt, *Personal Narrative,* 429.

9 Amunátegui, *Vida,* 76–9; Juan Germán Roscio, *Escritos representativos* (Caracas, 1971), 9; D. A. G. Waddell, "Las relaciones británicas con Venezuela, Nueva Granada y la Gran Colombia, 1810–1829. Primera Parte: en Londres," in *Bello y Londres* (Caracas, 1980), 1: 57.

10 Bello, *Resumen de la historia de Venezuela, OC* 19: 54–5. For a detailed bibliographical study of the *Resumen* see Pedro Grases, "El 'Resumen de la historia de Venezuela' de Andrés Bello," *Obras,* 1: 109–277; and his introduction to the edition of the *Calendario* (Caracas, 1959), 11–81, included in *Obras,* 1: 279–396. As Grases shows, Bello was preparing a complete history of the provinces of Venezuela at the time of the 1810 revolution, including civil, ecclesiastical, military, and commercial aspects. Of this project only the first part is known, the *Resumen de la historia de Venezuela.*

11 The impassioned defense of Venezuelan agriculture that characterizes the *Resumen* was not motivated entirely by Bello's public concerns. He and his family had been able to rent fifteen *fanegadas* of land (approximately 20 acres) from the government and started a coffee plantation. See *El helechal, posesión rural de los Bello,* preface by Manuel Pinto C. (Caracas, 1979).

3 Independence

1 [James Mill,] "Emancipation of Spanish America," *Edinburgh Review,* 26 (1809), 277–311; José Alberich, "Actitudes inglesas ante el mundo hispánico en la época de Bello," in *Bello y Londres,* 1: 128. On Miranda see William Spence Robertson, *The Life of Miranda* (New York, 1969); for his links with Mill and Bentham see John R. Dinwiddy, "Los círculos liberales y benthamistas en Londres, 1810–1829," in *Bello y Londres,* 1: 377–98.

2 Blanco White eventually abandoned Anglicanism and became the greatest authority among the Unitarian dissenters. For details of his life and works see *The Life of the Reverend Joseph Blanco White, Written by Himself* (London, 1845); Mario Méndez Bejarano, *D. José María Blanco y Crespo (Blanco White)* (Madrid, 1921); Marcelino Menéndez Pelayo, *Historia de los heterodoxos españoles* (Madrid, 1946), 6: 173–214; Vicente Llorens, *Liberales y románticos,* 2d. ed. (Madrid, 1968), passim; Martin Murphy, *Blanco White: Self-banished Spaniard* (New Haven, Conn., 1989). Also see Joseph Blanco White, *Antología de obras en español,* ed. V. Llorens (Barcelona, 1971).

3 John Allen, "Examen de la obra intitulada 'Essai politique sur le Royaume de la Nouvelle Espagne,' por Alexandre de Humboldt. Paris 1808–1809," *El Español,* 4 (1810), esp. 270–4; José María Blanco White, "Reflexiones políticas," *El Español,* 4 (1810), 315–34; Dinwiddy, "Los círculos liberales y benthamistas," esp. 380, 393.

4 Amunátegui, *Vida,* 88–90; "Borradores de Andrés Bello," *Revista de la Sociedad Bolivariana de Venezuela,* 27 (1967), 682–93; Grases, "Bolívar, ¿'diplomático atolondrado'?"; *Obras,* 4: 464–77.

5 *OC,* 11: 12; Waddell, "Las relaciones británicas con Venezuela," 62.

6 J. L. Salcedo Bastardo, "Bello y los 'Simposiums' de Grafton Street," in *Bello y Londres*, 1: 432–4.

7 William Burke, *Derechos de la América del Sur y México*, preliminary study by Augusto Mijares (Caracas, 1959).

8 C. Parra Pérez, *Historia de la primera república de Venezuela* (Caracas, 1959), 55–75; *Libro de actas del Supremo Congreso de Venezuela, 1811–1812* (Caracas, 1959), 134–202; Gil Fortoul, *Historia constitucional*, 191–216.

9 Julio Guillén, "Correo insurgente de Londres capturado por un corsario puertorriqueño, 1811," *Boletín de la Academia de la Historia*, 63 (1960), 155.

10 *Los libros de Miranda*, preface by Arturo Uslar Pietri and bibliographical preface by Pedro Grases (Caracas, 1979); Pedro Grases, "Los estudios de Bello en Londres sobre literatura medieval," *Bello y Londres* (Caracas, 1981) 2: 44.

11 Robertson, *The Life of Miranda*, 1: 151.

12 For Bello's deep admiration for Miranda also see John Robertson's response to a lost letter of introduction (original in French): "I am grateful to you for giving me the opportunity to meet Mr. M., and I thank you very sincerely; my opinion of this illustrious man agrees with yours, and it has not taken me very long to recognize in him the statesman, the warrior and the consummate legislator" (*OC*, 25: 20).

13 Amunátegui, *Vida*, 137: "In the end literary tastes solidified a friendship that had been first motivated by the analogy of their political goals."

14 This was suggested to me by Alamiro de Avila, the Bello scholar and former director of the library of the University of Chile.

15 J. Blanco White, "Contextación a una carta de la Junta de Caracas," *El Español*, 16 (1811), 302–3.

16 Dinwiddy, "Los círculos liberales y benthamistas," 393; Alberich, "Actitudes inglesas," 144.

17 Gil Fortoul, *Historia constitucional*, 1: 217–40.

18 Carlos Pi Sunyer, "Sobre la atribución a Andrés Bello de una obra publicada en Londres en 1812," *Patriotas americanos en Londres* (Caracas, 1978), 211–23.

19 Andrés Bello, "Preliminary Remarks," *Interesting Official Documents Relating to the United Provinces of Venezuela* (London, 1812); Pi Sunyer, "Sobre la atribución a Andrés Bello." These documents show the state of Bello's English prose after two years in London. He may well have published articles in English before, as suggested in the two letters from James Mill (*OC*, 25: 46–50), but these articles have not been found. For the progress of Bello's English see John Robertson's letters of February 2, 1809, and December 10, 1810 (*OC*, 25: 4–6, 19–22).

20 For the numbering and dating of Bello's manuscripts see the Appendix.

21 This fragment does not appear in the otherwise excellent edition

of Bello's poetic manuscripts in the second volume of *Obras completas*.

4 The reconquest

1 José Domingo Díaz, *Recuerdos sobre la rebelión de Caracas*, (Caracas, 1960), 98–9; Gil Fortoul, *Historia constitucional*, 1: 306–8.
2 The debate between Blanco White and Mier has been studied by Merle E. Simmons in "Una polémica sobre la independencia de Hispanoamérica," *Boletín de la Academia Nacional de la Historia*, 117 (1947), 82–125.
3 The Latin poem was first attributed to Bello by Ernesto Mejía Sánchez in "Don Andrés Bello y el Doctor Mier," *Anuario de Letras*, 10 (1972), 105–34.
4 See Miranda's account of the fall of the first republic published by Bello in *El Repertorio Americano*, 4 (1827), 265–6.
5 *Cautivo* was an epithet of Ferdinand VII that appears repeatedly in the writings of the time. Similarly, *tirano* was often used to refer to Napoleon, and in one of the variants of the passage cited here Bello describes the "Parca" as "*tirana*." These epithets also appear in Bello's *Resumen de la historia de Venezuela* ("*eterno odio al Tirano*") and in the poem he composed in Latin hexameters ("*captivus . . . Rex*"). For the use of *cautivo*, see also the oath of the 1810 junta: "a nombre de nuestro rey y señor don Fernando VII (que Dios guarde), injustamente cautivo por la traidora nación francesa," in Gil Fortoul, *Historia constitucional*, 1: 217. In Juan Bautista Arriaza's poem in celebration of Ferdinand's return, which I discuss in Chapter 6, the terms *cautiverio* and *tirano* are similarly used.
6 See *OC*, 2: 24, under "Otros intentos de redacción."
7 Cf. Dinwiddy, "Los círculos liberales y benthamistas," 390.
8 See Tulio Halperin Donghi, *Tradición política española e ideología revolucionaria de Mayo* (Buenos Aires, 1961), esp. 161–82.
9 Alamiro de Avila indicated to me that Bello probably used these books around 1814.
10 For Bello's *Cid* studies see Pedro Grases's introduction to *Estudios filológicos* (*OC*, 7).
11 "Notas a la Crónica," *OC*, 7: 75–6. These lines were part of an intended preface to the edition, finished before 1834. It is quite clear, however, that the reconstruction of the poem was from the beginning Bello's intention, and some of his most important contributions to medieval studies – the origins of the assonant rhyme, the epic source of the romances, and the relation between the epic and the Crónicas – are the result of this initial motive. Bello's reconstruction of the lost passages at the beginning of the *Cid* are, as Grases has observed, his most significant philological achievement (*OC*, 7: c–ci).

5 The decided revolution

1 See Grases, "Londres en la vida y la obra de Andrés Bello," *Obras*, 2: 79.

2 Mejía Sánchez, "Don Andrés Bello y el doctor Mier," 121. Very little of Palacio Fajardo's writings survive. His two best known documents are the letter to the government of Cartagena drafted by Bello and a letter in French to Bolívar, written on March 19, 1819, shortly before his death. These documents can be found in O'Leary, *Memorias* (Caracas, 1879), 9: 401–10. For Palacio Fajardo's participation in the first Venezuelan Congress see *Libro de actas del Supremo Congreso de Venezuela*, esp. 179. Letters from Palacio Fajardo to Aimé Bonpland have been published in *Londres, cuartel general europeo de los patriotas de la emancipación americana*, Archivo de Bonpland (Buenos Aires, 1940), vol. 4.

3 For a full account of the external evidence see the bibliographical note by Carlos Pi Sunyer in Manuel Palacio Fajardo, *Bosquejo de la revolución en la América española*, preface by Enrique Bernardo Núñcz (Caracas, 1953).

4 Jonte was an agent of Buenos Aires who, along with López Méndez and other patriots, was busy between 1817 and 1819 enlisting Irish and British legionnaires in the struggle for independence. No one has ever made much of the claim that Jonte was involved with the *Outline*; in the preface of the *Outline* there is frequent reference to only one "author."

5 After comparing passages of the *Outline* to Bello's poetry, Pi Sunyer concludes, "Those who link the name of Bello to the work of Palacio Fajardo are not totally off the mark" (xxxiii). Enrique Bernardo Núñez, in an article that tries to prove Palacio Fajardo's authorship, summarizes the contrast between Palacio Fajardo's career and the *Outline*: "When one reads this cool and well-argued presentation, one would think that its author is not the same man who has served the revolution with so many risky and perilous activities." Also see Grases, "Londres en la vida y la obra de Andrés Bello," *Obras*, 2: 80: "The parallelism between the events in Bello's poetry and the prose narrative of the *Outline* leads one to believe that Bello's thinking and cooperation [are] not absent from this work."

6 The Spanish translation of the *Rapport* was published by Angel Grisanti in *El informe de Palacio Fajardo a Napoleón, emperador y rey* (Caracas, 1961), 90–108. For Palacio Fajardo's mission to France also see C. Parra Pérez, *Una misión diplomática venezolana ante Napoleón en 1813* (Caracas, 1958).

7 For Bello's interest in Spanish colonial legislation during the early years of the revolution see Roscio's letters of June 29, 1810, and September 10, 1810 (*OC*, 25: 9, 15). In keeping with the spirit of 1810, in 1817 the author of the *Outline* was still offering a legal justification for independence. Notice the central significance in

the *Outline* and in Roscio's letters of ley 1. tit. 1. lib. 3. of the *Recopilación*. Bello may have kept in his library a copy of the *Siete partidas,* which is discussed in the *Outline; see OC,* 25: 59.

8 In contrast, in their *Rapport* Palacio Fajardo and Delpech state, "Thus, for three centuries, more than thirty million people have done nothing but obey and vegetate."

9 In the "Preliminary Remarks" to *Interesting Official Documents* Bello presented an identical argument and used the same evidence.

10 Bello often narrated the impact on the *caraqueños* of the fall of the Bourbons, and he emphasized the strong allegiance they showed toward Ferdinand. The account of the *Outline,* and even the significance of Beaver's letter, closely resemble the account of these events that Bello recounted to Amunátegui (see Amunátegui, *Vida,* 36–51). Conversely, the *Outline's* account of the effects of the French invasion clashes with that of the *Rapport,* which states that in 1808 the Venezuelans were ready to be free: "Americans broke away from their lethargic state; they all seemed ready to be free when French arms occupied almost all of Spain." Later the authors of the *Rapport* claim that the punishments inflicted by the Spaniards after the rebellions of 1749 and 1797 branded in the hearts of Venezuelans the implacable hatred they felt toward Spaniards.

11 The *Rapport* says nothing of the loyalist nature of the 1810 junta and even presents the events of that year in a sequence that could lead the reader to believe that the junta actually opposed Ferdinand: "A junta seized the reins of government, which was immediately entrusted to a Congress nominated by the majority of the people of Venezuela, with the exception of the provinces of Guayana, Maracaibo and Coro – these provinces were overpowered by the influence of Spaniards and remained faithful to Ferdinand VII."

12 Cf. *Rapport:* "The Spanish Creoles love the French on account of their religion, their customs, and their language, which everybody wants to speak, while nobody wants to have to listen to English. They all show an exalted enthusiasm for His Majesty, the Emperor of the French, they welcome the news that bring the victories of his armies, and they do not believe in his setbacks. Only the war has prevented Caracas from building a statue in his honor."

13 The *Outline's* clear backing of Miranda has traditionally been seen, even by those who favor the authorship of Palacio Fajardo, as proof of the presence of Bello's hand in the work. Indeed, Palacio Fajardo's enmity toward Miranda was notorious. See, for example, this passage of the *Rapport:* "The greatest order in all branches of the Administration was in place when the British government sent General Miranda to Caracas. Through intrigues, he quickly divides all the classes, he creates factions, parties, popular societies, and all the divisions that have contributed to the reconquest of

this country." The *Rapport* adds later that the republic would have been saved in 1812 "if Miranda had not planned to betray his homeland in order to turn it over to the British. With 12,000 soldiers [*sic*] it was easy for him to defeat inferior enemies who were lacking everything." Not even Bello was able to affect the strong animosity Palacio Fajardo held toward Miranda. In the letter to the government of Cartagena, Bello wrote these words about Miranda for the signature of Palacio Fajardo: "a General whose views were never shared with me." This tactful litotes allows Bello to show Palacio Fajardo's distance from Miranda (or Miranda's distance from Palacio Fajardo) without criticizing the general. It is a good example of Bello's refusal to express opinions that offend his own beliefs when he writes for the signature of others.

14 The *Outline's* portraits of the leaders of the revolution elicited this comment from the first review of the book (*Quarterly Review*, 17 [April–July 1817], 555): "The general bias of the author is in favor of the colonists, but he does not endeavour to conceal the misconduct of their leaders, to magnify their victories, or to diminish those of the Spaniards."

15 This campaign was directed by Bello's old friend and *compadre*, Luis López Méndez. See Eric Lambert, "Los legionarios británicos," in *Bello y Londres*, 1: 355–76.

16 The *Borradores* and the *Outline* also contain almost identical accounts of the following events: the celebration of the first anniversary of the April 19 junta (*Borradores*, ll. 690–702; *Outline*, pp. 112–13); the death of Ricaurte (*Borradores*, ll. 1426–51; *Outline*, pp. 153–4); the death of Ribas and Boves (*Borradores*, ll. 1452–70; *Outline*, pp. 158–9).

6 The new Augustus

1 Juan Bautista Arriaza, *BAE*, 67: 85. This volume contains biographical notes on Arriaza by Fernando José Wolf, Antonio de Iza Zamácola, and Antonio Alcalá Galiano.

2 *Pláticas doctrinales predicadas en la Santa Iglesia metropolitana de Caracas en los cinco primeros días de la Domínica de Pasión por el presbítero D. Salvador García Ortigosa de la Congregación del Oratorio de S. Felipe Neri en 1816* (Caracas, 1816), 25, 44, 66.

3 Simon Bolívar, "Discurso pronunciado por el Libertador ante el Congreso de Angostura el 15 de febrero de 1819, día de su instalación," *Obras completas* (México, 1976), 6: 236–325. The speech was first published in the *Correo del Orinoco*, between February 20 and March 13, 1819. Bolívar was certainly not the first "republican" to use *augusto*. The traditional royal epithet was often used in the most solemn declarations of the liberal congresses in Spain and Spanish America.

4 See Héctor Gros Espiell, "El derecho internacional en los años londinenses de Andrés Bello (1810–1829)," in *Bello y Londres*, 1: 320. The text of the encyclical can be found in Pedro de Leturia, *Relaciones entre la Santa Sede e Hispanoamérica, 1493–1835* (Roma–Caracas, 1959), 2: 110–13.

5 The letter to the Pope was signed by Peñalver and Vergara. We know that Bello was its author only because of a statement made by Peñalver that stands as a kind of accusation of Bello's delay in its composition. Upon his return from Europe, Peñalver told the Congress of Angostura, "A few days before I left London, I prevailed on Andrés Bello to finish a proposal in Latin addressed to the Pope that had been commissioned to him a long time before" (*OC*, 8: lxxix).

6 The reluctance to endorse republicanism is especially striking given the instructions of the two envoys, which had been drafted by Roscio. By 1819 Roscio was an ardent republican and a fierce enemy of Spain, a result of the horrors he suffered in Spanish prisons between 1814 and 1816.

7 See, e.g., Sergio Fernández Larraín, *Cartas a Bello en Londres, 1810–1829* (Santiago, 1968), 99: "The position of Blanco, that wandering sailor, is in contrast to the serene and firm position of Andrés Bello, surrounded as he was by a schismatic environment, in the very entrails of the Lutheran voice. And if he had doubts (who does not?), he preserved in the end that traditional and orthodox position that he propagated in our country [Chile]."

8 Photocopies of the letters of William Blair 1805–22, are filed in the Home Correspondence Inwards series of the Bible Society's Archives. Four unpublished documents signed by Bello are kept in the same correspondence series: one memorandum (dated January 18, 1818) and three letters (dated December 19, 1819; November 19, 1823; and November 27, 1823). For Bello's links with Blair and the Bible Society also see José María Fagoaga's letter of July 31, 1816 (*OC*, 25: 75); Carlos Pi Sunyer, "Andrés Bello y sus trabajos de correción de textos bíblicos," *Patriotas americanos en Londres*, 225–8; Dinwiddy, "Los círculos liberales y benthamistas," 378.

9 *The Life of the Reverend Joseph Blanco White*, 3: 356. In *Blanco White: Self-banished Spaniard* (108, 224) Martin Murphy identifies the "Mr. B." that appears in Blanco-White's autobiography as Bello and also claims that Bello is the "South American" who appears in a footnote to the first volume of this work (128): "There Blanco White asserts that Meléndez Valdés was the only Spaniard he had ever known 'who, disbelieving Catholicism, had not embraced Atheism. He was a devout Deist.'" In a footnote he adds, "I subsequently knew a South American in the same state."

10 Miguel Antonio Caro, *Escritos sobre Andrés Bello* (Bogotá, 1981), 66.

7 The campaign of the monarchists

1 The most complete work on Irisarri is Ricardo Donoso, *Antonio José de Irisarri: Escritor y diplomático, 1786–1868* (Santiago, 1966). Also see Guillermo Feliú Cruz, "Bello, Irisarri y Egaña en Londres," *Andrés Bello y la redacción de los documentos oficiales administrativos, internacionales y legislativos de Chile* (Caracas, 1957).

2 This letter and Blanco White's response were first published by M. V. de Lara, "Nota a unos manuscritos de José María Blanco White – I," *Bulletin of Spanish Studies*, 78–9 (1943), 116–18.

3 Donoso, *Antonio José de Irisarri*, 90.

4 *El Censor Americano*, 1 (1820), iv.

5 "Estado de la Revolución de América," *El Censor Americano*, 1 (1820), 5–22. This is Bello's translation of Pope's text:

> Extiende, oh bella Paz, tu dulce imperio
> De mar a mar; y la conquista cese,
> Y no haya más esclavitud. El Indio
> En su nativa selva exento, goce
> Los frutos de su suelo, y los amores
> De sus rojas beldades. Perú vea
> Otra estirpe Real, y se levanten
> Méxicos nuevas, coronadas de oro. (*OC*, 2: 629)

6 Manuel Salvat Monguillot has attributed to Bello the following articles in the *Censor:* "Examen de la obra intitulada *Voyage to South America* [. . .] by H. M. Brackenridge," (1 [1820], 62–750; 2 [1820], 138–47); "Topografía de la Provincia de Cumaná," a translation of a passage from Humboldt (3 [1820], 207–24), and "Vacuna," a translation of an article by Drapiez (4 [1820], 315–17). See "Vida de Bello" *Vida y obra de Bello* (Santiago, 1973), 37. One could also attribute to Bello "Estadística de la Gran Bretaña" (1 [1820] 37–61) and "Consideraciones sobre la primera población y las antigüedades de América," also an extract from Humboldt (4 [1820], 303–15).

7 Dinwiddy, "Los círculos liberales y benthamistas," 377–98, esp. 379–80; Dugald Stewart, *Philosophy of the Human Mind* (London, 1813). A document that corroborates Dinwiddy's findings is the book list Bello prepared for the university of the new Colombian government, published by Grases under the title "Andrés Bello y la Universidad de Caracas," *Obras*, 2: 249–57. Dugald Stewart is the only author to appear under two different headings, "Ciencias intelectuales y morales" and "Humanidades y ciencias intelectuales y morales." In the second list Bello adds a note to Stewart's *Philosophy of the Human Mind*, "obra digna de estudiarse." At the same time, Bello recommends only Dumont's translations of Bentham ("*Obras de Bentham*, en francés"), which suppress the more radical strain of the Utilitarian philosopher. For Bentham's contact with Spaniards

and Spanish Americans see Pedro Schwartz, "La correspondencia ibérica de Jeremy Bentham," in *Bello y Londres*, 1: 225–307.

8 R. A. Humphreys, *Liberation in South America, 1806–1827: The Career of James Paroissien* (London, 1952), chaps. 7 and 8; Guillermo L. Guitarte, "El papel de Juan García del Río en las revistas de Londres," *Bello y Londres*, 2: 59–73.

9 See Ernesto de la Cruz, José Manuel Goenaga, Bartolomé Mitre, and Carlos A. Villanueva, *La entrevista de Guayaquil (El Libertador y San Martín)* (Madrid, [1917?]); Vicente Lecuna, *La entrevista de Guayaquil* (Caracas, 1952); Humphreys, *Liberation in South America*, chap. 7.

10 Lecuna, *La entrevista de Guayaquil*, 312–13.

11 Gil Fortoul, *Historia constitucional*, 381–6.

12 Humphreys, *Liberation in South America*, 127.

13 Donoso, *Antonio José de Irisarri*, 119–20.

14 Humphreys, *Liberation in South America*, 123, 134–5.

8 Poetry visits America

1 For the influence of the term *"idéologie"* on Bello, García del Río, and other Spanish Americans see Arturo Ardao, *Andrés Bello, filósofo* (Caracas, 1986), 58–93, 98–109.

2 Juan María Gutiérrez, *América Poética* (Valparaíso, 1846), 11–16; Pedro Henríquez Ureña, "El descontento y la promesa," *Seis ensayos en busca de nuestra expresión* (Buenos Aires, 1928), and idem, *Las corrientes literarias en la América Hispánica* (México: 1978 [1st ed. in English, 1945]), esp. 103. For more recent comments on the "Alocución" as a milestone of *americanismo* see Donald Shaw, "'Americanness' in Spanish American Literature," *Comparative Criticism*, 8 (1986), 213, and Arturo Ardao, "Primera idea del americanismo literario," in his forthcoming *La inteligencia latinoamericana*.

3 Thomas Gray, *The Complete Poems*, ed. H. W. Starr and J. R. Hendrickson (Oxford, 1966), 15.

4 For the significance of this topos in the 1820s see Llorens, *Liberales y románticos*, 330.

5 Bello shared this aesthetic ideal with such Spanish contemporaries as Blanco White, Mora, and Alcalá Galiano. In a review article on Cienfuegos in the *Biblioteca*, he expressed this ideal in a memorable line: "Among the ancients [i.e., in the poets and dramatists of the sixteenth and seventeenth centuries] nature prevails, while art prevails among the moderns. In the former we find ease, grace, fire, fecundity, a frequently irregular and even wild exuberance, which carries nevertheless a seal of greatness and daring that is impressive even when it goes astray. Generally speaking, the poets who have flourished since Luzán do not show these traits" (*OC*, 9: 199–200). The article on Cienfuegos, incidentally, was the first

published writing of Bello's that he signed – but only with his initials, A. B.

6 Arturo Ardao, "La etapa filosófica de Bello en Londres," in *Bello y Londres*, 2: 158.

7 Cf. "Reflexiones sobre la presente constitución de España," *El Censor Americano*, 1 (1820), 33: "If the 1812 Constitution were permanently ratified (which is, fortunately, very unlikely), the Spanish chains would weigh over us more heavily than ever. A free people has always ruled with an iron hand over its distant possessions. The government of an absolute monarch, surrounded by an opulent nobility and by aging bureaucrats, is naturally less oppressive for the colonies than a popular congress."

8 *OC*, 25: 105; Alamiro de Avila Martel, *Dos elogios chilenos a Bolívar en 1819* (Santiago, 1976).

9 For the criticism of Augustus among the British poets of the eighteenth century, see Weinbrot, *Augustus Caesar in "Augustan" England*.

9 "Agricultura"

1 John Lynch, "Great Britain and Latin American Independence, 1810–1830," in *Bello y Londres*, 1: 46–7.

2 *Cartas del Libertador*, 2d ed., Vicente Lecuna, ed. (Caracas, 1966), 4: 188.

3 Amunátegui, *Vida*, 200; Waddell, "Las relaciones británicas con Venezuela," 80.

4 Humphreys, *Liberation in South America*, chap. 9; Lynch, "Great Britain and Latin American Independence," 75–81; John Ford, "Rudolph Ackermann: Publisher to Latin America," in *Bello y Londres*, 1: 204–5. For a more detailed description and analysis of the debt crisis see Jaime Rodríguez, "The Politics of Credit," *The Emergence of Spanish America: Vicente Rocafuerte and Spanish Americanism, 1808–1831* (Berkeley, Calif., 1975), 108–28.

5 Servando Teresa de Mier, *Discurso sobre la encíclica del Papa León XII* (México, 1825), 4, 14.

6 This description of the rise of anticlericalism in Colombia closely follows Mary Watters, *A History of the Church in Venezuela, 1810–1930* (Chapel Hill, N.C., 1933).

7 Guitarte, "El papel de Juan García del Río en las revistas de Londres," 59–73; *El Repertorio Americano*, facsimile edition with notes and preface by Pedro Grases (Caracas, 1971). For Bello's role in soliciting material for publication in the *Repertorio* see the first volume of his correspondence (*OC*, 25: 203, 213, 261, 270, 279, 310, 341, 343, 345, 350, 364, 377). Bello's leading role in the journal is confirmed by José Joaquín de Mora, who wrote in 1830: "[El] Repertorio Americano, publicado en Londres bajo la dirección de Andrés Bello," in Alamiro de Avila Martel, *Bello y Mora en Chile* (Santiago, 1982), 141.

8 "El campo americano" appears in *OC*, 2: 70–93, ll. 775–1305. The
   four manuscript sheets (14, 15, 16, 17) of this composite poem
   have watermarks of 1824 and 1825.
9 For the use of footnotes, especially of a scientific kind, in the
   poetry of the late Enlightenment see William Powell Jones, *The
   Rhetoric of Science: A Study of Scientific Ideas and Imagery in Eighteenth-Century English Poetry* (Berkeley, Calif., 1966), 186–7, 191.
   Many of the poems studied by Jones are descriptions of the nature
   of the New World.
10 In *Los censos en la Iglesia colonial venezolana*, a three-volume study
    published in 1982 (Caracas), Emilia Troconis de Veracoechea re-
    vealed the extensive use of the Church's mortgage financing not
    only during the colonial period, but throughout the wars of inde-
    pendence and beyond.
11 José Tomás Sanauria, *Fomento de la agricultura: Discurso canónico-
    legal sobre la necesidad de una ley que reduzca los censos en Venezuela*
    (Caracas, 1823), 18–19.
12 See Miguel Luis Amunátegui and Diego Barros Arana, *La Iglesia
    frente a la emancipación americana* (Havana, 1967), 137.
13 At the center of the turmoil was the publication in Caracas of *La
    serpiente de Moisés*, an orthodox pamphlet originally published in
    Bogotá in 1822 in which religious toleration is assailed. The liberal
    authorities accused the editors of sedition, and a public trial was
    held on March 13, 1826, in front of the Church of San Francisco.
    Objections to *La serpiente* were made in a number of pamphlets
    published in Caracas in 1826. In *Discurso teológico político sobre la
    tolerancia en que se acusa y reputa el escrito titulado "La serpiente de
    Moisés,"* José de la Natividad Saldanha charges that without a
    doubt the work in question promotes rebellion. In *Cartas de un
    alemán a S.E. el Vicepresidente*, the anonymous author charges that
    the clergy has placed the "torch of rebellion in the hands of fanati-
    cism." *La serpiente* was defended by its editor, Miguel Santana, in
    *Día que no se contará entre los de Colombia: El 18 de marzo de 1826, en
    que se comenzó a hollar en Caracas la libertad de imprenta*.
14 For the influence of Tibullus on the "Agricultura" see Manuel
    Briceño Jáuregui, "Andrés Bello, humanista latino," in *Bello y la
    América Latina* (Caracas, 1982), 317–36.
15 Jacques Delille, *Les Géorgiques de Virgile*, 4th ed. (Paris: Bleuet,
    1770), note to the poem.

10 Bolívar's poetics

1 O'Leary, *Memorias*, 4: 382–3.
2 Ibid., 383.
3 José Joaquín Olmedo, *Victoria de Junín: Canto a Bolívar* (London,
   1826), 3–4.
4 O'Leary, *Memorias*, 4: 387n.

5 Ibid., 389–90.

6 *Cartas del Libertador,* 4: 329; Manuel Pérez Vila, *La biblioteca del Libertador* (Caracas, 1960).

7 Bello's review was first published in *El Repertorio Americano,* 1 (1826), 54–61. Another contemporary review of Olmedo's poem appeared in José Joaquín de Mora's journal *No Me Olvides: Colección de Producciones en Prosa y Verso, Originales y Traducidas* (London, 1827), 272–5.

8 Miguel Luis Amunátegui and Gregorio Victor Amunátegui, *Juicio crítico de algunos poetas hispanoamericanos* (Santiago, 1861), 30.

9 Amunátegui, *Vida,* 259; O'Leary, *Memorias,* 4: 390.

10 Cf. *Cartas del Libertador,* 4: 334, 344, 421, 447, 517–18, 523, 535; 5: 40, 66, 121, 122, 134, 205, 213.

11 Gil Fortoul, *Historia constitucional,* 1:471–4.

12 *Cartas del Libertador,* 5:97–102.

13 Pedro Grases, "Proyecto de Constitución para la República Boliviana, por Simón Bolívar," *Estudios bolivarianos, Obras,* 4: 404–16.

14 Bolívar, *Obras completas,* 6: 412.

15 On May 3, 1827, Bello apparently wrote just the beginning of the "Carta." The original manuscript of the poem shows only the first thirty-seven lines crowded in a page, to which is appended "etc., etc., etc." Details about the publication of the "Carta" can be found in Amunátegui, *Vida,* 267–77; Amunátegui, Prologue to *Poesías, Obras completas de Andrés Bello,* ed. Miguel Luis Amunátegui (Santiago, 1888), 3: xxv–xxvi; and *OC,* 1: 93. The "Carta" was probably written between 1827 and 1829.

16 The "Carta" is written in terza rima, following the model of the epistles in verse composed by the Argensola brothers, who in turn follow Dante. The main inspiration for the Argensola brothers and Olmedo, however, is Horace. As Pedro Grases has observed in a study of Bello's translation of Virgil's second eclogue, the Venezuelan poet imitates the Roman classics but through the perspective of the Spanish golden age. See his article, "La elaboración de una égloga juvenil de Bello," *Obras,* 2: 186–203.

17 Amunátegui, *Vida,* 298–9.

18 Ibid., 300–1.

19 Louis Perú de Lacroix, *Diario de Bucaramanga: Vida pública y privada del Libertador* (Caracas, 1976), 114–17.

20 During the first seven weeks that Perú de Lacroix kept his diary, that is, from April 1 to May 25, 1828, Bolívar discussed the wars only once, on April 16, according to the index of the lost portion of the diary (April 1 to May 1).

21 Perú de Lacroix, *Diario de Bucaramanga,* 118.

22 Amunátegui, *Vida,* 309.

11 The liberal poets

1 For the authorship of the article see Amunátegui and Amunátegui, *Juicio crítico de algunos poetas hispanoamericanos;* Pedro Grases, "La primera colaboración escrita de Bello en Chile," *Obras,* 2: 258–73. The article has been published in *OC,* 9: 289–98. The most important argument advanced by Grases is that Bello announced this article in his letter to Fernández Madrid. But there Bello says he has made announcements of the book in the Santiago newspapers ("He dado noticias de ella a los periódicos") and that a review, not necessarily his, will appear ("saldrá otra más completa en el próximo número de *El Mercurio Chileno*").

2 In 1824 Mora published a free translation of a song by Béranger, and in 1826 he mentioned Moore and Lavigne in the company of "el inmortal Byron." See Luis Monguió, *Don José Joaquín de Mora y el Perú del ochocientos* (Madrid, 1967), 82, 328.

3 Amunátegui, Prologue to *Poesías,* xxvii. Like other letters to Fernández Madrid, this one has been published only in fragmentary form. I have not been able to locate Fernández Madrid's archive.

4 This debate has been studied by Alamiro de Avila Martel, *Mora y Bello en Chile* (Santiago, 1982). Also see Miguel Luis Amunátegui, *Don José Joaquín de Mora: Apuntes biográficos* (Santiago, 1888), chap. 13, and Diego Barros Arana, *Historia general de Chile* (Santiago, 1898), 15: 612ff.

5 As is well known, Dumont's "Bentham" did not disclose the radical strain of the Utilitarian philosopher. Bello recommended the study of Dumont's translations even when he opposed Bentham's support of the Spanish liberals (see Chapter 8).

6 Alamiro de Avila Martel, "Londres en la formación jurídica de Bello," in *Bello y Londres,* 2: 211–42; Monguillot, "Vida de Bello," 59; Guillermo Feliú Cruz, *Andrés Bello y la redacción de los documentos oficiales administrativos, internacionales y legislativos de Chile* (Caracas, 1957).

7 Barros Arana, *Historia general de Chile,* 15: chap. 39; *OC,* 1: 251–5.

8 Cf. "La introducción de libros perniciosos," and "Los inconvenientes de la censura," *OC,* 9: 719–22. It is said that Ventura Marín, a devout man, proclaimed throughout Santiago and even in front of Bello, "This is the man who corrupts our youth, this is the man who fosters the destruction of religion" (Amunátegui, *Vida,* 388–9).

9 Amunátegui, *Vida,* 468–73.

10 "La estatua de Bolívar," *OC,* 23: 195; "Memoria histórico-crítica del derecho público chileno desde 1810 hasta 1833," *OC,* 23: 323–35. On Bello's ideas about a multilateral congress of states, see Amunátegui, *Vida,* 367–78.

11 Cf. Monguió, *Don José Joaquín de Mora,* 223.

12 "La acción del Gobierno," *Obras completas de Andrés Bello,* ed.

Amunátegui, 8: 27–76. This article was originally published in *El Araucano* and was therefore anonymous. It was not included in the Caracas edition, though the traces of Bello are unmistakable.

13 The spelling *jente,* for example, replaced *gente.* The new spelling was simpler to learn, since the confusion arising from two different spellings for the same sound (*je* and *ge*) was eliminated, but it increased the distance from the root *gens.* The 1844 orthographic reform was less radical than the 1823 project. The old ideal of a "perfect" orthography was preserved, but it was a distant ideal, one that could be reached only after several moderate reforms had been instituted. Bello's experiment to reform the alphabet brought him recognition throughout Spanish America, especially in Argentina and Uruguay, where his reforms were applied. Even Funes the Memorious, that great parody of the Enlightenment devised by Borges, followed the rules of Bello's orthography.

12 The exile

1 Edward Gibbon, *The History of the Decline and Fall of the Roman Empire,* with notes by Dean Milman, M. Guizot, and Dr. William Smith (New York, 1880), 1: 486.
2 Arístides Rojas, "El poeta virgiliano," 128.

Bibliographical note

In this book I have used the standard Bello bibliography, Agustín Millares Carlo, *Bibliografía de Andrés Bello* (Madrid, 1978), and the more recent one found in Fernando Murillo Rubiera, *Andrés Bello: Historia de una vida y de una obra* (Caracas, 1986). The fundamental work on Bello is Miguel Luis Amunátegui, *Vida de don Andrés Bello* (Santiago, 1882). Most of Amunátegui's research is based on Bello's own recollections, on the few letters Amunátegui had at his disposal, and on the letters Bello received in London. The majority of these letters are quoted in Amunátegui's text, and many that were omitted or appeared in fragmentary form have been published by Sergio Fernández Larraín in *Cartas a Bello en Londres* (Santiago, 1968); this book is a valuable contribution not only for having made available many important documents, but also for giving a detailed account of Bello's correspondents. Oscar Sambrano Urdaneta has published all the known correspondence of Bello in vols. 25 and 26 of the Caracas edition of the complete works, adding many documents that are missing in Amunátegui and Fernández Larraín. A detailed account of Bello's relationship with the ambassadors of Chile in London is given by Guillermo Feliú Cruz in "Bello, Irisarri y Egaña en Londres," which first appeared in the *Revista Chilena de Historia y Geografía* (1927); this work presents a significant number of documents that clarify Bello's role as a diplomat and his services for Chile. Other scholars who have to be singled out for their contribution to Bello, particularly to his London years, include Alamiro de Avila, Arturo Ardao, and Emir Rodríguez Monegal, though the work of the last (*El otro Andrés Bello* [Caracas, 1969]) exaggerates, in my view, Bello's connections with British romanticism. Despite their undue emphasis on Bello's Catholicism, Miguel Antonio Caro's studies on Bello, collected in *Escritos sobre Andrés Bello* (Bogotá, 1981), and Marcelino Menéndez Pelayo's study of

Bello in *Historia de la poesía hispanoamericana* (Santander, 1948; first published in 1911), establish important connections between Bello and his classical sources.

Rafael Caldera and Pedro Grases have been the major forces behind the Caracas edition of Bello's complete works (26 volumes published between 1951 and 1988). Grases's own studies on Bello have been collected in vols. 1 and 2 of his *Obras*. Grases has also organized the congresses that celebrated Bello's bicentennial between 1979 and 1981. The articles delivered at these congresses have been published in *Bello y Caracas* (Caracas, 1979), *Bello y Londres* (2 vols., Caracas, 1980, 1981), *Bello y Chile* (2 vols., Caracas, 1981), and *Bello y la América Latina* (Caracas, 1982). All six volumes include excellent studies. John Lynch published a selection of the articles contained in *Bello y Londres* in *Andrés Bello: The London Years* (London, 1982).

Index